U0092555

生活法律漫談
Law about Life

輕鬆學習
美國法律

鄧穎懋
王承守　編著

三民書局

國家圖書館出版品預行編目資料

輕鬆學習美國法律 / 鄧穎懋,王承守編著. －－初
版二刷. －－臺北市：三民，2004
　　面；　　公分. －－(生活法律漫談)
參考書目
ISBN 957-14-3224-5 　(平裝)

　1.法律－美國

583.52　　　　　　　　　　　　　　89006326

網路書店位址　http :// www. sanmin. com. tw

© 輕鬆學習美國法律

編著者	鄧穎懋　王承守
發行人	劉振強
著作財產權人	三民書局股份有限公司 臺北市復興北路386號
發行所	三民書局股份有限公司 地址／臺北市復興北路386號 電話／(02)25006600 郵撥／0009998-5
印刷所	三民書局股份有限公司
門市部	復北店／臺北市復興北路386號 重南店／臺北市重慶南路一段61號

初版一刷　2000年6月
初版二刷　2004年9月修正
編　號　S 584830
基本定價　陸　元
行政院新聞局登記證局版臺業字第○二○○號

有著作權　不准侵害

ISBN　957-14-3224-5 （平裝）

序

　　深感國人對美國法律認識不足及臺灣留學生對留美攻讀法律之最新資料欠缺，近年承辦國際商務案件之際並於大學兼授英美法課程，對美國基本法律之研究偶有心得。英美法課程中，學生上課表情多茫茫無辜，考試更不知如何準備。筆者在紐約大學(NYU)唸書時，臺灣來的商學院學生，亦常求助如何準備商事法(Business Law)，美國會計師考試(CPA)亦指定商事法為必考科目之一（包含Contract, torts等科目）。臺灣留學生感覺唸美國法律仿如唸天書，其中主要原因為英文與法律均是臺灣學生之致命傷。英美法是一種比較科學，藉由比較法學必能辨其優劣、擇善固執、改進我司法制度並提供我司法借鏡，因此拋磚引玉，簡介法律人如何順利申請美國法學院及如何利用本書準備英美法考試，俾使他日多一些留學生或攻讀美國法律之人才，投入社會、國際律師事務所或學校，不但能貢獻自己法學專業素養，更能共同切磋改進我司法體系制度。惟筆者才疏學淺，趕稿謬誤多處，敬請不吝指教。最後藉此機會感謝我的父親鄧火星先生，也要感謝東吳大學法律系之栽培。至於本書之校稿則有賴王承守博士及三民書局編輯部校稿，特誌謝意。

鄧穎懋

一九九九年十月二十日

承聯國際法律事務所

輕鬆學習美國法律

目　錄

序

第一章　美國法學院

第一節　導　言

　　自從洛城法網(L.A. Law)在美播出以來，申請入學美國法律系之學生激增一倍以上，在臺灣的「法律人」亦同時感染了L.A. Law中美國民刑法之活潑。由於中美司法制度之迥異，美國法院所著重之「先前判例」(precedent)和臺灣的「法條」(code)更明顯突出其相異之處。美國電視上不時有陪審員(juror)參與審判場面之出現，第一審法官所扮演之角色，似乎較被動而不若律師們積極主動針鋒相對的主動姿態；反觀我國法官則較積極主動詢問當事人，而律師不若美國律師可扮演較積極主動之角色。因此研究美國法律不論從何種觀點切入，對法律人均提供了一個重要之比較方向，某一法條或判例面臨新的社會現象而無法適用時，例如愛滋病、安樂死、墮胎等問題，若能參酌他國判例或學說，擇善從之，辨其異同，比較優劣，思考方向將可有新的創意參考。此種比較法學之方法，對律師、法官、學者而言，無異是提供解決方案之思考，公平正義得以伸張。

　　美國之法律錯綜複雜，其中有聯邦法律(Federal laws)和五十州法律(State laws)，大部分雖承襲了英國之習慣法(Common law)，但美國仍獨自發展出一套改良式聯邦和州法律的雙軌系統，舉凡

世界前衛之爭端(issues)，皆無所遁形於美國法律之規範之內。美國係一民族大熔爐，特秉公平正義原則，否則族群間難和平相處，故美國依賴這一套複雜完整的法律，始能發揮最大公平正義之境界。

　　本書藉由導言引述如何申請美國法學院，如何接受美國法律洗禮，進而結合大陸法系之法律，使個人之法學素養提昇之際，調和整個國家社會法益，邁入一個更公正法治的社會。

　　目前臺灣已有些學校法律系開設英美法課程，諸如英美法導論、英美契約法、英美侵權行為法、美國憲法、英美刑法與刑事訴訟法等。開此風氣之先的學校首推東吳大學法學院，國人留學喜歡至美國英國留學，若能於出國前已修習該課程，他日必減少許多異鄉苦讀法律之辛酸。惟並不是很多法律系之學生都有緣一窺英美法之浩瀚淵源，其中原因之一只是該校並無該英美法課程之設計或僅將上述課程列為選修。其實留學不留學是一回事，日後有人考上律師、法官、檢察官等，辦案之餘，莫不思考如何能有一套公正之判斷標準？英美法課程之訓練並能提供您一個很好的思考方向。東方的思維方式有時與西方之思維方式大異其趣，藉由了解其中之奧秘與差異，必能試探其立法意旨、判例主旨，二者合而為一，融入中西方世界主客觀思想，必能悟出一個具有國際觀的合理解決方式。雖然很多人一碰上英文即閃躲不及，更遑論學習英美法，英美法入門固需有英文基礎，但英美法之精華並不在其表面上之英文，而是法律本身之合理設計。故能藉由學習英美法並訓練自己，一方面提昇英文程度，另一方面了解英美法系之法律，一舉數得，何樂而不為？

第二節　美國法學院簡介

　　美國有法學院的學校大約有二百多所。其中又可分為美國律師公會(American Bar Association Approved or ABA)承認之學校和未為美國律師公會承認之學校（大部分在加州）。若無特殊理由，絕對不要唸美國律師公會不承認的學校，因為ABA不承認的學校只能獲當州(例如加州)之承認，卻未能如其他ABA承認之學校，為全美各州所承認。若唸了非ABA承認之學校，幾乎無法轉學或要求承認或抵免在非ABA承認學校所修之學分，故不可不慎！

　　ABA承認之學校為我教育部承認之學校，非ABA承認之學校，我教育部則不予承認其學位。例如在加州，若唸了加州承認但非ABA承認之學校，則只能在加州考律師，不得至他州考律師執照，即使考上了加州律師，出了該州，只是一般人而已。美國有些法律系學校規模較小，只是一個獨立學院(school)，大約只有一棟大樓，而沒有校園。例如California Western School of Law, Dickinson School of Law, Washington School of Law, New England School of Law等。美國大學生畢業不論主修為何，均可申請進入法學院，只要有好的LSAT成績和好的GPA。美國大學並無法律系，這點與臺灣大不相同。因為美國的法學院是栽培專業學位(professional degree)的地方。

　　美國學生唸的法律系其實就是臺灣學生唸的基礎法律課程，不同的是美國學生申請入學應具有大學文憑，臺灣學生有高中文憑即已足；另美國學生攻讀的學位為法學博士(Juris Doctor/J.D.)，臺灣學生攻讀的學位為法學士(Bachelor of Law/LL.B.)。在美國，

外國學生只要具有大學文憑即可申請美國法學院，但大部分外國學生因英文程度不足關係，多直接申請攻讀碩士學位(Master of Law)，唸完碩士之後，再攻讀博士學位。尤以臺灣學生，若唸完碩士除直接攻讀正式之法律科學博士學位(例如S.J.D或J.S.D等)，亦有人攻讀一般美國學生唸的法學博士(Juris Doctor)。

美國法學院基礎課程(Juris Doctor)的學生，幾乎全部為美國人，其他研究所課程(LL.M或M.C.L.)則多為外國學生攻讀，亦有美國學生夾雜攻讀LL.M學位(M.C.L或M.C.J僅開放給非英美法學之外國學生攻讀)。美國法律學生因每個人均具有大學文憑，故成員背景多元化，有唸電腦、會計、理工學科，甚至醫生、會計師、工程師亦不乏其人。很多英文系的學生，因有不錯的英文程度亦選擇法律系為第一志願。雖然美國人常開律師的玩笑(Lawyer's Joke)，但事實上私底下每個人仍然對唸法律系的人有幾分敬重。因為在美國唸法律是一種驕傲與榮耀。

欲赴美留學攻讀法律或學習美國法律，下列參考書是必備之捷徑：⑴*Emanuel law outline*；⑵*Siegel's*；⑶*Legal lines*（附有案例與法律實體內容，為最有效之參考書）；⑷*Case note legal brief*（詳細的將case事實、爭議、分析與結論濃縮，為留美不可或缺之參考書）；⑸*Finals*（期末考之複習參考書）。欲考美國律師執照者，得參加BAR/BRI之複習課程。

第三節　申請流程

美國法學院很歡迎任何人去唸其研究所(Graduate School)，但對於基礎法學的課程(Juris Doctor課程)，則寧願選擇本地美國人，而且所有申請Juris Doctor (J.D.)者，必需考法學院入學考試(Law School Admission Test or LSAT)。對於研究所，大部分學校只要求托福(Toefl)即可。進了法學院並不保證畢得了業，但大部分通過托福考試的人且成績達550分以上者應可順利過關，故美國法律系之申請，應不若國內研究所困難，只要英文程度達一定標準。有心想唸J.D.的人不妨從碩士班(LL.M.)先唸，因為一來，J.D.課程非常嚴謹，英文寫作和聽力會話不佳時，會造成出師未捷身先死，常使英雄淚滿襟之田地！二來，有了碩士班課程之基礎，對美國法律已有基本認識後再出發，較不會手忙腳亂，壓力重重；三來，J.D.班上幾乎為老美，英文未臻至一定水準，第一年準被當掉（大部分學校約10～30%）。有心唸J.S.D.或S.J.D. (Science of Juridical Doctor)的人，更必需由研究所(LL.M.)唸起，茲分述申請碩士班、博士班的流程，如下頁所示：

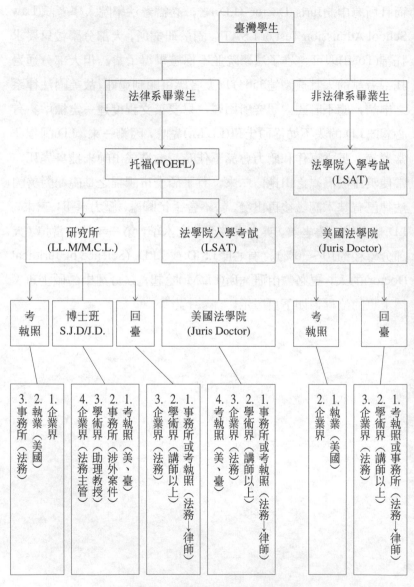

圖：申請法學碩博士流程

一、碩士班之一(M.C.L.)

　　美國的法律碩士大致可分為兩大系統，第一種稱為比較法學碩士(Master of Comparative Law or M.C.L.)的課程。此種課程只提供給非美國人的外籍學生來唸，大部分攻讀M.C.L.的外國人幾乎來自全世界，而且幾乎所有學生來自大陸法系的國家，其班上成員有年輕律師、法官、教授，或法律系畢業學生。這種課程大多規定學生修畢20至24個學分，有些學校另要求一份碩士論文(thesis)；大部分的學校則不要求，只要修畢學分即可。M.C.L可謂是攻讀碩士最快的捷徑，因為課程雖規定一年，實際上大約10個月即可修畢課程。有些課程併在傳統法學院之J.D.課程裡，有些另聘老師教授單獨授課；有些則和LL.M.或J.D.之課程選修夾雜一起。由於修畢學分即可取得學位，比起國內研究所，大約可節省一年時間綽綽有餘，此種學位只需要看托福成績(500～600分之間)。M.C.L.因班上同學來自全世界，故生活多采多姿，成員中有來自法國、德國、日本、南美國家等，跟他們一起更具國際觀且易了解該國民俗風情。但每個外國學生略有當地國家口音，跟他們在一起，較難學到正統的美國英語。對有心攻讀J.S.D.或S.J.D.博士班的人，最好選擇另一種碩士班(LL.M.)，因為J.S.D.或S.J.D學位均要求先有LL.M學位與不錯之成績。唸了M.C.L.後，如果考了一個不錯的LSAT成績加上不錯的G.P.A.，亦可申請攻讀J.D.學位。有些學校不稱M.C.L.而稱M.C.J. (Master of Comparative Jurisprudence)，例如昔日紐約大學(N.Y.U.)和德州大學(TU-Austin)，紐約大學已將M.C.J.改為LL.M. (Comparative Jurisprudence)。由於M.C.L.名氣不若LL.M.眾所皆知，故為了減少M.C.L.學生名稱之劣

勢（大部分美國人不知M.C.L.為何，甚至美國法律系學生根本不知S.J.D.或J.S.D.，美國法律系最熟悉的學位僅是J.D.與LL.M.而已），最好改唸LL.M.。想繼續留在美國的人，尤建議唸LL.M.，若是欲回臺就業者，M.C.L.即已足。

二、碩士班之二(LL.M.)

碩士班(Graduate Studies)的另一種選擇稱為Master of Law，美國人簡稱為LL.M.。跟美國談M.C.L.，幾乎大部分的美國法律人不知你所云為何，因M.C.L.係開放給外國人唸，而沒有任何美國人會去唸M.C.L.，故LL.M.之名稱，雖與M.C.L.位階相等，但知名度全美皆知，M.C.J.則佔劣勢。LL.M.學位亦只需考托福（550～600分之間）。欲唸名校(Top 15)則需達600分以上。

LL.M.的課程相當活潑廣泛，得依興趣選擇專長領域，常見的專長領域有公司法、貿易法規、稅法、國際公法、國際商法、刑法、比較法學、憲法與一般專長等。LL.M.亦要求修業約一年左右的課程，其學生成員，有些學校只願意開放給美國人，如稅法研究所；有些則完全開放給外國人；有些則外國人和美國人均可。目前美國法學院傾向全球性之開放。

不過美國人唸LL.M.，並不是很多，除非他(她)想進入教職，大部分的人唸完基礎法學的課程，即「法學博士」(Juris Doctor)即告停止。故選擇唸LL.M.的人，空間很廣，自己最好先規劃好將來走向再申請，當然想唸J.D.或J.S.D.的人，最好先修畢一個LL.M.（或M.C.L.）較佳且成績不能太差（至少B+以上）。LL.M.課程學生大抵修J.D.課程裡二三年級的高階課程(Advanced Study)，而非傳統J.D.法學院的一年級課程，如美國契約法、侵權行為法、財產法、民刑訴訟法、憲法、法學寫作等。故英文聽力和寫作需格外加強，方能生存過關。想唸J.S.D./S.J.D.，其LL.M.之成績需達B+以上或一定標準之漂亮成績，否則根本無法進入該校博士班。若LL.M.成績不理想，欲唸J.D.時，則必需考LSAT重新申請學院。由LL.M.唸至J.S.D.或S.J.D.大抵是相同學校，由LL.M.唸J.D.學位，由於需加考美國法學院入學考試(LSAT)，故大抵LL.M.的學校與將來J.D.之學校不同。有J.S.D./S.J.D.之學校大多是知名學校(Top 25)，J.D.之學校較多，故並非每個人均能申請到名校。其中原因是臺灣學生之英文程度不如在地的美國人，故LSAT之成績通常不好，而影響到申請名校之資格。欲唸J.S.D./S.J.D.，不用考LSAT，只要找好指導教授，並注意研究所(LL.M.)成績應維持一定程度，否則將前功盡棄！

三、碩士班之三(MIP)

智慧財產權法(Intellectual Property Rights Law)為目前頗流行之研讀科目，智慧財產權涵蓋了營業秘密法、商標法、專利法、著作權法、積體電路布局法及相關半導體法律。由於智慧財產權法之管理已與企業管理結合一起，因此有興趣者，得花一至二年時間攻讀智慧財產權法碩士(Master of Intellectual Property Law or MIP degree)。美國近年來陸陸續續有很多學校已開設此種課程，供學生攻讀，足見其需求擴大中。

有人說二十一世紀是智財權之世紀，跨國性之國際企業觸角已延伸至國外，法律系學生不應將自己的研究領域侷限於傳統之民刑訴訟，將法律與管理結合是一種更高的境界。商業法律之活潑，貴在與企業經營息息相關，修習MIP之學位，將使你跨足高

科技業界，專利與營業秘密為企業致勝之法寶，即使有了律師執
照亦可轉入企業界，專研專利與研發(R&D)成果之保護，恪盡職
守作好一位智慧財產工程師(IP engineer)，必能獲企業界重用。
MIP是碩士班的另一類選擇。

四、博士班之一(J.S.D.或S.J.D.或Ph.D.或D.C.L.)

欲攻讀法律科學博士的人，必需先修畢LL.M.之課程且成績
(GPA)達某一標準(通常B+以上或3.3以上)方能申請J.S.D./S.J.D.，
經過寫論文的型態取得該博士。申請J.S.D./S.J.D.最好同校，因為
碩博士的課程在同一學校可抵免學分,而且找指導教授比較方便。
J.S.D./S.J.D.大致等於所謂的Ph.D.。有了LL.M.學位後欲攻讀另
一個學校之J.S.D.或S.J.D.博士班時，大部分學校仍會要求欲攻讀
J.S.D./S.J.D.的同學，再修另一個LL.M.，因為此一LL.M.是你將來
欲攻讀J.S.D./S.J.D.的預備課程。申請之前先備妥一份計劃書(proposal)及擬修課程，而且必需先行找一位主要指導教授接納你。托
福成績在此時已不被要求了。因此在唸LL.M.時，即必需邊唸邊找
指導教授。J.S.D./S.J.D.的風險之一是，萬一指導教授對你的計畫
書不感興趣，則你很可能無法拜師學藝，只有嘗試另一條攻讀J.D.
的方向了。S.J.D.的學生大多是外國人而非美國人。另Washington
大學有Ph.D.的博士學位；Georgetown大學則有D.C.L. (Doctor of
Comparative Law)的比較法學博士。全美有J.S.D./S.J.D.的學校大
概只有十幾所。由於S.J.D./J.S.D.多由外國人申請，故美國人大多
不知。J.S.D.或S.J.D.，他們只知J.D.而已。故S.J.D./J.S.D.之博士多
回臺往學術界發展，反而是唸J.D.的人多往律師事務所與實務界
發展。

五、博士班之二(J.D.)

欲攻讀J.D. (Juris Doctor)亦絕非易事，有J.D.的學校大約有200多所，但正式為全美國律師公會(ABA-approved)所承認者，大約只有180所。美國人唸的法學院，即是J.D.的學位，而非S.J.D.學位。有些美國人認為J.D.非博士學位，如同M.D. (Medical Doctor)一般，但因其學位有Doctor一字，故仍被很多人認為是博士學位。基本上J.D.是一種專業的學位(professional degree)，它和MBA不同，因要求修業年限至少三年，其學生成員幾乎清一色美國人，美國人是先唸J.D.後，再唸LL.M.。臺灣學生則反過來唸。有人認為到底唸J.D.或J.S.D./S.J.D.那一個好？很難定論，端視你的方向目標。在臺灣J.D.仍被教育部視為博士學位，若能擁有J.D.學位加上碩士學位或論文，即可被學校或教育部認定助理教授資格。在唸J.D.期間，你的競爭對手是美國人，你必需有超人的意志和決心，過五關斬洋將及苦撐三年精力時間和壓力換取畢業J.D.。不用寫博士論文，但有專題研究報告之要求。欲唸J.D.的所有人，必需要先考法學院入學考試，即LSAT (Law School Admission Test)。並綜合自己大學或研究所的成績，提出申請，錄取率必需視你的LSAT成績和在校GPA成績。大部分之學校要求你參加法學院資料彙整服務，即LSDAS (Law School Data Assembly Service)，該報告將記錄你的大學或研究所的成績(G.P.A.)，LSAT之成績與LSAT之作文(Writing sample)。故LSAT/LSDAS已成進入美國法學院之必備資料之一。J.D.學位大部分不要求外國學生托福成績，只要求LSAT。大部分的臺灣學生考LSAT時大多考不高，因為其題目比托福還難，托福600分的人，其LSAT充其量只有在後面算來的10

～20%，因為你是和美國大學生在同一考試桌上競爭。臺灣補習LSAT之補習班很少，如有，建議你先惡補後再考。

LSAT裡沒有如GRE之簡易數學或幾合單元可以拿分，只有硬碰硬的邏輯推理、英文分析、閱讀的題目。大部分的人成績多不理想，故申請J.D.常常會有挫折感。但欲窺美國法律全貌，則惟有唸J.D.，因為J.D.課程教你美國的基本法律如下：Contract, Torts, Property law, Civil procedure, Criminal law, Criminal procedure, Legal writing, Constitution, Evidence等理論和實務課程，不若J.S.D./S.J.D.偏重某一專業領域。唸完J.D.可參加律師考試或踏入教職，經過至少三年以上和美國人生活，提昇英文對話最快，並可充分了解美國法律和美國人的生活點滴。選擇J.D.學校必需切記，申請ABA承認的學校為宜。否則將來若欲參加本州以外的律師考試，則只有乾瞪眼的份！

Juris Doctor (J.D.)學位依專科以上學校以國外學歷送審教師資格作業需知七及〈附錄二〉，採認原則如下：（教育部）

(1)凡在國內外大學法律系畢業獲有法律學士學位或曾修讀法律輔系並於畢業證書載明輔系名稱，繼續在法學研究所進修獲有法學碩士學位，再繼續在美國律師公會認可之法學院進修獲得J.D.學位者採認為具有助理教授資格。

(2)凡在國內外大學法律學系畢業持有法律學士學位，再繼續在美國律師公會認可之法學院進修獲有J.D.學位者，得以專門著作送審助理教授資格。

(3)國、內外大學畢業取得美國J.D.學位者，至少可認定相當碩士同等學力送審講師資格，若欲認定具博士同等資格仍須符合前述㈠㈡之認定原則，且依教育人員任用條例，必須有學位論文或發表於學術期刊之論文。

因此最好先唸個LL.M.或M.C.L.再唸J.D.，否則欲回臺任教必需先備有專門著作，即以著作送審方式送審較麻煩。J.D.學位並未要求博士論文，S.J.D./J.S.D.則需博士論文。J.D.大概是唯一不用寫博士論文之博士。

另非具有法學士之人，若直接攻讀J.D.學位，回來臺灣可能無法獲教育部採認為助理教授資格，亦不被承認為法律博士。例如英文系或化學系畢業後赴美攻讀J.D.，畢業後若欲回國擔任教職，則依據現行教育部規定，無法視為法學博士而不能順利獲認助理教授以上之資格。若欲往學術界發展，最多大致以相同於碩士學位而僅聘任為講師。

六、心　得

不管你的方向是如何，只要你有心留美攻讀法律，或研究美國法律，英文是一項非常重要的工具，美國人認為欲唸法學院，最好大學的主修是英文。若大學的GPA已成定局，只有加強托福或LSAT，而這二種考試均測驗你的英文實力。因此國人欲留美攻讀或研究美國法律，平時必需特別加強英文寫作、聽力、會話表達之能力，只要你這三方面均衡訓練，留美學法律必能勝任愉快。若能在臺灣修一些英美法課程，則助益更多，必能減少他鄉的艱苦奮鬥。律師、法官、檢察官與學者尤更應利用閒暇空檔，出國充電一下，必能扭轉既定之思維，對工作崗位必有助益。

美國的基本法律如契約法(Contract)、侵權行為法(Torts)、財產法(Property law)、刑法(Criminal law)和刑事訴訟法(Criminal procedure)。由聯邦民事訴訟法(Federal rule of Civil procedure)流程，

可透視其他州的程序法。證據法(Evidence)涵蓋了整個民刑訴訟的案件。法律人欲留學美國攻讀法律,若能在出國前對基本之美國法律有所認識,殆進入美國司法體系之殿堂,必能不畏其複雜龐大而且必能事半功倍,成為一個優秀的比較法律師、法官、學者或法律人。第二章即將帶領你巡弋美國司法殿堂,接受美式法律洗禮。

第二章　美國基礎法律概述

第一節　司法程序(Judicial Process)：民刑程序法

一、導　言

　　全世界有二大司法體系。其一為大陸法系國家；其二為英美法系國家。大陸法系國家以歐洲大陸的國家為主，如德國、法國等。英美法系國家以英國和美國為主。臺灣因仿德國等國家之法律而立法，故屬大陸法系國家。中國大陸、日本和拉丁美洲國家大部分同屬大陸法系國家。美國因襲了英國的習慣法(或普通法)，但卻發展成另一套習慣法(Common law)。 雖然均是英美法系國家，不過基本上，有很多制度並不相同，例如美國境內的路易斯安那州，則不採習慣法，而以法國的大陸法系司法制度為主。

　　大陸法和英美法系國家，在法律之適用有極大的不同。大陸法系國家係以成文法典(codification)為法律之依據，而英美法國家則以判決或判例(precedent)為法律之依據。美國本身有聯邦成文法典來管轄依憲法所授權之標的，例如聯邦證據法、聯邦刑事訴訟法、聯邦民事訴訟法等。其主要優缺點，乃是大陸法系和英美法系之法律人常爭執的正反面論點。以下就大陸法和英美法重要

相異之處指出，以期使學習英美法之人，有開門見山的震撼，並於學習案例過程中，反覆思考，加以自我反擊和挑戰司法之公允，對我法律加以比較分析，我想這應是學習英美法之重要目標。

二、中美刑法和刑事訴訟法之異同

臺灣沿襲大陸法國家的體系，基本上以法典(法條)為審判之主要依據，英美國家則以判例為審判之主要依據。近來大陸法國家已有逐漸重視判例之趨勢，如臺灣大法官釋憲或最高法院之判例，已扮演舉足輕重的地位；英美法國家，不約而同已慢慢制定統一的法典，以期消弭眾多法律適用之衝突，如美國聯邦證據法(Federal Rule of Evidence)和統一商法典(Uniform Commercial Code)或模範刑法典(Model Penal Code)。故世界主要法源和綜合原理，似有經比較分析而漸漸發展出一套全世界可接受的司法原理與法則。惟各國法制，仍因地理、國情淵源或社會條件而各異其趣，筆者依比較法學的原理，對我刑事法律提出對話，俾使我司法檢討革新，呈現新氣象。茲分述中美主要法制之異同：

㈠大陸法（臺灣）versus 英美法（以美國為主）

臺灣的判決以法條(statute)，而英美國家則以先前判例(precedent)為判決依據。在法官的扮演上，大陸法國家採糾問制度，故法官常一人扮演獨角戲，經常處於主動狀態；英美法之法官則因雙方對造律師辯論，而退居成一個較被動的看戲者，只在有嚴重錯誤或必要之情形之下，方會主動維持法庭秩序並詢問雙造，因英美法國家有陪審制度，讓法官無形中扮演另一個陪審員(第十三個陪審員)，而大陸法國家(如臺灣)大多無陪審員；大陸法國家因採用法條(典)制度，其法律不會經常變動，故其穩定性和預期性頗佳，不會一法律朝令夕改，使人民無所適從，但也因法條太具穩定效果，常使老舊的法條，無法滿足或適應新的社會環境變遷，故常產生與時代脫離或不公平的判決；英美法雖具有適時反映社會潮流和人民需求之判例，例如「司法造法」(Judge-made laws)，但法律之穩定性不若大陸法國家，常有朝令夕改之風險，故如何衡平二者之優劣，乃當今各派法學之務，現時大多數國家作法，即採法條和判例合一，只是以何者為主或輔，而有不同或透過修正改善其不足。

㈡聯邦制度(Federal Government)

臺灣只是一個海島，故只有一個中央法律，地方與中央之法律適用，因其統一性而有規則；美國有一個聯邦法律和五十個不同州法律，故美國其實共有五十一種法律，每一州的法律均有不同，聯邦有聯邦管轄的法院，採三級三審，即地方法院→巡迴上訴法院→聯邦最高法院。聯邦最高法院對於大使、領事之案件有初審權，聯邦法院有權管轄州與州之衝突或不同州民訴訟案件，舉凡商標、專利、著作權、破產法與海商案件等；另有特別法院，如聯邦海關法院，聯邦稅務法院；州亦採三級三審：第一審→上訴法院→州最高法院(但紐約與馬里蘭州，稱州最高法院為上訴法院)。 聯邦最高法院對於州最高法院， 得頒發覆審令(Writ of Certiorari)，即命該州案件移送聯邦最高法院。美國憲法規定美國司法權， 屬於聯邦最高法院(U.S. Supreme Court)且國會得隨時制定與成立下級法院。州與聯邦法律衝突時，聯邦法律優先適用。

惟臺灣目前之制度會不會因與大陸統一或獨立分離而可能出現聯邦(或邦聯)或其他制度，例如一國三制，此亦是將來司法設計的另一重點。

㈢陪審團(Jury)

臺灣目前沒有陪審制度，但孫中山先生於清光緒時曾主張陪審制度，且於民國十八年八月十日設有「反革命案件陪審暫行辦法」，但於進入訓政時期被廢止，期間甚短。❶

美國之陪審制度沿革於英國，惟英國現行民法中漸無陪審制度。美國的陪審主司調查「事實」，充當陪審員是美國公民的義務。陪審又分大陪審團與一般陪審團。大陪審團限於聯邦案件，通常在偵察階段，約由十六至二十三位非法律專業人員組成，協助檢察官秘密偵察工作，調查死刑犯或不名譽罪的嫌犯，其評決不公開審判：大陪審團員表決過半數時，即可對該犯人提起公訴(indict-ment)；一般陪審團則分別適用於聯邦和州法院。在聯邦法院，應由十二位非法律專業人員組成陪審團，對被告公開審查事實並依法官的法律指示(instruction or charge)，經評議 (deliberation)而下評決(verdict)。聯邦評決需十二人一致全部通過；州之陪審團原則上亦由十二或六人組成，評決方法本應有十二人一致全部同意，惟近日已有寬鬆至九人同意即可，但在六人組成之小陪審團(petit jury)，則必需六人一致全部評決有罪方能定罪。

陪審的優點在：⑴反映各階層民意，集思廣益增進人民對司法的認識和信心，透過人民監督司法，促進司法民主化，使法理情三者兼顧；⑵阻卻法官專橫獨斷主觀之自由心證裁判，使被告之權益多一層保障。其缺點為：⑴若陪審員意見不一或生病時，拖延訴訟且耗財費時；⑵陪審人員法律專業素質不齊，易受影響而產生違誤之判決。既有檢察官又有大陪審團，無異是司法資源

---

❶ 蔣耀祖，《中美司法制度之比較》，臺灣商務公司，民國六十五年，頁372～379。

之浪費，既有專業法官，又何需不懂法律的陪審外行人審理案件；
⑶陪審員易受被告脅迫，而主張被告為無罪。

㈣自由心證 versus 法定證據（事實一次審）

　　臺灣法界最為人訴病者，乃在法官的自由心證漫無限制。刑
事訴訟法第一百五十五條第一項規定：「證據之證明力，由法院自
由判斷。」第一百六十三條第一項，又規定「法院因發見事實之必
要，應依職權調查證據」，但證據能力並無等級程度之分，只賴法
官心證決定之。

　　美國證據調查，以聯邦證據法為多數州採用，例如傳聞證據
已實質上的自由化。基本上美國對證據法之法定舉證責任有三種：
⑴優勢證據(evidence of preponderance)；⑵清晰可信或清晰具說服
力證據(clear and convincing evidence)；⑶無合理懷疑證據(beyond
reasonable doubt)；「優勢證據」適用於一般民事，即一般證據能力
超過50% (more probable than not)，通常意謂較大的相信程度與較
多的證據數量；「清晰可信之證據」，則介於優勢證據和無合理懷
疑證據之間，目前很多民刑事案件，已依其性質，把無合理懷疑
之標準降為清晰可信之證據，藉以補救無合理懷疑之嚴格適用。
例如主張安樂死者生前表意不受植物人狀態，需符合清晰可信的
證據；❷「無合理懷疑之證據」為刑法之證據原則，意即被告所
犯之罪名，法官與檢察官必需在其所犯之罪的構成要件中，逐一
證明被告無合理懷疑理由犯罪，若其中或僅一構成要件不符無合
理懷疑證據，即該構成要件之一有合理懷疑，法官應依證據法及
經驗與論理原則，不能判定被告犯罪，且應諭知被告無罪開釋。

❷　Cruzan v. Director, Missouri Dep't of Health, 109 S.Ct. 3240, 106 L.Ed.
　　2d 587 (1989).

　　由此可見，無合理懷疑證據之標準，乃超過合理懷疑標準，可說幾乎接近100%之證據。此舉對被告權益之保障，可謂更週詳且實現了被告「推定無罪前提」，即每一被告未起訴前，均為無罪(presumption of innocence)。

　　美國的陪審員在第一審，只負責審查被告犯罪事實，法官不作事實之審理，只作法律之審理，且此事實審僅此一次，除非有重大瑕疵，法官大多尊重陪審團之評決，第二、三審的法官只負責法律審。反觀臺灣之法官於第二審仍有權審理事實，對於當事人一造事實之捏造，沒有嚇阻作用，且又增加法官辦案額外負擔。我刑事訴訟法第一百六十六條第一項規定，證人鑑定人之詰問，經聲請亦由審判長為之，故想減輕法官負擔，其實只要把法官退居第二線，採當事人雙造辯論主義，一來可減輕法官負擔，二來雙造當事人較不畏法官包青天神化的威脅，真理事實愈辯愈明，故事實審以一次為限，可有效防止日後一造有多餘時間杜撰新事實。比較上，臺灣只有法官一人審查第一審之事實部分，而美國包含法官在內，共有十三人共同監督審查事實，較我方慎重。

　　另美國對於證據之提出採預審會議(pretrial conference)集中審理，當事人只能依預審會議所提出之證據攻擊防禦，不得另行提出其他證據；反觀我國在第二審還能提出新事實，常令對造措手不及(unfair surprise)。

㈤認罪之協議(Plea Bargain)

　　我國已有輕罪認罪的協議方法，為防止被告或檢察官之間曖昧行為，如賄賂行為，故以前乾脆沒有立法。陳進興在挾持南非武官之際，即要求與檢察官或立委達成認罪協議，我國現引進此制度，當時之間很多單位不知如何是好。此制度眾說紛紜，其優劣各見。

　　美國允許被告和檢察官之間，得進行認罪的協議，但非被告與法官間的協議，除非有正當理由，法官得禁止被告和檢察官之協議，而變為法官和被告之協議。被告認罪供出某一事實行為，得使案情早日偵破結案，但檢察官必需保證減輕被告刑責，此節省了法官辦案時間，檢察官和被告應訂立一個類似公法之契約，如建議法官酌情減刑，若將來法官不依認罪協議履行條件時，被告可撤回認罪之協議，其認罪之事實，視為自始不存在。❸

㈥保持緘默權與受律師幫助之權利（刑法）(Silent Right and Right to Counsel)

　　臺灣目前已修正此法，惟在衡平被告期待隱私權和公法利益是一大學問。在二十世紀，被告期待隱私權，若不觸犯公共利益，自應受憲法之合理保障。

　　美國規定警察人員在搜索、逮捕、羈押犯人之前，必需告知下列義務(Miranda warning)。犯罪嫌疑犯(suspect)有權保持：⑴緘默權(right to remain silent)；⑵任何其告知緘默權後，所說不利自己的話，得成為在庭上控告自己之證據(self-incriminating statements)，又稱呈堂證供；⑶有權請律師協助(right to assistance of counsel)；⑷若無錢請律師時，政府會指派律師（公設辯護人）給付不起律師費的人(appointed counsel)。❹由此可見，美國對被告保障勝於臺灣，尤其在憲法所保障的緘默權和受律師幫助之權利。而且警察人員若無可能的原因(probable cause)，不可對人民的身

❸　Santobello v. New York, 404 U.S. 257, 30 L.Ed. 2d. 427, 92 S.Ct. 495 (1971).

❹　Miranda v. Arizona, 384 U.S. 436, 16 L.Ed. 694, 86 S.Ct. 495 (1971).

體、財產、住宅進行搜索和扣押，此亦在美國憲法第四修正案所保護之範圍之內。在臺灣，檢察官得發拘票、羈押票等，對被告逮捕或羈押；在美國，檢察官仍必需向法院(治安審判法官或行政官)申請方能為之。所以，人權維護之保障，臺灣似不如美國。現在臺灣擴大了檢察官不起訴職權(如逆子殺父、公職人員侵占公司財產、恐嚇勒索取財、夜間竊盜、投票受賄等)，表面上在減輕法官負擔，避免司法資源浪費，但對人民三級三審之權利可能是又一剝奪。

(七)新聞傳播自由與限制(Freedom of Press)

臺灣並未採電視審判，但新聞審判則司空見慣，惟尤其是被告的權益是否可獲公平審判，殊難謂社會輿論或新聞人員沒有絲毫影響法官日後之判決。若偵察不公開的案件，每每因新聞電視人員的公開轉播，則整個案件變成了「新聞審判」或「電視審判」，對公平公正之司法審判，常產生負面的影響，因有些新聞人員或電視播音員(記者)常不知不覺或在故意的情況下，誤導了整個案情。雖表現自由與報導自由，係憲法所保障，但侵害到他人權益時應受刑事限制。陳進興案即成為一個負面的新聞自由報導。

在英國，通常法院會有禁止報導法律層面的命令，規定上述人員只能傳達或轉播事實，否則會惹上「藐視法庭罪」(contempt of law)；在美國，因衡量新聞傳播人員，在憲法第一修正案保障的新聞傳播言論自由及禁止事前限制(prior restraint)之前提下，只在其言論足妨礙司法行政，始構成藐視法庭罪。洛城的金恩(Rodney King)於審判時，即因新聞審判之干涉因素而造成洛杉磯黑人大暴動。故新聞審判之限制，不可忽略，宜制定有關新聞人員專業道德責任方面的法律。❺

㈧釋憲權(Interpretation of Constitutionality)

臺灣的憲法法庭誕生不久，其憲法所保障的權益常與刑事訴訟法規範衝突，故在衡量上必需有專門人員，即大法官解釋是否違憲。目前有人提議減少大法官人數，但筆者認為千萬不可，美國大法官僅九人，但每州法院有司法造法權，故能釋法者恆多。但臺灣的法院並無釋憲權，故仍需要至少十七人的大法官負責重大違憲事由解釋。既然法院不能釋憲，至少維持大法官目前人數，以維人民權益。

在美國，普通法院對於憲法之違憲有解釋權，不限單由聯邦憲法法院釋憲，故對人民有雙重保障，即使在確定判決後，有任何對被告身體之不法侵害，州及聯邦系統均有人身保護令(writ of habeas corpus)，要求除去侵害和賠償。

我國刑事訴訟法雖有再審與非常上訴制度，但其適用機率非常微小，故當人民生命自由財產受侵害或人民對法律有疑義時，不得且不能逕行向法院請求釋憲，只能向大法官請求釋憲，惟此必需藉由中央或地方行使之。人民與最高法院之距離本來已有間隔，若人民或地方公共團體不能透過法院解決人民最基本權益，而必需請高高在上的大法官主持會議，對人民的基本權利及時間法益，亦是一項打擊與剝奪。行政訴訟方面常由各機關訴願委員審理，而非法律專家審理，因其審理為書面審理，必需經過訴願，方能進行行政訴訟，對人民法益之保障，恐有不公之虞。

❺ Rodney King為一名黑人，因受白人警察毆打，遭人用V8現場錄下，後因評決毆打黑人之二位白人無罪，造成洛城暴動。最後重審(retrial)評決二名白人警察有罪，方平息此一風波。但有人批評違憲，即雙重危險之禁止。

　　另外，美國的憲法由聯邦政府制定，在整個政治體系包括三個獨立系統：⑴美國聯邦法院(Judicial Branch)；⑵總統行政(Executive Branch)；⑶國會(Legislative Branch)。三者之間各有各的管轄權限，三者互相監督互相制衡，人民的基本權利在憲法修正案(Article four)第一條至第十四條方能有週全之保護。❻

三、結　論

　　比較法學為研究法學之重要方法，當法條或判決面臨無法解決某一社會現象時，若能比較分析他國判例或學說，擇善從之，辨其異同，比較優劣，常會令執迷者頓然清醒，仿如注入新血，思考不再偏限於死角。

　　鑑於國內英美法教科書不多，且均以英文印刷，筆者以教授英美法課程經驗，發現大部分臺灣學生仍無法適應全英文版之教科書；每每講至重點之處，若非以簡單明瞭之中文輔助教學，學生理解力不甚良好。因此，若能以中英文搭配教學，必能提高學習興趣，減少學生對英美法課程之排斥。法律貴在「法」而非法律本身之外文，若選讀案例配合中英文上課，必能克服語言障礙，事半功倍，並增進法律英文書寫和對話之實力。在參加WTO後，國人對於國際間的法律必日漸耳熟，但卻未必能詳，故此書提供非傳統之中英文教學方式，盼以簡潔中英文互用，節省閱者之時間，提昇對英美法之理解力。鑑於法官或律師辦案時，可能對於美國法律或判決有遙遠陌生之距離感，故筆者希提供給法律人士，於本國專業法律領域外，參酌另一套外國的司法模式，以俾共同

---

❻　本文部分內容曾於八十三年八月十七日承當時總統府第一局顏慶章局長力邀，於總統府發表司法革新建議。

改進我國法律。

第二節　法律研究(Legal Research)

一、如何解析案例

　　美國係大量採用習慣法(Common law)的一個國家，故先前的判例(prior precedent)常被用來作為法院判決之依據，維持先前判例(Stare Decisis)成為大部分法官心中之準則，惟法官之附記意見(dictum)並非拘束之判決，不得作為判決之依據。若依先前判例，會造成極不公平的判決，英美法官可能利用司法(法官)造法(Judge-made laws)之功能，推翻原先的判例，重新作了一個領導性的判例(Leading case)。

　　在西元1960年的案子，在2020年可能會有不同的判決。因此我們必需對美國的司法作一巡迴的認識。如何解析一個案例，有賴於法律之尋找或研究。一般的法源有(1)習慣法(Common law)：以案例(case precedent)為主；(2)法典(statutory law)：由聯邦或州制定成文法典，尤以美國聯邦法律和美國法典(United State Code or U.S.C.)制定的法律，最引人注目。每一個案件會有官方正式的引證處(citation)，例如1 U.S. 20 (1997)，指最高法院的判決報告書第一冊(Volume)中第二十頁(page)可找到本案，除了官方的引證外，私人出版機構亦有彙編法院的判決，例如1 N.E. 20，N.E.指North East(東北，一家法律出版公司)亦有出版相同的案例。常見電腦網路工具有West law、Nexis/Lexis及Lawyer edition (L.Ed.)等。

　　一個案件時，最主要目的，在找出爭議點(Issue)，然後把重要

事實應用於法律(Rule of Law)。其應用的過程，經過分析過程，得到結論。美國法學院大多採用下列「爭議—法律—分析—結論」之模式，即IRAC公式，剖析案例，即Issue(爭議點)，Rule of Law(法律)，Analysis(分析)，及Conclusion(結論)。下一項將有深入之介紹。

二、如何寫案例摘要(Brief)

一個案件事實必定繁雜，法官律師的攻擊理論更是天花亂墜，如何於數頁的冗長文章中，精簡扼要寫出真正的摘要，闡明事實、爭議、分析與結論，是學習英美法的精髓，這與學大陸法(civil law)的過程，截然不同。

首先我們必需把事實部分濃縮成重要事實，不需無謂冗長地敘述全部事實。第二，必需把爭議點或爭端找出，如原告理論和被告抗辯(contention)之對立立場。第三，把法官依據的法律找出，大部分的法官會以先前的判例，或以經驗論理原則，發展出一套具有邏輯的司法言論(judicial opinion or statement)，判決文中閃閃發光的字(Buzz words)，是法官經典之作。唸英美法之判決即在尋找這些優美之詞。第四，把重要事實引用於上述之法律，看看是否得以比較分析適用。英美法以類比(Analogy)或比較來作案件的判決理論，若1993年P v. D案子的原告，很類似1995年本案之原告，且1993年P v. D的判決是原告勝訴，原告的律師，即可以引證1993年案件之判決，請求法院或陪審團在本案判決或評決時，判原告勝訴。以下是BRIEF之撰寫技巧：

HOW TO READ A CASE AND BRIEF

You will learn legal reasoning and substantive law in law school by analyzing the appellate decisions included in your textbooks. This teaching device is called the case method. （案例教育）

To prepare for class you will be expected to brief assigned cases. A brief is an organized, written summary of the important elements of a judicial opinion. In addition to class discussion, briefs will be helpful in review and exam preparation.

This discussion is introductory in nature and designed to help you during your first few days of classes. Be sure to look up all terms you do not understand in a legal dictionary. The leading one is *Black's Law Dictionary*.

After you have read the case, go back and begin to identify the different elements. A case brief will usually contain the following main elements: facts, issue, rule of law (ruling), analysis (reasoning), conclusion, concurring opinion (optional), dissenting opinion (optional). The elements are explained below.

CITATION （引證）：必需正確引證出處

P v. D, 36 N.Y. 2d. 63, 174 N.E. 2d. 881 (1961).

N.Y. 2d. stands for official reporter, while N.E. 2d. unofficial reporter; 36 indicates volumes of New York Reporter, second series, while 63 indicates page in that volume. The following is an example of BRIEF:

1. FACTS: State only the facts essential or material to the decision. The case may say "a fat thirty-nine years old man slipped and fell on a wet floor in So-Go shopping mall on NanGin E. Road." Your brief needs only to state that "a man fell on a wet floor in a shop-

ping mall."

2. ISSUE: Framing or forming a statement of the issue involved in a decision is probably the hardest part of briefing a case. The issue should be relevant without being too broad or too narrow. For example: (1) Did the Defendant (D) assault plaintiff (P)? Is there a contract? (too broad); (2) Can the P, a tenant in D's apartment, recover for assault when the D threatened to shoot movers with a pistol he was carrying if they moved any furniture and also threatened to shoot the P (too narrow)?; (3) Does a threat, that the P has reason to believe the D has ability to carry out, constitute assault? (Good issue-framing a Yes/No decision or answer)

3. RULE OF LAW: The precedents (prior binding decision/stare decisis), logic, and policy the court relied upon to make its decision.

4. ANALYSIS: Applying the facts into rule of law. The part should be the longest part in your brief. By analyzing the facts, a relevant ruling can be achieved. Both P's (pro) and D's argument (con) should be discussed separately. A critic (comparative method) is welcome to be part of your brief. Please be sure to discuss the merits of case. The merits of case shall cover the arguments of both side.

5. CONCLUSION: State a judgment for P or D and give a concise reasoning.

6. CONCURRING OPINION (same judgment but concur/agree with different reasons)

7. DISSENTING OPINION (disagree with a reverse judgment)

8. NOTE: Supplement the points you learn in class.

三、如何寫一個A的考卷和法律備忘錄(A Answer & Memo)

考試時或於事務所上班時，教授或資深律師合夥人，可能會要求你寫一個案件評估。如何迅速抓著案件真正的重點，而不必辛勤日夜待在圖書館或辦公室K書。這種濃縮案件之功力，有賴平日不斷練習IRAC之架構。

正式的寫法，應該於IRAC前上陳述簡短的小結論，把IRAC的C先搬至開頭，方便讓閱卷人或資深律師先一目了然，把握重點。茲將二大類型：⑴一般考試案件(case)和⑵法律備忘錄(memorandum)，分述如下：

考試情形／事務所備忘錄

Instruction

This essay exam is an open-book test. You may bring the text-book and any material prepared by your own efforts. You do not have to know the exact rule of law. However, a well-organized IRAC analysis (issue-rule-analysis-conclusion) is necessary no matter what conclusion you draw. USE YOUR COMMON SENSE AND LOGIC.

FACTS （事實）

P had a business in Los Angeles and wanted a branch in San Francisco. C and D, both of whom P knew, each owned property in San Francisco on which a branch could be located. After looking over

these possibilities, P returned to Los Angeles. On March 2, P received and read the following letter from D: "I enclose my proposal in the attached lease and the beginning date. You said if interested, you would take the premises either on May 1 or August 1. If the former, the rent would be $650 a month, if the latter, $700. P.S. I need to know at least by March 15."

On March 5, Arnold, a salesman, who is acquainted with P and D, told P while D had not yet sold it, he (D) was "now offering the property you want to Jack." P then "immediately" signed the lease and mail it in a letter to D which stated that "the May 1 date and the $650 rental are what I am electing." D received this letter and enclosure on March 6. Also on that date, P received a letter from D postmarked March 4 stating "THE DEAL IS OFF!"

Does P have a binding contract with D? Please discuss the elements of contract.

TYPE I: TEST(考試)

CONCLUSION (short opening statements)＋ISSUE

(#1) P should probably prevail in this case under the xx theory. In the alternative, even if no xx rights, she/he can argue under yy theory. The (first) issue is whether Offeree's acceptance is valid when Offeree learns Offeror's indirect revocation of offer from reliable source? The (second) issue is ＊＊＊?

(#2) The court was (partially) correct and partially wrong in Ruling (1)The issue is whether ＊＊＊ (Given a court's ruling, the essay you to tell whether the judgment is correct or incorrect).

RULE OF LAW (elements)＋

ANALYSIS (apply facts into rule of law)

A. Acceptance v. Indirect Revocation

In determining whether there is a valid contract, three elements/factors to be considered as a contract are (1) offer (2) acceptance (3) consideration. Here, D learned the information concerning revocation from both P's and D's friend, this constituted an indirect revocation. P should/may/might/could argue that ....

D could rebut that .... Although the fact (one particular fact) favored D, P could allege that .... Even if (though) D might argue in rebuttal that .... Since (Because) the facts indicated that .... This demonstrates that the element (2) analysis favors P. Besides, the element (3) analysis weights against D. In addition (also), ... The mere fact that D accepted within the offer's stipulated time is not sufficient (decisive) to constitute the acceptance. Suppose/Assuming ..., ... However, the element (2) must be justified on the basis of no indirect revocation. Thus (Therefore), the contract was terminated and there was no contract because of no meeting of mind between the parties. This issue favors P.

B. Reliable Information v. Hearsay

(same analysis) This issue analysis also favors P.

CONCLUSION (concise if time allowed)

(#1) In conclusion, P should prevail on this case because .... If I were the judge, I would reach a judgment for P because ....

(#2) Therefore, I would advise P to ... because ....

TYPE II: MEMO (court or law office)[備忘錄](事務所)

CONCLUSION (short opening statements)

(#1) You have asked me to advise you whether the contract is valid. I conclude that elements of a contract can be established against D. My analysis follow:

    X (issue #1)

    Y (issue #2)

(#2) The legal theories potentially available to P are A, B, and C. These legal theories, together with D's defenses, will be examined in order.

以上範例提供你下筆前之沉思，應盡量有完整架構再下筆。

四、結　論

　　一般英美的法律由普通法、成文法典、判例或判決組成，作為適用或解釋法律的依據。主要原則應遵守先前判例(case precedent or stare Decisis)。主要依據或權威的法源(Primary authority)如法條或判例。輔助之權威法源(Secondary authority)如所有關於法律之文章、法律學報等。如何引證判例、法條、學說(citation form)，非常複雜，具有一定之格式，最有效的一本書稱Blue Book (A Uniform system of Citation)，這本書對如何引證有非常詳細之規定。基於篇幅，常見的引證方式，請參見第三章美國法律大綱第二節法律研究之解說部分。

第三節 聯邦巡迴上訴法院(Circuit Courts)

　　美國聯邦法院之中級法院，即巡迴上訴法院，由幾個州共用一個巡迴上訴法院，除了排列方式由東至西由北至南共十一個巡迴上訴法院，另有聯邦巡迴上訴法院及華盛頓D.C.巡迴上訴法院，其區域之劃分如下：

(1)第一巡迴上訴法院：Maine, NH, Mass.

(2)第二巡迴上訴法院：NY, Conn.

(3)第三巡迴上訴法院：Penn., Del., NJ

(4)第四巡迴上訴法院：W. VA, VA, N. Carolina, S. Carolina

(5)第五巡迴上訴法院：Miss., Louisana, TX

(6)第六巡迴上訴法院：Michigan, Ohio

(7)第七巡迴上訴法院：IN, IL, WIS

(8)第八巡迴上訴法院：N. Dakota, S. Dakota, Nebraska, Minnesota, Iowa, Missouri, Arkansas

(9)第九巡迴上訴法院：WA, OR, Idaho, Montana

(10)第十巡迴上訴法院：Utah, Wyoming, Colorado, New Mexico

(11)第十一巡迴上訴法院：Alabama, Georgia, FL

　　聯邦巡迴上訴法院及華盛頓D.C.巡迴上訴法院為獨立之巡迴法院。巡迴上訴法院為聯邦法院管轄，對聯邦地方法院之判決若有不服，得上訴聯邦巡迴上訴法院。對聯邦上訴法院不服，得向

最高法院聲請覆查(Certiorari)，需經九位大法官中至少四位之同意接受該案之上訴。九位聯邦最高法院大法官的名字常見諸於判例中，諸如Byron White（現由Ruth Bader Ginsburg取代）、Harry Blackmum、William Rehnquist、John Stevens、Sandra O'Connor、Antonin Scalia、Anthony Kennedy、David Souter 與 Clarence Thomas。

第四節 契約法(Contract)

一、簡 介(Preview)

契約(Contract)是債發生的原因之一，舉凡中外債權與債務的關係有賴契約的條款作一明細的規範。債(Obligation)之概念拘束契約當事人作為或不作為。由於英美契約法多由不成文的商業交易習慣組成，其構成要件大多由⑴要約(Offer)；⑵承諾(Acceptance)；⑶約因或對價(Consideration)；⑷當事人能力(Capacity)；⑸標的物(Subject matter)組成。當事人之合意(meeting of mind)是英美法契約很重要的一個概念。其發生的原因來自直接或間接同意書(Agreement)、侵權行為(Tort)、違約(breach of contract)或準契約行為(Quasi in law or in fact)而來，因此可以說契約衍生之債，與侵權所生之債均是債的發生原因。惟我民法把侵權而生之債納入債編。❼

美國的契約法由習慣法(Common Law)演繹而來，由於美國共有五十州，各州法律各異其趣，故有美國統一商法典(Uniform

---

❼ 何孝元，《中國債法與英美法之比較》，頁5～6。

Commercial Code or U.C.C.)之出現及法律彙編。但非具強制拘束力，例如契約法彙編(Restatement of Contract, 2nd edition)。契約是一種法律行為，由早期的口說無憑契約至防止詐欺條例(Statute of Fraud)之出現，契約必需有二人或二人以上之當事人(Contracting parties)，互為意思表示之合意，藉由要約與承諾，多次的磋商(negotiation)，雙方同意簽下契約條款，合意互相約束對方。

契約大抵可分單務契約(Unilateral Contract)和雙務契約(Bilateral contract)。前者(單務契約)指一方為意思表示(promise)，而他方以行為(act)或不作為(omission)承諾契約內容；後者(雙務契約)指要約人(offer)與承諾人或要約相對人(offered)，經雙方意思表示之合意合致，契約即成立。此契約係以明示(express)或默示(implied)構成契約種類，另有可撤回(revocable)或不可撤回(irrevocable)契約。

英美法與大陸法有關契約法的差異，除了約因對價觀念外，還有承諾之發信主義(Dispatch rule)。一般而言要約，要約之撤回(revocation)，選擇契約(option contract)及承諾之拒絕(rejection)，均採到達主義(arrival or receipt rule)。承諾人或要約之相對人只要把非對話之承諾信件丟入郵筒，而且信件適當住址無誤，則已構成有效承諾之法律效力(Effective upon posting or dispatch)。故理論上美國法律沒有撤回承諾的可能，但實務上，可至郵局填寫一張攔截信件申請書(Form of interception)，阻止承諾之寄出，惟動作要快。要約基本上均可撤銷或撤回，只要要約相對人未承諾前，好比要約人與相對人握手(shaking hand: master offer)，在相對人還沒有伸手與要約人之手接觸前，要約人得隨時撤回。若信函之要約，經發出但未到達要約相對人時，要約人得以最快速且相同或

相類似之傳播工具，例如傳真、電話、掛號信等撤回要約。美國的撤回要約，不但包括了直接撤回(direct revocation)，有些州甚至容許間接撤回，即要約相對人從可靠消息人或處所得知要約人已撤回(Indirect revocation)。❽惟單務契約，要約人不得隨意撤回，一旦要約相對人因有正當理由信賴要約人要約或已行使選擇權(option)契約時，法院得以衡平法的禁止反言(Promissory estoppel)原則， 解釋相對人法律地位是否實質變更或影響， 決定契約效力。❾

二、契約之解釋(Interpretation of Contract)

契約之訂立附帶口頭的補充或有不清楚的條款時，到底如何探知當事人真意，除了以法律規定來排除當事人真意，下列方法常會被用來闡明當事人之真意，當事人之真意不若刑法，側重主觀犯意，而以信賴、善意與客觀原則，推論是否成立有效契約。茲分述契約解釋適用順序如下：

㈠法律強行規定(Rule of Law)

若法律有所規定，不論當事人如何規定，違反法律強制規定，其約定無效。很多外商到大陸(PRC)投資簽定的契約，常與法律規定不符而失效。因此，法律之規定得部分或全部排除當事人真意。

㈡契約明示的條款規定(Plain Meaning Rule)

在不違反法律強行規定之下，我們只斟酌契約條款的明文規定解釋，有規定者方適用，無明示規定，則無適用之餘地。此種明示條款是一種嚴格解釋方法(strict interpretation)，只解釋契約條

---

❽　Dickinson c. Dodds, 2 Ch. Dir. 463 (1876).

❾　Ryer v. Wescoat, 535 S.W. 2d. 269 (1976).

款中，四個框框角落之內容而已(Four Corner rule)。擴充或限制解釋是禁止的。

㈢當事人真意(Party's Real Intent)

當事人之真意可能涉及擴充或限制解釋，這是較自由的解釋(liberal interpretation)。但當事人之真意也可能由履行交易過程和商業習慣之一致性，而被排除適用。

㈣履行過程(Course of Performance)

契約條款的一致性解釋，得依履行期間之交易次數而有不同。若當事人已有好幾次的商業往來，每次履行的過程條件均同，若發生糾紛時，法院或當事人得依過去幾次履行過程，判決或主張履行過程中一貫作法之解釋。美國統一商法典(U.C.C.) 2-208 (1)對此作了下列的說明："Where the contract for sale involves repeated occasions for performance by either party with knowledge of the nature of the performance and the opportunity for objection to it by the other, any course of performance accepted or acquiesced in without objection shall be relevant to determine the meaning of the agreement."

㈤交易過程(Course of Dealing)

交易過程指在一次交易中有好幾次階段或時期。每一個的階段或時期交易均相同或類似之行為。交易當事人得依據該契約其中某個階段交易，說明解釋其他階段性時期的交貨條款，應具相同解釋等問題。UCC1-205 (1)對此亦有說明：Course of dealing is a sequence of previous conduct between the parties to a particular transaction which is fair to be regarded as establishing a common basis of understanding for interpreting their expressions and

other conducts."

㈥商業使用習慣(Trade Usage)

當踏入新的領域或行業時，我們必需特別注意當地或世界性商業使用習慣，例如國際信用狀統一條例(Uniform Customs & Practice for Documentary Credit or U.C.P.)；例如某國或該當地亦有其特別的交易使用習慣等。UCC1-205 (2)亦有說明："A usage of trade is any practice or method for dealing having such regularity of observance in a place, vocation or trade as to justify an expectation that it will be observed with respect to the transaction in question. The existence and scope of such usage is embodied in a written trade code or similar writing the interpretation of the writing is for the court."

㈦主要目的說(Main Purpose Rule)

契約的成立有其主要目的。法條之解釋常溯及立法之主要目的和原意(Legislative Purpose and Intent)。

㈧實質和程序的合致與不合致(Substitutive and Procedural Meeting of Minds)

一契約條款若有隱藏性的不明確點(Latent ambiguity)，則無當事人之合致(No meeting of minds)，因為雙方當事人在訂約當時，均不知此隱藏不明確點(latent ambiguity)，這是一種實質上的不合致；程序上的沒有合致(procedural no meeting of minds)，指原告未能舉證當地的交易習慣等，而導致整個契約沒有合意。

三、要約和撤回(Offer and Revocation)

要約(offer)之當事人稱為要約人(Offeror or Offerer)，其相對人為要約相對人或承諾人(Offeree)。要約得向特定人(specific one)或向不特定人為之(general public)。通常要約以言詞、行動或書面為意思表示。要約和要約之引誘(Invitation to offer or treat)不一樣，在未進入正式要約前，有些動作只稱得上要約之引誘而已，引誘承諾人（或要約相對人）與之交易。例如，報紙廣告引誘不特定承諾人與之交易，若原承諾人提議承諾時，其法律地位變成要約人，而原要約人之地位變成承諾人。要約之引誘至多屬於一種準備工作，是否達成雙方意思表示之合致，有賴更進一步之要約。要約價錢、履行時間、標的物、交貨條件和方式等皆需明確。例如自動販賣機之設置，拍賣(auction)只是引誘路人來觀賞並非要約，等路人進場喊價時，這旁人所說的價錢方視為要約。因此很多從事商業活動的生意人，常利用廣告或拍賣，化被動成主動，使自己原本位居要約人的身分，透過要約之引誘，轉換為決定權之要約相對人或承諾人。常見要約之引誘廣告，如價目表之寄送(quotation)、傳單(circulars)、貨物之陳列(display of goods)[我國視為要約]、標售(bid)、拍賣(auction)等。另火車表和國際貿易之預約（期）發票(Proforma Invoice)，則視為正式之要約。國際貿易裡除了fax order外，最好應有確認書和再確認書(Confirm and reconfirm by purchase order)，賣方應要求一份正式書面契約，以防日後法律問題之滋生。

　　要約一定要通知或到達要約相對人之處所。非對話要約採到達主義(receipt or arrival rule)，信件承諾則採發信主義(Dispatch rule)。交錯之要約(或承諾)不能視為意思表示之合致。要約之直接撤回，必需在要約相對人未承諾前撤回（銷）(revocation)，且該撤回必需通知相對人(communication)。因此要約人得隨時在承諾

人未承諾前撤回要約。間接撤回(indirect revocation)有時亦發生撤回效力。例如要約相對人由可靠之消息中獲知要約已被撤回。若承諾人欲拘束要約人，則可運用選擇權(option)來行使之，惟該選擇權必需付出「對價或約因」，例如支付一些錢，要求要約人於某期間內，不得撤回要約。除了要約之撤回，下列原因為要約消滅的原因：⑴承諾期限已過(lapse of time)；⑵要約人死亡(death of offeror)；⑶要約人間接之撤回(Indirect revocation)；⑷要約相對人死亡(death of offeree)；⑸要約之拒絕(rejection by offeror)。 ❿

　　要約之拒絕包括⑴直接明示的拒絕；⑵暗示的反要約(counter offer)。反要約為一新要約(new offer)，原承諾人（相對人）變為要約人，而原要約人變為承諾人。常見要約相對人即承諾人於承諾時，條件式承諾(conditional or qualified acceptance)。不同條件承諾是否為契約之一部分或反要約，需視條件或增加新的不同條款(additional terms)， 是否為契約重要之點(essence or root of contract)，若是重要之點，一般被視為反要約，不得為契約之一部分；反之若條件或新增條款非重要之點，則得視為契約之一部分。若兩邊當事人均為個人時(Individuals)，條件或新增條款會被視為反要約，若交易人為商人，則有可能新增條款為契約之一部分，但該新增條款不公平損害至一方的經濟利益(unduly burden)時，通常該部分不得成為契約之一部分。

四、承諾與拒絕(Acceptance and Rejection)

　　承諾需依要約所提示的方法來承諾，不得附有其他的條款或條件或為不明確的承諾。一個承諾附帶不明確且存有其他目的，

---

❿　何孝元著：《中國債法與英美契約之比較》，頁34～36。

則此承諾並不拘束要約人，因此承諾必需視其主要要約內容，不得附加條件，方符合要約明示所要求之內容(unequivocal refer-able)。 若承諾附有其他條件，則稱為附條件承諾(conditional or qualified acceptance)。此時附條件承諾，視為要約之拒絕(rejection)或新要約(new offer)。在個人間(Individuals)之交易中，附條件的承諾常被視為新要約； 商人間(merchants)之交易裡，如附加條款為非必要之點或並無使對方承受經濟負擔，得視為契約之一部分。

　　沉默(silence)不得推定為承諾，但在履行或交易過程中或商業使用習慣，曾視沉默為默示承諾者，則從其約束。原則上，沉默不得視為承諾，但下列情形不在此限：⑴履行過程中有「沉默即承諾」之事實(course of performance)；⑵交易過程中有「沉默即承諾」之事實(Course of dealing)；⑶商業使用習慣(Trade usage)；⑷行為明示「沉默即承諾」(Assent manifested by conduct)；⑸明白表示願受「沉默即承諾」之拘束(intent to be bound)；⑹沉默時已佔人便宜或已受領利益(receive benefits)。 例如業務員將洗髮精置放你家中門外，留言三日後再回來拜訪。你拿回並於沐浴時使用之，此時你並未為承諾，惟此時承諾之沉默即等於承諾，因你已受領利益，將洗髮精消耗了。

　　承諾原則上需通知對方(notice of communication)。 但非對話間的承諾，尤以書信之承諾，美國採發信主義(Dispatch rule)， 即只要把正確住址之承諾信投入信箱，即承諾生效(Effective upon posting or dispatch)， 有人稱為信箱規則(mail box rule)。 除非在要約裡，已指示排除發信主義之適用，例如承諾必需採到達要約人辦公室為生效條件。若承諾前附有選擇權(option)時，承諾人得拘束要約人對於某時期內不得撤回要約(irrevocable offer)，此時承諾

人若能證明已經部分履行契約(partial performance)或已開始履行(begin to perform)或甚至提出履行(tender to perform)，則選擇權可依合理信賴(justifiable reliance)與禁止反言(promissory estoppel)等公平原則，使要約人不得撤回要約。若於選擇權期間內，先撤回選擇權後復表明欲再行使選擇權時，法院承諾只要在選擇權契約所指定的期限內，並不損承諾之效力。

承諾得依下列方式消滅：⑴承諾人之拒絕(rejection by offeree)；⑵要約期限屆滿(expiration of time in offer)；⑶要約人或承諾人之死亡(death of offeree or offeror)；⑷要約人撤回或撤銷要約(revocation by offeror)；⑸標的物之滅失(destruction of subject matter)。 ⓫

五、約因或對價

約因是一種法律對價交換，一方可能獲有利益，他方受有損失之情形。若一方引誘他方從事某一種行為或不作為，要求一方放棄法律上之權利，即為對價或對價之一種。約因或對價可能是一種容忍，例如，經妥協或和解不以訴訟解決。約因會造成每個人法律上之地位變動。無約因的契約，即使有承諾和要約，契約亦為無效。情愛因素(love or affection)所為之要約，沒有對價要約，過去的約因(past consideration)，亦不能支持契約對價之完整性。贈與、假約因例如一元之給付、道德上義務(moral obligation)、履行自己本來就應該做的事(do what one is obliged to do)，亦無約因。除非依當時情況，有不可預測之事件或合理正當之原因，否則任

⓫ Ryer v. Wescoat, 535 S.W. 269 (1976); Lively v. Tabor, 341 Mo. 352, 107 S.W. 2d. 62 (1937).

何事後的修改契約內容(subsequent modification without consideration)，均視為沒有約因。

六、過去之約因(Past Consideration)

約因是一種相互間現時的對價交換，一方拘束他方作為或不作為的交易。此相互間交易並非無償贈與或一方純獲經濟利益，是否有彼此的交換承諾條件，導致他方喪失現時具有法律價值的犧牲，此稱為對價或約因。若要約誘使交換過去的對價(past consideration)，無實際之約因。例如，老闆為了感激員工過去的忠貞，願在聖誕節給付$5,000的贈與金。此承諾尚不得強制執行，因贈與係建立在過去的勞務上；警察幫忙遺失物所有人找回遺失物，遺失物所有人承諾之獎金約定，仍因無對價而為無效。❷例如，同意替他人償還已破產後之債務(promise to pay indebtedness discharged in bankruptcy)為欠缺約因或對價之承諾。

道德的約因(moral consideration)，亦不得強制執行。基於道德的考量，子女為父母的親戚償還債務，亦同。但若有部分履行且具有過去的約因，則可能會使該要約成為得強制執行的標的。

過去的約因多為過去存在的交換條件，並沒有新的約因介入，除非雙方當事人合意舊的契約已經廢除(old contract abrogated)或過去的約因，因道德的考量而故意回復舊的約因(revived)，❸該新的要約或承諾，仍得視為具有拘束力。

---

❷　Gray v. Martino, 91 N.J.L. 462, 103 A. 24 (1918).

❸　Angel v. Murray, 113 R.I. 482, 322 A. 2d. 630 (1974).

七、 口頭證據(Parol Evidence)

一般人總以為口說無憑，因此有很多人常以對方沒有書面證據，故意或惡意規避契約之效力。因此有防止詐欺條例(Statute of Fraud)之出現，舉凡保證(Surety)、為第三人償還債務之承諾、結婚、不動產買賣、動產逾$500之買賣(U.C.C.規定)、租賃逾一年之租約、遺囑等，均規定必須以書面為主。沒有書面，不得約束其契約效力。但往往在完整契約訂立時或訂立前，當事人可能有口頭或書面的約定，這部分的約定可否成為完整契約之一部分？訂約時或訂約以前口頭或書面部分(prior or contemporaneous statement)，是否與此完整契約衝突或抵觸(contradiction)，若有抵觸時，該部分不得視為契約之一部分；若沒有抵觸時且此約定係用附帶以補充說明完整契約(integration)之一部分或模糊不明條款， 該補充或釋明約定(口頭或書面)得視為該完整契約之一部分，不需新的約因或對價。 口頭證據(parol evidence)不得視為完整契約之一部分，除非該不同條款有新的約定或對價支持。因此，口頭證據得被視為契約的一部分，不需新的獨立約因介入。口頭證據常被用來解釋交易過程、履行過程和商業使用習慣，亦得被用來證明當事人之詐欺(fraud)、脅迫(duress)、惡意(bad faith)、欠缺約因對價(lack of consideration)等情事。

八、交易過程和習慣(Course of Dealing, Performance and Trade Usage)

契約交易過程中，若有先前之交易行為或交易中，有數階段時，法院會以交易過程、履行過程及商業使用習慣之一致性，加以判斷是否為有效之契約。實務上之推定行為，若一交易中有好幾次的交易，而且交易雙方彼此認知交易之條款或慣性，任何先前交易中承諾或默示的事實，均得被法院依相關主題，探討該交易之有效性。若一交易中有數階段的交易，則每階段的交易過程，亦可被法院用來解釋本契約之效力。商業使用習慣常被用來決定本契約是否有效的指標。這些解釋係以推定(construction)的方式，解釋該契約之有效性與否。

九、錯誤、不可能及虛偽不實之陳述(Mistake、Impossibility and Misrepresentation)

錯誤是規避契約效力的一種抗辯事由。倘雙方當事人的錯誤，涉及契約重要之點(heart of subject matter or essence/root of contract)，則該契約欠缺雙方之合致合意，契約不生效力。單方面錯誤，則不能構成解約事由，除非該錯誤係雙方面的錯誤。

不可能事由，基本上有二種。第一種為客觀不可能(Objective impossibility)，第二種為主觀不可能(Subjective impossibility)。主觀的不可能，不得為抗辯事由之一，因為契約的構成要件，建立在客觀的情事上，主觀不能不是客觀不能，只要客觀上可能的話，具有一點點可能仍是可能，並非完全的不可能。客觀不可能涵蓋不可預見的天災、人禍與事變。常見的有經濟上極不可能原因(economic impracticability)及目的不能(frustration of purpose)。前者指標的物因天災而減少或滅失；後者指買賣主要目的已消滅。訂約人於訂約時，皆無法預見該介入的原因事實，致使買賣標的之給付不能。

例如，蝗蟲吃掉了整田的稻米；國王因病取消了遊行，致使

觀賞人取消飯店陽臺之房間預約。

另有一些不可能事由，係因主觀不滿意所致，但該不滿意須為主觀善意的不滿意，方能構成抗辯事由(Dissatisfaction in good faith)。

錯誤時得撤銷其意思表示。若單方面錯誤，不得為撤銷之事由。例如自己一方估價錯誤，仍須負擔商業上之損失風險。但若錯誤涉及實質上或目的上的不可能，則得構成解約或撤銷事由，除非依照公開調查，一方應可明顯發現對方的標的物有瑕疵或不符其需求；投資人以股票市場之評論作為投資之指標，不得以實質財務報告錯誤理由而要求撤銷買賣，因評論只是一種「言論」而已。假設錯誤並未涉及必要之點，更不得視為實質錯誤。

虛偽不實之陳述有下列三種：(1)無心的不實陳述(Innocent misrepresentation)；(2)過失之不實陳述(Negligent misrepresentation)；(3)故意不實陳述。這三者中以(3)最為嚴重。例如，房屋明明有白蟻，賣主卻隱藏，在美國不動產買賣中，都會有一項關於白蟻條款，由於美國的房屋大多是木造的，因此惡意隱瞞白蟻事實，可構成故意不實虛偽陳述。❹若一方與有過失，但非惡意虛偽不實陳述，則損害賠償責任，得相對減低。但故意或惡意隱藏事實，則如同瑕疵擔保責任，須負通知義務，否則應負損害賠償。

若雙方當事人均合意重訂契約，則得以書面重新簽定契約(Reformation)。故有錯誤、詐欺、脅迫，亦可行使撤銷(revocation)權，解除契約(rescission)。

---

❹　Obde v. Schlemeyer, 56 Wash. 2d. 449, 353 P. 2d. 672 (1960).

十、情事變更事宜(Changed Circumstances)

情事變更涉及危險負擔問題(Risk of loss)。危險負擔到底在那個時候轉嫁，需視契約的規定與一般法律見解。標的物滅失時，若買方已接受貨物標的物，買方應負擔危險責任；若買方未接受交付標的物前，危險負擔仍在賣方。❶財產法中以買方是否占有(obsession)或法律所有權(title)是否移轉，來判斷危險負擔點。買賣中，倘買方係一般人，在未占有標的物前，不負危險負擔。若買方為商人時，則於準備履行時(tender)或指示交付，危險負擔已轉嫁之。

情事變更有時係因法律不能，雙方遇有不可預見之事件，致使履行契約非常困難，危險負擔由一方轉嫁至他方時，這種不可抗力的事件(force majurer)，得構成解約之原因。不可抗力原因，通常為契約中未明示，且該不可抗力原為商業上極不可能發生的原因事實。因此如何規避這些不可能事由，當事人在簽約時必須注意。以下方式可供參考，以避免危險負擔：⑴多問幾家廠商(shop around)；⑵以書面明定不可抗力條款，載明有關危險負擔時點；⑶明定雙方互相分擔危險負擔；⑷隨時注意履行過程；⑸多利用商務仲裁(arbitration)解決紛爭；⑹利用管轄法院及準據法適用法律來控制履行過程；⑺仔細審閱法律文件，以期減少法律上之錯誤。

十一、契約之實質履行(Substantial Performance)

當契約已接近完全履行階段前，可能構成實質履行，對方若

---

❶ Stees v. Leonard, 20 Minn. 494 (1874).

在此時違約，應負擔損害賠償。若僅部分履行時(Partial performance)，得依準契約(quasi contract)行為，請求原告提供之勞務報酬
(services rendered)，以避免被告不當得利。實質履行指信賴對方要
求，持續履行契約，直至接近完成，但不一定以百分比(%)是否過
半，來計算是否具備實質履行階段，基本上已逾契約重要之點時，
得視為實質履行，但必須以善意為原則。實質履行原則另一目的，
在避免他方違約，致使經濟上浪費(economic waste)。例如建築營
造契約得採實質履行原則。若契約涉及個人主觀滿意或美感觀點
時(personal taste or aesthetic)，而非有關物之實用性(thing of utili-
ty)，實質履行原則不適用之。若有一方已屆實質履行該契約階段
時，他方之損害賠償為若非違約時之價值與完全履行契約間之價
值之差額(difference in value)。大多數的建築營造契約，均採實質
履行契約原則，此因建築營造係一工程複雜的雜項綜合工作，定
作人(owner)不得因一點點不滿意或瑕疵，要求承攬人(contractor)
重新再建，故一般建築工程契約，只要符合實質履行階段，該契
約即為有效(substantial compliance)，但其他非建築營造契約，如
以個人主觀滿意為契約條款之重要之點，應符合履行至100%主觀
滿意為生效要件(strict compliance)，即附停止條件，契約履行義務
人不得以已符合實質履行階段，要求對方給付報酬。

十二、條　件(Condition)

條件可分為下列四種：⑴附停止條件(Condition precedent)；
⑵附解除條件(Condition subsequent)；⑶附同時履行條件(Condition concurrent)；⑷滿意及不滿意條件(Satisfaction and dissatisfaction condition)。附停止條件指某一事件(contingency)或條件(condi-

tion)發生成就時，契約生其效力。訂約當時，契約已簽訂，但效力尚未發生，必須等該條件（即該事件）成就時，效力方真正生效。例如，若考上東吳大學法律系，我給你100萬，契約已簽訂，但效力尚未發生，100萬之贈與必須等你考上東吳大學法律系方生效。附解除條件，指某一事件（或條件），在簽訂契約時已發生效力，但等該條件成就時，失其效力。例如，我先給你100萬，若被大學退學，則退還我100萬。契約效力在簽約時已發生，但在該條件（被退學）成就時，整個契約失效，先前贈與之100萬之法律行為失效。附停止條件大多為正面或積極肯定的條件，而附解除條件多為負面或消極否定的條件。附同時履行條件，是一種同時履行推定的條件，一方交付貨物時，他方推定同時履行交付價金。雙方的義務是同時的，具有同時履行抗辯之權利義務。滿意和不滿意條件為一種主觀的條件。一方欲主張不滿意時，主觀上必須是善意的。❶主觀上的滿意或不滿意(personal taste or aesthetic)方能構成解約之原因，否則一方主觀上惡意或故意佯稱不滿意，如該物仍具實用性時，常造成規避法律責任的藉口，此時會造成很多不公平情況，即所謂的Illusory promise or naked promise。例如，上餐廳時與老板約定，若我覺得牛肉麵很好吃，我才付錢。契約基本上採客觀標準(Objective standard)探測當事人之真意，但在不滿意條款中，法院允許個人主張主觀善意不滿意(subjective dissatisfaction in good faith)作為抗辯事由。例如，一個鋼琴家於試彈鋼琴時，主觀上不滿意，因而決定不買。實務上，法院多以utility(實用性)或個人之善意主觀滿意度，判斷契約條件。

---

❶　Morion bldg. Products Co. v. Baystone Construction, Inc. 717 F. 2d. 413 (1983).

違反條件得要求解約(recission)或拒絕履行契約(repudiation)或要求損害賠償。但違反契約條款時，只能要求賠償(damages)。回復原狀之救濟(Restitution)，不適用已逾實質履行之契約。明示的附停止條件，又稱明示同意條件(Express permitting)，該條件所要求的事件必須先發生，契約方生效力，但被告先拒絕履行或原告自動放棄權利(forfeiture)，不在此限。若被告在訂約後履行契約前，先行表明事前違約(anticipatory breach)，原告有下列選擇權利求償：⑴勸對方不要違約；⑵不理會對方；⑶馬上向被告訴訟；⑷等契約期間屆滿，再告被告違約。

附解除條件通常有隱喻暗示允許不可能因素為解約事由，例如實質上商業不可能原因(房屋經火焚成平地致無法交屋)及天災人禍事變等(implied condition subsequent on impracticability or impossibility)。

十三、履行順序(Order of Performance)

履行契約之順序，法院通常以探討履行過程(course of performance)為契約解釋之第一順位，次而探討交易過程(Course of dealing)，再探討商業使用習慣(Usage of trade)。例如，判斷沉默是否為承諾時，法院以履行過程中有否相同或相類似的沉默即承諾情事，若無，則再看交易過程中，有否相同或相類似的情況，最後如不能探求當事人之真意時，再視商業上是否有特別之使用習慣，來解釋契約條款或適用法律。

十四、法律賠償(Damages)

一般司法救濟可分二種，即法律上的救濟，如金錢賠償(monetary damages)及衡平法的救濟(equitable remedy)，例如強制特別履（執）行(Specific performance)及禁止令(Injunction)。一般損害賠償區分為三大類：⑴回復原狀(Restitution damages or status quo)；⑵信賴所受之損害賠償(reliance damage)；⑶期待利益(Expectation damage)。回復原狀為一般的賠償原則，即雙方當事人恢復訂約前的地位(precontract status)。若一方信賴他方所付出的實際損失，得要求對方損害賠償，又稱實際的損失(actual or out-of-pocket loss)，這種損害賠償，借用侵權行為(tort)原則，填補損失為前提，以實際損失作為信賴賠償計算方法。期待利益係一種對方可預見將來之違約，致使他方遭受本約和本約相關衍生的損失之損害，作為賠償計算方式。若要求之期待利益太浮濫或以想像力(speculative)為依據，法院多不會判決期待利益。這三種計算方式因州而異。大部分的人，喜歡以期待利益作為損害賠償請求。茲舉一例，A產品的賣方廠商，向買方堅稱A產品價值$100，而實際契約價格，卻以$80成交，買方付$20訂金後，發現市價才值$90，若賣方違約時，買方之損害賠償，依上述之計算方式，買方得選擇⑴恢復原狀：即賣方返還買方訂金$20;⑵信賴所受之損害賠償:$10 ($90–80)；⑶期待利益賠償: $20 ($100–80) 。其計算式如下：

Represented price	$100	Deposit: $20
Actual price (contract)	90	
Market price	80	
Restitution:	$ 20	
Reliance:	$ 10 ($90–80)	
Expectation:	$ 20 ($100–80)	

綜上，回復原狀，類似於準契約，回復到契約未訂前之地位(pre-contract status)，一方獲有不當得利時(unjust enrichment)，他方受有損害(detriment)，受利益者應返還所得利益，例如，返還訂金等。信賴利益以契約彷若沒有執行，來計算損害賠償基礎(Had the contract never performed or existed)。期待利益賠償，則以彷若該契約已被履行來計算損害賠償基礎(Had the contract performed or existed)。有些人以Consequential damages涵蓋間接可預見損害賠償，包含附帶賠償(incidental damages)。約定違約賠償又稱逾期違約賠償(Liquidated damage)，指雙方無法於訂立契約當時，精準計算出違約金時，而以成數(通常以總價金之10%)或公式計算違約金。但倘該違約金之比例，佔總金額過高比例時，法院得視為懲罰性違約金(punitive damages)，而將該違約金賠償條款，解釋為無效條款(void)。

十五、特別履行(Specific Performance)

強制特別履（執）行令(writ of specific performance)在早期英國時，法院認為，若沒有其他救濟方法可供救濟或標的物非常的特殊(specific or special)時，或個人勞務提供案件，法院通常給予特別履行令，而非給予法律賠償(damages)。一般不動產交易，均被視為特別或特殊之標的。不動產買賣的糾紛中，法院極可能會判給買方強制特別（執）履行令，強制執行該不動產買賣。這是一種衡平法的救濟。另一種救濟為禁止令(writ of Injunction)。禁止令通常禁止違約者(breaching party)不得某些作為或要求其不作為(omission)。一般的勞務契約，法院通常不會給予強制特別履（執）行令，而改以禁止令代之。因為勞務之提供，涉及專業或提供勞務之人，具有非常特殊身分或具有不可代替性時，該違約勢必影響契約之信賴利益。若提供勞務之人，因緊急事情或生病，無法履行契約時，法院強制特別履（執）行，於法於理均不公平。例如，Michael Jackson答應來臺作危險之旅(dangerous tour)的演唱會，屆時通知因病無法前來臺北，法院可否強制Michael Jackson到臺履行演唱會？若強制特別履行對一個真正生病之人，要求其抱病參加演唱，有違公平原則。因此最好的方式，是向法院改聲請禁止令，若Michael Jackson根本沒有生病，且故意違約，得聲請禁止令，禁止他在亞洲其他地區的演唱會，這種救濟應較可行。

　　若一方於他方違約時，可藉由其他管道獲有救濟時，例如金錢賠償(Damages)，即使是不動產之交易，法院亦不會給予特別履行令，因為已有足夠其他方式彌補損害賠償之救濟，另一原因，為法院根本很難隨時監督不動產建築之整個過程。

十六、瑕疵擔保(Warranty)

　　除了物和權利之瑕疵擔保外，一般物之瑕疵擔保責任區分三種：⑴明示的瑕疵擔保(Express Warranty)；⑵一般商品的瑕疵擔保(Warranty of merchantability)；⑶特殊目的的瑕疵擔保(Warranty of fitness for particular purpose)。茲分述如下：

　　⑴指明示的保證，例如經由樣品(Sample)，清楚表示與樣品相同性質產品而承受瑕疵擔保責任;⑵指一般商品適用的瑕疵擔保，例如，菜刀的一般用途或功能應能切菜，若此菜刀不能切菜，則違反一般商品的瑕疵擔保責任;⑶指特殊目的的瑕疵擔保，例如，買方要一把特殊能砍木材的刀（開山刀），係一種特殊功能的刀，而非一般的菜刀，其目的是砍木材之用，若開山刀經賣方擔保，

能適合某特殊目的（砍木材），但卻無法用來砍木材，賣方即違反特別目的的瑕疵擔保責任。

以前的瑕疵擔保責任，常常建立在「貨物出門，概不退換」之立場，因此早期的買方購物時，要特別注意，注意該物是否有瑕疵，否則一拿回貨物，則回天乏術，甭想換貨。那個階段稱為「買方注意」(Caveat emptor)的時代。直到最近方有一些法律，例如消費者保護法、民商法把瑕疵擔保責任加諸在賣方身上，因此又稱「賣方注意」(Caveat venditor)的時代。通常賣方於出售物品後，在某個期間內，仍需負擔產品無瑕疵之責任。歐美早已有「無過失」之產品責任(no-fault product liability)，消費者不論是否有過失，得在指定的期限內，無條件退回該物，不必說明任何理由。臺灣目前的消費者保護法第十九條，對於街頭訪問或郵購物品，亦改採無過失主義，買方得於買入物品後七天內任意退回。

十七、債權讓與和債務承擔(Assignment & Delegation)

一般的債權讓與，指讓與人(Assignor)將對債務人(Obligor)之債權（權利與義務），概括轉讓給受讓人(Assignee)。但該債權讓與涉及當事人特約禁止轉讓、債之性質不得讓與、債權禁止扣押、相當特別的個人勞務、專屬需求契約(Requirement contract)、專屬供應契約(Output contract)或讓與將導致債務人實質過度負擔時，則不得債權讓與。債權讓與應有明確的表示，受讓人應向債務人為債權讓與之通知。債務承擔，指原債務承擔人(Obligor or Delegator)把債務（義務）轉給受讓承擔債務人承擔(Delegate)。

原則上契約上之權利均得讓與，義務債務均得受讓承擔。當事人亦得以特約禁止轉讓，但法律明文禁止承擔者，不在此限。

例如特殊債權性質或足以實質改變債權人期待利益的債務承擔，不得任意轉讓承擔。債權人若沒有正當理由，必須接受原債務人將債務(義務)讓給第三人承擔，除非該承擔實質改變契約內容。債務承擔人(Delegate)於承擔債務和契約義務後，變成第一順位之主債務人，原先債務人(Delegator)，則變成第二順位之保證人(surety)。臺灣民法第二九四條規定，當事人間禁止轉讓之特約不得對抗善意(good faith)第三人，常滋生法院認定「善意第三人」之困擾，於此一併說明。

十八、結　論

　　契約是一種雙方當事人意思表示之合致及合意。明確之要約創設接受承諾之拘束力，明確的承諾使要約人不得任意撤回要約。任何撤銷或撤回均以通知與到達對方為主。但非對話之書信承諾，美國採發信主義。構成要件中，若要約和承諾均無問題後，法院再依是否有對價關係，決定效力。若交易標的間並無對價或根本是贈與或假的對價時，整個契約因沒有對價而失去效力。除非對價有代替物，如衡平原則、法律損害性的信賴、書面契約、部分履行或禁止反言原則等替代對價約因要求，則可免除對價或約因之構成要件。除此之外，若契約條款不明時，法院得透過交易過程，履行過程或商業使用習慣，兼採論理解釋和文理解釋，於必要時擴充，限制解釋契約條款。如何訂立一份完整契約，應考慮訂約當時或之前之口頭證據(parol evidence)，若口頭證據並不與本契約抵觸，而係補充說明疑義或本契約尚未到達完整階段(integration)，致使有些條款需口頭或書面的補充或說明，則該口頭證據仍是有證據力。因此，附帶之口頭證據有時仍具效力。約因中

必需有獨立的對價，但若有不可預測的事由，基於公平原則，如
訂約後的善意變更修定原契約條款，仍得視為契約之一部分，並
不需新的或獨立的約因來支持訂約後的修改事宜。約因或對價建
立在要約和承諾間的互換，致使雙方地位在法律上發生變動。其
實，努力去找的話，約因在整個契約簽立時，應該可以覓尋得到。

　　臺灣僅在民法債編各論，分述各種契約型態，但根據契約自
由原則，可發展出混合型態契約，例如，租賃買回契約。如何寫
一份好的契約書，則有賴於平日之IRAC訓練、輔以經驗，深思當
事人權益，熟慮每一種可能之突發事變之預防和違約處理模擬，
必能擬定一份完美之契約，降低法律風險之發生。當簽擬一份契
約，於簽名前，應先仔細閱讀違約條款及損害賠償金額之計算方
式，而非匆匆簽名蓋章了事。英美法之契約與大陸法之契約之差
異，除了口頭證據、完整條款、發信主義、對價觀念等外，其實
仍見共通之處，即不論是國際商務契約或國內契約，每人均應仔
細閱讀每一條款，以免一失足成千古恨。

第五節　侵權行為法(Torts)

一、侵權行為

　　侵權行為法其實為債編之一種，但美國法律特別將侵權行為
與契約法區分之。

　　侵權行為法為民法之一種，美國侵權行為法，特別由契約法
中獨立出來。任何人若違反下列構成要件，即屬侵權行為之過失
(Negligence)：(1)法律義務責任(duty)；(2)違反法律義務責任(breach

of duty)；⑶損害及行為具有因果關係(Causation)；⑷損害結果發生(damages)。過失以「相對過失」及「與有過失」作為損害賠償依據。自願性承擔風險亦是抗辯事由之一。

二、侵權行為之種類

侵權行為之種類,得依對人身體之侵權與非身體之故意侵害,分類大致如下：(若情節重大，法院得給予懲罰性賠償) [punitive damages]

⑴威脅攻擊(Assault)：恐嚇他人致使其心生恐懼。

⑵毆擊(Battery)：對他人施以直接之肉體上之侵害。

⑶非法監禁(unlawful imprisonment)：①一定區域內②明知為要件③時間長短不相關。

⑷不動產之故意侵害(Intentional trespass to Land)←→動產之故意侵害(trespass to chattel)。

⑸危害(Nuisance)：①個人騷擾②公共騷擾（社區健康、安全或財產之公害）。

⑹毀謗(Defamation)：①口頭(slander)②書面(libel)。

⑺侵害隱私權(Invasion of privacy)：①非法使用他人姓名或照片供商業之用②侵入私人不願公開之事件③不實事實經公開④任何合理人(reasonable man)均會反對公開私人事件之情形⑤法律因果關係（抗辯事由：同意及豁免權）⑥得要求非財產（精神）損失⑦人死後繼承人不得提出侵害死人的隱私權。

⑻虛偽不實之陳述(Misrepresentation)：①無心②過失③故意（參見契約法）。

⑼非法致人於死(Wrongful death)

⑽非法致人於身體殘廢(Wrongful life)

⑾雇用人及場所主人責任(Respondent superior)：①受邀請人：invitee②被授權人：licensee (friend)③非法入侵者：trespasser。

⑿產品責任(Product liability)：①明示②默示③特殊目的（參見契約法）。

⒀故意造成他人精神沮喪(Intention infliction of emotional distress)：①加害人具有故意行為②加害人過失造成受害人等精神沮喪間具有因果關係③受害人具有親屬關係④加害人為惡意知情受害人之精神沮喪情形。

⒁過失造成他人精神沮喪(negligent infliction of emotional distress)：①旁觀者(bystander)必需證明在危險區域內②過失造成精神沮喪間具有因果關係存在③受害人間之親屬家屬關係已不重要（僅少數州採用）。

三、過　失

　　侵權之行為，行為人必需負連帶責任，損害賠償以金錢賠償為原則，填補被害人身體及精神賠償。行為人之過失之要件，為⑴法律上課以責任義務；⑵義務責任之違反；⑶行為與損害結果有相當之因果關係，即事實之因果關係（若非關係：but for test與實質因素關係：substantial factor）與法律因果關係（法律政策與公平原則決定是否為獨立之替代介入原因抑是非替代介入之法律原因）；⑷損害結果發生。目前美國對產品之責任已採無過失之產品瑕疵擔保責任（參見契約法第十六項）。消費者不需證明產品具有瑕疵，得於一定期間內，退回購買物，且不需說明原因或理由。注意義務在美國法律採可預見原告(foreseeable plaintiff)原則，　場所主人需負一定的義務。對非法侵入者，基本上不用負責，但對無知之小孩，應有特別告知危險之義務(child nuisance)，例如：游泳池應有警告或防護措施以避免小孩侵入；對於被授權人(licensee)，由於多為朋友，場所主人應主動「告知危險」之情況予不知情之被允許人或被授權人；受邀請人(invitee)，由於場所主人對受邀請人具有金錢往來之期待利益者，故責任與注意義務較高，除了「告知危險」外，應「修理檢查」其缺失之場所是否有安全標示。這些場所大多為公共場所。違反上述義務者，均屬侵權行為構成要件之過失。

四、因果關係

㈠民事之因果關係

一般的因果關係可分為：

1.事實原因的因果關係(cause in fact)

通常係指發生原因和結果有直接的關聯,若非該行為之介入,其結果可能會和不介入時不相同(But for test)。另原因和結果有二個以上的外力或因素(一般指人或行為之因素)介入時，但無法分辨究竟是那一因素造成時，如法院認定實質造成結果的人或因素負責(substantial factor test)。刑法的因果關係和侵權行為的因果關係相類似，但刑法之因果關係，則採較直接之因果關係說。

2.間接原因（或法律原因）之因果關係

此時外力因素以人之介入為主。間接原因可分為可替代的介入原因(superseding cause)和不可替代的介入原因 (non-superseding cause)。 通說以是否預見結果來判斷因果關係(foreseeability test)，但在實務上因果關係之運用，則常依立法政策，考量公平正

義來解剖複雜的因果關係。

　　原則上第三人之不法行為(criminal activity)、天災(act of God)與故意侵權行為(intentional tort) 為替代性的介入原因，得切斷原始第一個因素歸咎的責任，即這些介入人或物之行為(第二個介入因素)吸收取代了第一個原始因素的行為。但是有些原始第一因素行為若可預見，即使不能預見其特別結果，但可預見一般的結果(例如一般之傷害)， 則這些原因稱之為不可替代的可預見的原因，此時原來第一個原始因素的行為並未被後來介入之人或行為所吸收或取代，亦即原來第一個被告對其所造成的傷害或死亡結果仍需負責，例如預見他人自殺。

　　在間接或法律原因中如立法政策考量不切斷原來第一個侵害人之行為時,即視原來第一個侵害行為人對可預見結果發生行為,必須自負其責。常見的有因傷痛苦而自殺(commit suicide)； 旁人過失的解救(rescuer's negligence)， 但仍造成死亡結果； 車禍後傷勢加重而導致死亡結果(post-accident injury or post-accident aggravation of wound)； 高度危險之行為(highly dangerous act)。醫生之誤診(medical malpractice or wrong medicine given)， 則較眾說紛紜(split)。有學說認為誤診致死行為並不替代切斷原來第一個侵害人的行為。有學說認為醫生誤診為一替代性法律原因，切斷了原先侵權人的行為或原因。受害人得分別起訴原先的侵害人和後來疏忽誤診之醫生， 或起訴他們二者為共同被告。如何舉證誤診與死亡結果沒有因果關係， 是醫生之間的問題。但多數說認為，如傷口之發炎導致死亡之結果， 非醫生之誤診或藥物因素，基於立法理由，政策傾向不切斷原來侵害他人之因果關係責任。醫療過失多引用疫學因果關係判斷之。

綜上，死者受傷後本身的行為（例如被送入醫院後，自己把插管拔除而導致死亡；女受害人受到性攻擊，雖未至被強姦地步，但最後飲毒藥自殺），若在行為後但死亡或受傷結果前，不可能有外力或第三種替代行為或第三人之行為原因，則第一個侵害人仍依可預見推論，認定應受刑法制裁。若原始第一因素行為，而產生自然和可能的結果(Natural and probable of the result within chain of causation)，則符合因果關係之構成要件。刑法所要求的法律原因通常比侵權行為(tort)的法律原因還要嚴格，即要求更多直接的原因(more direct causation)。

　　事實原因(cause in fact)是以邏輯、實際經驗或哲學來判斷與行為之關連性，若非這個行為或不作為，結果可能會完全不一樣(But for test)。間接原因或法律原因(Legal or proximate cause)，則建立在立法政策之考量，即基於立法政策考量決定是否來聯結原因和結果是否具有因果關係。綜上，行為人可否預見未來發生的一般結果判斷。因果關係之存在，輔以立法政策、考量公平原則判斷其因果關係。以下實例揭示了因果相當性之複雜關連：

(1)甲射殺（打）乙，乙受傷躺在路上，一小時後乙被閃電擊斃，試問：乙之死亡結果和甲之行為是否具有因果關係？

　解析：無；因閃電為任何人皆不可預料之事件。

(2)甲射殺（打）乙，乙受傷躺在路上，丙之車於三分鐘後不小心壓到乙而造成乙之死亡結果，試問：乙之死亡結果和甲之行為是否具有因果關係？

　解析：有；受傷之人躺在路上，其死亡之危險性是高度具有可預見性。

(3)甲射殺（打）乙，乙受傷躺在路上，丙為醫生，見狀馬上為乙

做人工呼吸，由於搶救CPR不當，結果造成乙之死亡結果，試問：乙之死亡與甲之行為是否具有因果關係？

解析： 有；因為危險情形會引發急救情形，基於公共政策考量，宜鼓勵救助受傷路人，故因果關係不能切斷，甲仍需負責。惟丙是否因重大過失造成死亡之結果，屬丙之醫療過失問題。

(4)甲射殺（打）乙，乙受傷被送往丙醫院，最後死因是傷口細菌感染，試問：乙之死亡和甲之行為是否具有因果關係？

解析： 有；因為受傷病人被送往醫院是可預見的，且在醫院診療中發生死亡結果亦是可能預見的。

(5)甲射殺（打）乙，乙被送往醫院，乙因宗教信仰拒絕醫治而致死，試問：乙之死亡和甲之行為是否具有因果關係？

解析： 有；因為甲之射殺（打）行為為乙死亡之直接原因。若甲是故意殺人，則有殺人罪之嫌。

(6)甲射殺（打）乙，乙受傷，痛不欲生，拿起手術刀割腕自殺，試問：乙之死亡與甲之行為是否具有因果關係？

解析： 有；因為醫院發生死亡結果為自然可能之原因而導致死亡。

(7)甲射殺（打）乙，乙受傷而痛不欲生，乙之太太丙見狀於心不忍，將乙身上人工維持生命養份之插管拔起，而導致乙死亡，試問：乙之死亡與甲之行為是否具有因果關係？

解析： 無；因拔管行為乃不法之行為，故替代原因切斷了甲之行為，丙之行為非為一般人所預見。

(8)甲和乙在高雄東帝士85樓決鬥，乙被甲拋下，掉至第60層樓時，剛好丙從窗戶丟一石頭準備打小鳥,石頭恰巧撞擊乙之太陽穴,法醫鑑定死亡原因是先頭部受創後再摔地而死，試問：乙之死亡與甲之行為是否具有因果關係?

解析： 有；因為把人從85樓推下，其死亡結果是可預見的。縱然人不可能死二次，即使丟石頭是不可預見的，基於公共政策考量人身安全，將人從高樓丟下，其不法行為造成極高死亡率，是自然可能預見的。

㈡刑事之因果關係

刑法上之過失，其過失行為與結果間，在客觀上應有相當因果關係，始得成立。所謂相當因果關係，係指依經驗法則，綜合行為當時所存在之一切事實，為客觀之事後審查，認為在一般情形下，有此環境、有此行為之同一條件，均可發生同一之結果者，則該條件即為發生結果之相當條件，行為與結果即有相當之因果關係。反之，若在一般情形下，有此同一條件存在，而依客觀之審查，認為不必皆發生此結果者，則該條件與結果並不相當，不過為偶然之事實而已，其行為與結果間即無相當因果關係(七六臺上一九二)。在法學上之因果關係並非自然科學上之因果關係，而係法律上之概念而指行為與結果之聯絡關係。⑰

我刑法以行為和結果是否有相當之因果關係判斷關連性，美國則要求結果是否係自然且可能由於該行為所造成(Natural and Probable results)判斷關連性。若肯定者，原始行為人或行為必須對其行為負責，即使未能很精確預測產生之狀況，但法律推定他能預見一般由於他的故意或過失行為，有可能造成一般之傷害即足。上述例子雖可能發生民法侵權與刑法罪名競合，基於刑法之

---

⑰　蔡墩銘，〈醫療犯罪與因果關係〉，《法令月刊》，民國八十四年，第9期，46卷，頁7～9。

推定人是無罪的假設，故刑法之因果關係遠較民法侵權行為嚴謹及慎重。

五、結　論

　　侵權行為以故意或過失為構成要件，有些情形得不證自明(things speak for itself)，藉由表面證據(prima facie case)推定損害之產生。對故意侵害之抗辯如下：(1)同意(2)正當防衛(3)防衛他人(4)防衛財產(5)必要之情況。因果關係區分(1)事實原因：①若非說(直接關係)、②實質因素說：若有實質因素時，由實質因素為真正直接原因；(2)法律原因：利用公平正義原則或公共政策評定是否為獨立法律原因。第三人之侵權行為或犯罪行為及天災人禍得為介入替代之原因(intervening superseding cause)，惟醫生護士誤診，被害人自殺，他人過失救助致使他人受有損害，仍不得謂介入替代之原因。

第六節　憲　法(Constitution Law)

一、美　國

㈠導　言

　　美國自1776年宣布獨立，建立民主共和國，於1787年制憲，通過第一部美國憲法，這是一部民有、民治和民享的政治制度。政府只是人民的服務機關，根據三權分立(separation of power)與制衡原理(check and balance)，行政立法司法三單位互相牽制且互相平衡。三權分立來自洛克、盧梭與孟德斯鳩之想法，總統、國會與法院三者共同治理國家，美國總統(President)為行政最高首長，政策法案需經國會參議院(Senate)和眾議院(House of Representative)表決通過，方得實行。最高法院(Supreme court)具有司法審核權(Judicial review)，國會雖依職權得通過法律，條約締結及預算削減為國會權限，但法院亦宣布任何法律違憲。

㈡聯邦政府(Federal Government)

美國是一個聯邦(Federal government)，而非單一國家。共有50州(states)組成美國。依據州自治原理(State autonomy)，全美除了聯邦法律之外，尚有50州的不同法律。聯邦和州各司其管轄權。聯邦管轄權，如宣戰、媾和、締約、外事政治活動、國際貿易、徵收稅款、郵政、商標、專利、著作權、海商案件、破產案件、訴訟標的逾$50,000元以上之案件、涉及聯邦問題、移民歸化、聯邦法院、武裝部隊之設立時，均屬聯邦管轄。其餘未規定事項，依美國憲法第10條修正案規定，本憲法所未授與中央或未禁止各州行使的權力，由各州或其人民保留之。州法院亦有解釋違憲之權，州本身亦有州的憲法和法令規章。

美國係採總統制之國家，總統為國家元首和行政首長，具有否決權(Veto right)。美國的政黨，主要有民主黨(Democratic party)和共和黨(Republican party)，每四年舉行一次全國代表大會，推舉各黨總統候選人。北方之州多屬共和黨，南方則一向為民主黨。民主黨主要政治理念，以尊重州權為主，認為最好之政府，是管事最少的政府，一切人民至上，例如自由貿易、開放關稅同盟、援助非洲、亞洲、觸角延伸歐洲大陸；共和黨則以工商人士為主，主張堅強的政府，高壁壘關稅、擴展國力至世界每一角落。每個人得自由選擇政治立場，全民強制醫療保險由民主黨提出，但導

致大部分的醫生步入共和黨之員。

二、國會(Congress)：立法部門(Legislative Branch)

美國的國會(Congress)採取兩院制，由參議員(The Senate)和眾議員(The House of Representatives)共同組成。參議員代表州，眾議員代表人民共同參加表決議案，相互制衡。例如，WTO案之表決應經二院表決通過。當兩院三分之二表決通過時，議案方能通過，再經總統公布後生效。眾議員必需滿25歲，且為美國公民七年，方得為眾議員，眾議院以各州人民每兩年所選舉之議員組織之，任期二年。參議員由各州州議會選舉，每州選舉參議員二人，任期六年，參議員年齡需滿30歲，且為美國公民滿九年。

兩院議員，除了犯有叛國罪(Treason)、重罪(Felony)、和妨害治安罪(Breach of peace)外，在各該院開會期間及往返途中，不受逮捕，各該院議員不得因其在議院內所發表之言論，於議院外負責。此所謂之「言論免責豁免權」。

凡兩院通過之法案，於成為法律前，需送請總統公布，總統如批准該案，即應簽署，否則應異議，交還提出該項法案之議院，該院應於接到異議書，詳載異議於議事錄，進行覆議。如有該院三分之二人數，同意通過該項法案，應即把該法案及異議書送交另一院以供覆議，如該院議員以三分之二人數同意時，該項法案即成法律。如法案於送達總統10日內，未經總統退還，即視為總統簽署，該項法案即成法律。惟國會因休會致該項法院不獲交還時，該項法案不得成為法律。例如，援外法原需經國會通過，但總統可以不公布使之失效，即行使否決權，但國會得再以三分之二的多數通過覆議案,最高法院亦可行使司法審查決定是否違憲。

國會的權限大致上有立法權、預算批准權、貨幣權、州與州之間的商業活動權、外交權（與總統共有）、執行管理權、司法權（下級聯邦法院之司法程序）、宣戰權、調查權、彈劾權、增加稅收權（眾議院才有）及同意權等。

三、總統(President)：行政部門(Executive Branch)

美國係採總統制的一個國家，內閣只是其參謀的一環，要當上美國總統，必需有赫赫有名之黨政經歷，例如州長或將軍，而且必需財力雄厚，如此人士方能透過黨之提名，不論是共和黨或是民主黨推舉總統候選人(President Candidate)，各代表以各州之名義，向大會提出候選人，最後看誰得到全體代表之大多數票源，即可被選為總統候選人，開始進行州際間之宣傳、演講和競選活動。

總統資格必需滿三十五歲及住在美國境內達十四年以上者，方能競選總統。其權限為三軍之統帥(commander in chief)、提名任命各行政部門長官、大赦權(pardon)、締結條約權、填補空缺職位、建議國會立法權、召集特別會議、接見外賓、處理國際事務、代表美國、彈劾文官等。惟美國總統並無宣戰權(declare war)，但有權製造戰爭(make war)，即如以三軍之統帥身分派兵至伊拉克或越南。

四、最高法院(Supreme Court)：司法部門(Judicial Branch)

美國的司法權，屬於最高法院及國會得隨時制定與設立之下級法院。所謂司法權，指法官在審判時，作成判決和執行法律之

權力。聯邦的法院有憲法的法院，例如最高法院、上訴巡迴法院、地方法院、海關及上訴法院、國家求償法院和海關法院等。另一種為立法性質的法院，例如軍事上訴法院和哥倫比亞特區之地方法院（兼具立法和憲法之性質）等。

最高法院有九位大法官(justice)，最高法院之判決為終局判決，為沒有陪審的法律書面審。其下的上訴巡迴法院，一共有十三個，每一上訴法院有三位法官（至少兩位法官聽審），亦不採陪審。聯邦地方法院為最下面的法院，共約九十七個，院內至少有一法官聽審。聯邦法官皆由總統提名經參議院同意任命。

聯邦法院之管轄權擴及外交官案件、海事與海商案件、涉及聯邦政府與州的案件、州際間的訴訟案件(diversity of citizenship)、州與外國間的訴訟、原始和上訴法院之管轄。

陪審制度(Jury)為美國之法律特色，刑事第一審法院由陪審員十二人組成，共同對被告犯罪之事實，經法官指示後，加以調查而作成評決(verdict)，而非由法官(judge)作成判決(judgment)。這十二人必需全體一致評決被告有罪或無罪；民事若系爭標的超過$20，得要求陪審評議(deliberation)。州之陪審，若輕罪得以六人陪審決定事實，若由十二人組成之陪審，有些州並不要求全數一致之評決，而以絕對多數評決，例如11:1或10:2或9:3來判斷事實。在美國法律，法官適用法律，為法律之終結者(law finder)，陪審員尋找事實，為事實的終結者(fact finder)。

五、司法審查(Judicial Review)

㈠聯邦司法審查：正當理由

聯邦最高法院對相關政府部門有司法審查權(Marbury v.

Madison (1803))。州法院若涉及聯邦問題，聯邦最高法院亦有司法審查權。因此法院是憲法最後之仲裁者。根據三權分立原則第三章(Article III)，聯邦法院僅處理由聯邦引發之案件(case)或爭論(controversy)。所謂案件或爭論係指當事人雙方對其法律權利有真正的衝突利益，且該利益對彼此會有拘束力。聯邦法院不得回答假設(hypothetical)或抽象(abstract)之法律問題，也不得提供諮詢意見(Advisory Opinion)。即便當事人雙方，彼此同意管轄權，聯邦法院仍不得行使管轄權。聯邦法院必需自我設限(self restraint on judicial review)，以免逾越了憲法第10條所保留賦予州之權利。

(二)不具爭議主義(Mootness)

聯邦法院不得決定不具爭論之紛爭。一案件被視為不具爭論時，法院得不對雙方當事人已不見任何影響之爭議判決。若爭議點不在，而只是一種學術或假設問題，法院若遽下斷言，則如同給予諮詢意見(advisory opinion)，有違憲之嫌。案件或爭論必需具爭議點，在每一階段均具有爭議性。

惟於集體訴訟(class action)中，雖然該集體訴訟案件之聲明已不具爭議，就相當大量的集體訴訟成員，仍視為具有爭議性；另一種例外為重覆出現之爭議，雖可暫時規避爭議，但此一問題爭議隨後再度發生，即具有爭議性。在Roe v. Wade (1973)之案例，雖然懷孕之原告在抗辯德州墮胎法違憲後，已產下子女，但該問題爭議，於訴訟繫屬中原告已不再懷孕，仍得視此爭議問題具有爭議性(Capable of repetition)。

(三)成熟主義(Ripeness)

聯邦法院不會去聽審任何未至成熟的案例。當一個紛爭不具成熟度，預見的損害將來不可能發生，其損害純屬臆測。故聯邦

法院得不予理會。

㈣適格主義(Standing)

　　適格指誰具有資格並以當事人能力參加訴訟。當事人是否適格，需以當事人對訴訟結果是否有影響力。憲法Article III§2要求當事人證明，該行為可能或由被告的行為，將會造成個人明顯之損害。

　　假使原告已證明其適格能力，他或她不得以第三人之權利支持其理論，但該原告與主張權利之人有充分之代表，而且有些問題涉及非當事人表達自己之能力將可能受損，不在此限(Barrows v. Jackson (1953))。

㈤政治問題(Political Question)

　　在Baker v. Carr. (1962)的案例，法院認為政治問題之特性在於憲法的明示規定，例如彈劾、修憲程序、軍隊事宜。司法不得干涉(non-justifiable)。但法院仍得對政黨選舉權劃分有管轄權(Davis v. Bandemer (1986))；法院對行政特權亦有決定範圍之權(United States v. Nixon (1974))。

㈥聯邦自制(Abstention)

　　基於禮讓原則(comity)，聯邦給予州自治(state autonomy)一個空間。若州法律尚未解決某一問題癥結，而且此一癥結解釋紛歧時，聯邦法院應自我抑制，應把當事人在聯邦的案件移至州法院去解決該州之尚未解決的問題。[18]最近美國的案例，顯示似乎允許聯邦法院關於未解決之爭端尋求州之證實(certification)，例如，要求州證實新修正禁止販賣成人書刊給未成年的法令相關範圍。[19]

---

[18]　Waldron v. McAtee, 723 F. 2d 1348 (7th Cir. 1983).

若聯邦法院被要求宣布州法律失其效力時，聯邦法院得考量聯邦與州之利益。例如：若州司法程序尚未繫屬，但問題已產生不可彌補之傷害(irreparable injury)，聯邦法院得依一般原則，發布確認判決(Declaratory Judgment)，並得發布預先禁止令補救(preliminary injunction) (Doran v. Salem Inn. (1975); Steffel v. Thompson (1974))；若州的利益在繫屬之中，上述二種方式不得發布，但有極大和直接的不可彌補損害發生，不在此限。例如州政府官員之惡意(bad faith)或騷擾(harassment)。 (Young v. Harris (1971); Middlesex Ethic Com'n v. Garden State Bar Ass'n (1982).) 另外聯邦法院不得介入州行政聽證會(State administrative hearing)。 (See Ohio Civ. Rights Com'n v. Dayton Christian School (1986).)

六、國會權限

依Article I第8條第3及第18款規定國會有權規定商事活動，並制定任何必需且適當的法律(necessary and proper)以便執行。這即所謂的商業條款(Commercial Clause)。 任何商業活動之變動或任何州際間，足以影響商業活動，國會均得立法管制。因此只要有合理的基礎(rational basis)用以支持國會立法，而且國會立法的手段可合理達成既定目標，這些制定的商業活動影響州際間之商業往來，國會均得立法。根據1938年合理勞工標準法令(Fair Labor Standards Act)，國會即立法州際間運輸貨物生產勞工的最低工資(minimum wage)或超工作時(working excess hour)相關法令。

㈠實質影響(Substantial Effect)

藉由必需及適當條款，國會得依商業活動具實質影響為由適

---

❶⑨ Virginia v. American Booksellers Ass'n, Inc. (1988).

時立法。(NLRB v. J. & L. Steel (1937); United States v. Darby (1941)). 國會並得依累積性的影響結果(Cumulative effect)對相關事宜立法。例如，國會立法小麥的生產力。(Wickard v. Filburn (1942)) 國會得以商業條款立法任何旅店、飯店,利用歧視性規定,足以影響州際間的商業活動。 (Heart of Atlanta Motel v. U.S. (1964))

惟在Nat'l League of Citics v. Usery (1976)的案例中,法院曾判決國會不得介入立法州勞工的薪資和工作時, 因該立法足以剝奪限制、州重要主權的完整性(essential sovereign integrity)。但此一原則已在 Garcia v. San Antonio Metropolitan Transit Authority (1985)被推翻。

㈡州商業之立法規定

州雖然有權立法該州的商業活動, 不過有下列限制: (1)優先及最高條款(Preemption and Supremacy Clause, Article VI); (2)商業條款之否定禁止解釋(The negative implication of the Commercial Clause); (3)州際間特權和豁免條款(The Interstate Privileges and Immunities Clause, Article IV, Section 2); (4)契約條款; (5)徵收條款(Taking Clause)。

1.優先與最高條款

若州法律和聯邦法律直接抵觸, 則依最高條款(Supremacy clause), 州法律為無效。即使州法律和聯邦法律並無直接抵觸或衝突, 國會依其立法意旨足以解釋其為管轄權, 則州法律亦會被解為無效(Pre-emption)。(C.T.S. Corp. v. Dynamic Corp. of America (1987)) 但若州法律提供比聯邦法律更有好的懷胎婦女的保護時, 則聯邦法律不會優先州法律, 因聯邦法律主要目的亦在保障懷孕婦女的權益，不會因為州法律提供比聯邦法律更優厚條件而把州法律解釋成無效。 (Calif. Federal Sav. & Loan Ass'n v. Guerra (1987))

2.商業條款之否定禁止解釋

國會商業條款主要目的，在避免州的經濟單位，因分歧而鬆散無力，故為求經濟利益的完整性，統一其經濟活動，俾使其發揮最大利益。但如此的規定並不得否定州關於提昇公共福利(public welfare)、公共道德(public morality)和公共健康(public health)之警察權(police power)目的。

假使國會的商業條款對於某些商業活動保持沉默，並任意放棄立法的權限，任何州立法足以引起不合理的歧視或造成他州經濟之不利益影響，依反面或否定禁止解釋，為維國家一致性的完整經濟利益，國會得禁止州立法(local affair against the national interest in uniformity and an integrated economy)(Cooley v. Bd. of Wardens. (1851))。

3.州際間特權及豁免條款

係建立在不得歧視美國公民（自然人）之立場。

4.契約條款

政府不得有立法任何損害當事人合法之契約權利(Contract clause)。

5.徵收條款

政府徵收應有合理之補償報酬(Taking clause)

㈢法律程序(Due process of law)

美國憲法賦予人民基本之權利，例如投票權、隱私權之保護，有限制之墮胎或安樂死、性別之喜好（同性戀）、自由旅行權利。

美國憲法對於種族、外國人及男女性別，不得未經一套合法之法律正當程序(due process of law)，專斷損害美國憲法所保障之權利。

㈣平等保障(Equal protection)

若人民之權利涉及重要之權利時，不得以種族(race)差別待遇，但政府若能提出調和州公共利益時，則不在此限(state compelling interest)。相同的，基本權利，如同法律程序保障之選舉權與旅行權，若有歧視則為違憲。憲法對基本權利，採用非常嚴格之監視(strict scrutiny)。對於外國人小孩之就讀美國學校權利之剝奪或性別之待遇歧異，憲法得以保護州重要利益(state important interest)，為適當之區分與限制(intermediary scrutiny)。對於外國人，薪資，智障，貧富問題，憲法賦予州得以合理之利益保護為由(rational basis)，適度立法限制之。綜上，本條款不得對上述權利有所歧視，但每一權利得適用不同標準分類，決定是否違憲。

七、美國憲法法條

刑事訴訟法的規定不得抵觸憲法之規定，任何抵觸之條文，皆為違憲(unconstitutional)。茲把美國保障被告權益相關憲法主要條文分述如下：

AMENDMENT I（第一修正案）

Congress shall make no law respecting an establishment of religion, or prohibiting the free exercise thereof; or abridging the freedom of speech, or the press; or the right of the people peaceably to assemble, and to petition the Government for a redress of grievance.

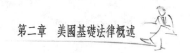

國會不得制定創設任何法律提倡宗教、禁止限制宗教信仰、自由行使權利、限制言論、新聞自由、禁止和平聚會及向政府請求損害賠償之權利。

AMENDMENT II（第二修正案）

A well regulated Militia, being necessary to the security of a free State, the right of the people to keep and bear Arms, shall not be infringed.

為維護自由國家安全，必要時得建立軍隊，使人民擁有軍械的權利，不得被侵害。（本條為美國人得擁有槍枝之憲法權利）

AMENDMENT III（第三修正案）

No soldier shall, in time of peace be quartered in any house, without the consent of the Owner, nor in time of war, but in a manner to be prescribed by law.

任何軍人在和平或戰時，不得未經其本人或所有人同意徵召入伍，但依法規定者，不在此限。

AMENDMENT IV（第四修正案）

The right of the people to be secure in their persons, houses, papers, and effects, against unreasonable searches and seizures, shall not be violated, and no Warrant shall issue, but upon probable cause, supported by Oath or affirmation, and particularly describing the place to be searched, and the persons or things to be seized.

任何人的住處、文件、及東西，應受到安全保障，不得受到

未具理由之搜索與扣押，此權利不得被違反而且未經可能原因或未為宣誓或證實前，不得發出搜索狀，搜索狀必需明確指定欲搜索之地、人或事。

AMENDMENT V（第五修正案）

No person shall be held to answer for a capital, or otherwise infamous crime, unless on a presentment or indictment of a Grand Jury, except in cases arising in the land or naval forces or in the Militia, when in actual service in time of War or public danger; nor shall any person be subject for the same offense to be twice put in jeopardy of life or limb; nor shall be compelled in any criminal case to be a witness against himself, nor be deprived of life, liberty, or property, without due process of law; nor shall private property be taken for public use, without just compensation.

任何人未經大陪審團提起公訴不得受死刑宣告或不名譽之罪，但因軍中服役陸軍或海軍而引起的犯罪案件，因戰爭或公共危險之服役，不在此限；任何人不得受二次相同的罪名宣告，即受二次危害；任何刑事案件，不得強迫證人陳述對其不利之言詞；任何人之生命、自由和財產，未經法律正當程序，不得予以剝奪。

AMENDMENT VI（第六修正案）

In all criminal prosecutions, the accused shall enjoy the right to a speedy trial and public trial, by an impartial jury of the State and district wherein the crime shall have been committed, which district shall have been previously ascertained by law, and to be informed of nature and cause of the accusation; to be confronted with the witness against him; to have compulsory process for obtaining witness in his favor, and to have the Assistance of Counsel for his defense.

在所有的刑事案件，被告有權要求迅速審判，接受州和地方法院之公開迅速審判，地方法院應依法確定並告知被告被控罪名性質及原因；並得要求當面對質；並得要求對他（她）有利之證人，強制傳喚出席；並得要求律師幫助之權利。

AMENDMENT VII（第七修正案）

In Suits at common law, where the value in controversy shall exceed twenty (20) dollars, the right of trial by jury shall be preserved, and no fact tried by jury, shall be reexamined in any Court of the United States, than according to the rules of the common law.

依普通法之訴訟，若訴訟金額逾美金二十元，得要求陪審評決。事實依習慣法原則，經陪審評議後，不得再向任何法院，提出相同事實告訴。

AMENDMENT VIII（第八修正案）

Excessive bail shall not be required, nor excessive fines imposed, nor cruel and unusual punishments inflicted.

不得有不相當高額之保釋金，不得有鉅額之罰金，不得有殘忍及不尋常之處罰。

AMENDMENT IX（第九修正案）

The enumeration in the Constitution of certain rights, shall not

be construed to deny or disparage others retained by the people.

憲法所列舉的權利，不可被解釋為否定或輕視貶抑他人之權利。

AMENDMENT X（第十修正案）

The powers not delegated to the United States by the Constitution, nor prohibited by it to the States, are reserved to the States respectively, or to the people.

任何依憲法未授權委任美國聯邦政府管轄之權限，州亦無明文禁止時，其權限保留給州或其人民。

AMENDMENT XIII（第十三修正案）

Neither slavery nor involuntary servitude, except as a punishment for crime whereof the party shall have been duly convicted, shall exist within the United States, or any place subject to their jurisdiction.

任何人不得在美國境內或管轄範圍內，為奴役或非自願性之奴役行為，但該人依法被起訴且處罰者，不在此限。

AMENDMENT XIV（第十四修正案）

All persons born or naturalized in the United States, and subject to the jurisdiction thereof, are citizens of the United States and of the State wherein they reside. No State shall make or enforce any law which shall abridge the privileges or immunities or citizens of the United States; nor shall any State deprive any person of life, liberty, or property, without due process of law; nor deny to any person within its jurisdiction the equal protection of the laws.

任何在美國出生或歸化之人且受美國管轄之人，皆為美國公民和當地居民。州不得制定或強制頒佈任何法律，侵害美國人民權利或免責權；州亦不得任意剝奪任何人民之生命、自由或財產，但經正常法律程序，不在此限；亦不得否定在其管轄內，任何人法律上之平等保障權。(國人婦女同胞常於快生育前赴美生產，其目的乃於出生小孩得馬上取得美國公民資格)

第七節　刑　法(Criminal Law)

一、刑　法

㈠刑法之分類(Classification)

美國刑法之分類採重罪(Felony)與輕罪(Misdemeanor)之分，重罪為一年以上有期徒刑，輕罪為一年以下有期徒刑，重罪有級數分別，如一級謀殺(first degree)與二級謀殺(second degree)等。其構成要件為⑴行為(包括不行為)；⑵犯意：特別犯意與一般犯意；⑶因果關係(較侵權行為之因果關係還嚴格，即要求更直接之因果關係)；⑷行為與犯罪同時競合；⑸伴隨狀況；⑹結果。

㈡懲罰之性質(Nature of Punishment)

四種普通法(Common law)常見的懲罰目的：⑴報應 (retribution)，以牙還牙用以彌補過去所造成之邪惡行為。⑵嚇阻(Deterrent)。⑶使失去行為能力(restraint or incapacitation)。⑷教化(rehabilitation or reform)。

1. 報　應(Retribution)

當我們思考為什麼人應該被懲罰？是因為他們造成別人的傷害？報復理論支持以牙還牙之基礎。通常應衡量相當性，來論被告應得之罪。

2. 嚇　阻(Deterrent)

預防犯罪是一重要課題。我們自問，預防別人犯罪，是為了保護我們自己抑保護其他團體或為了宗教道德的約束？通常一般的預防犯罪，得由一般的嚇阻作起，但有時候一般的嚇阻，起不了作用，因為法律無法制定道德的法律(Law cannot legislate morality.)。法律和道德或宗教終究二回事。道德或宗教的標準，通常高於法律之規範，即使法律來自道德或宗教，或者即使法律對道德有拘束，預防未來的犯罪，一般的嚇阻，僅能提供部分嚇阻功能，而非全部嚇阻功效。

3. 使失去行為能力(Restraint or Incapacitation)

使失去行為能力，例如，剝奪個人權益或褫奪公權，實質上是一種處罰或者限制一個人的權利，無異對其權利和義務之限制。

採用上述之單獨方式，常使個人失去行為或權利能力，懲罰將無限制的侵害人的權益。故把上述三種方式，配合教化效果一併使用，以期對懲罰有一正確認識，使違法者不會重蹈覆轍。

4. 教　化(Rehabilitation or Reform)

此種方式可分⑴特別的個人教化：目的在使其日後成為更好更守法之人；⑵一般的教化：係向不特定的多數人行使教化，例如在上課灌輸學生守法的觀念，以免觸犯法律之效果。

綜上，報應(retribution)係以造成傷害為判斷懲罰之標準(harm-focused)。例如，普通法要求未遂(attempt)階段，必需達到若非警察或第三人之及時阻止，其犯罪已接近成功既遂之地步，但美國刑法典(Model Penal Code)，則以該行為必須逾越實質危險地步，方構成未遂階段，故Model Penal Code係以犯意為懲罰未遂犯之標準(intent-focused)。目前的趨勢(Current trend)，則不願輕易限制具有危險之人之行為，因其限制將嚴重侵害憲法所保障人民之基本權益。況且刑法所採取的原則是推定被告無罪(presumption of innocence)，除了有犯意之外，我們仍需視其行為之違法性與傷害，是否相關或具有因果關係或有責性，而論定其刑責。 **❷⓿** 單單只有犯意而沒有履行犯罪的行為，不可能構成刑法之罪責。因此，通說認為犯意(mens rea)和行為(Actus rea)競合(Concurrence)時，必需嚴加探討因果之相當性。

(三)舉證責任(Burden of Proof)

1.舉證責任在州政府(State)

刑法採取的責任標準為「**無合理懷疑**」標準(beyond a reasonable doubt)，若有合理懷疑關於被告的罪嫌，法院應宣告為無罪之判決。刑法推定所有被告均無辜或無罪(presumption of innocence)。在每一個構成要件中，若有其一個要件，代表人民之政府無法提出無合理懷疑證明時，被告應被喻知無罪之判決，縱然有部分要件，已符無合理懷疑之標準。但只要有一部分構成要件，有合理懷疑(reasonable doubt)之處，被告必須被無罪釋放。

2.舉證之證據力(Burden of Proof in Evidence)

美國因採法定證據主義，除了刑法採無合理懷疑證據標準外，民法尚有優勢證據(evidence of preponderance)和清晰可見之證據(clear and convincing evidence)。政府必需以無合理懷疑標準，證

---

❷⓿　甘添貴著，《刑法總論講義》，頁46(1992)。

明被告犯罪之構成要件，若某一要件沒有證明出來，被告應被釋放無罪。反之，被告得僅以優勢證據或清晰可見之證據，加以反駁答辯。以下為美國證據法之規定(BURDEN OF PROOF in PLEADING)：

I. **BURDEN OF PRODUCTION** (burden of going forward) [judge]（提出證據責任）

  A. Who must present evidence to prove existing facts (adverse party may rebut)

  B. How much evidence must be presented (prima facie case—reasonable jury verdict)

  C. If P establishes xx evidence, burden of production shifts to the other party. The burden may shift back and forth. Affirmative defense (e,g., statute of limitation, alibi, self-defense, contributory negligence) may be introduced to shift burden to the other party.

比較: Presumed facts—a reasonable juror could infer from the basic facts (civil cases) [推定事實]

Directed Verdict—no reasonable jury would find for the other party (direct proof) [指示評決]

Circumstantial evidence—evidence which infers existence of fact at issue [情況證據]

II. **BURDEN OF PERSUASION** (who wins the case)（說明證據責任）

  A. Once the burden of persuasion has shifted, it usually remains on that party.

B. Persuade trier of facts that facts at issue exist.

C. Burden of proof concerning facts for P, while defenses for D. Standard of proof:

1. PREPONDERANCE EVIDENCE (more probable or likely to exist than not to exist) [beyond 50% creditability]

2. CLEAR AND CONVINCING EVIDENCE (more than preponderance evidence)

   a. facts at issue is highly probable or reasonable certain.

   b. between evidence of preponderance and beyond a reasonable doubt.

   c. apply to civil cases, while few in criminal cases.

3. BEYOND A REASONABLE DOUBT (up to 100%):

   a. criminal standard: sufficient to overcome presumption of innocence of D

   b. burden of proof is on state/government to prove all elements of crime. Failure to prove one of the elements, jury must find for the defendant.

比較: Summary judgment—there is no genuine material facts that exists, the summary judgment as a matter of law should be rendered for the moving party. (pre-trial in civil cases) [法院簡易判決，得不經陪審評決]

3. 自由心證(Discretion)

自由心證是一種法官依職權可在冥冥之中殺人的武器。但大多數的我們卻不知它的可怕性。我們常聽的一個司法笑話:「一審

有罪，二審無罪，三審免罪」。這是「有錢判生，無錢判死」的根源所在，這也和自由心證有極大的淵源。最近大家常發現某一案件，尤其是刑事案件(例：O. J. Simpson與陳進興案件)，未審先轟動。偵察階段，依法不公開，但媒體之傳播，常常造成報紙或電視審判，而刑法所要求證據之公平公正，難有不受報紙或電視之「預審」干涉而受影響。刑法和憲法實為一體之二面，二者之間如何尋求平衡點，是社會動盪關鍵。舉證責任之所在，敗訴之所在。在英國和美國一些州，被告只需舉證「清晰具說服力」之證據能力(clear and convincing evidence)，證明被告精神異常或心神喪失。在美聯邦和一些州，則要求州以「無合理懷疑」(beyond a reasonable doubt)證明被告係精神正常。有些州要求被告方面提出「實質證據」(substantial evidence)，證明被告精神異常，但州應證明被告之精神狀態無合理懷疑正常。

二、行　為(ACT)

㈠行為(Actus Rea)或不作為(Omission)

行為必須是出自內心的自願性(voluntary)或出於自己的意志(free will)。通常行為和犯意(mens rea)相互關連。單純自願性的傷害行為，並不一定是刑法所咎責的範圍，若有阻卻違法事由，得免除其刑責。例如，夜間夢遊者的行為在Model Penal Code(MPC)，並不算是自願性的行為。非自願性的行為通常有：

⑴心智無法控制之行為，例如反射動作、痙攣、沒有知覺的行動。

⑵心智部分控制的行為，例如腦震盪、催眠狀態、夜遊等行為，亦包括不作為(omission)，作為與不作為關係到法律的責任義

務和法律效果。法律責任(Legal Duty)之發生，茲有下列6種方式：

①身分關係(status)：例如，父母親小孩的身分關係。

②造成危險的狀況(creation of peril)：朋友結夥登高山之危險。

③控制他人之關係：例如，有控制權的僱用關係及僅有部分控制權的承攬關係，其法律責任，因其有否控制關係而有不同。前者法律責任重，後者法律責任較輕。

④房東對被邀請者之責任(landowner to invitees)。

⑤民事法定責任：例如，提供充足食物給同居人。

⑥刑事法定責任：例如，未餵食自己的小孩或逃稅。

綜上，美國法律基本上，只處罰違法行為，故不作為並非刑法之罪，除非法定責任義務或契約規定，需履行該責任。

(二)犯　意(Intent)

犯意通常具有階段性。開始時可能僅有邪惡的思想(guilty mind or bad thought)，這不構成犯罪，因為犯罪須有實質傷害造成。一個人的犯意必須是合理正常能預見結果，方能構成犯罪。通常包含了一個人的故意目的(purpose)、明知(knowledge)、草率魯莽(reckless)和過失(Negligence)行為。

1. 主觀犯意(Subjective Mens Rea)

　(1)殺人罪(Homicide)：美國普通法謀殺罪(murder)的犯意形態，種類如下：

　　①明知或故意殺人(intentional killing)。[直接故意]

　　②明知或故意造成他人嚴重身體傷害(intentional inflicting serious bodily injury)。[間接故意]

③漠視生命而為草菅人命之冷血殺人行為(depraved heart killing)。

④重罪謀殺(felony murder)，前二項指有意圖之故意或明知行為，後二項意謂著隱示的惡意，很多州視前二項罪名為自願性殺人罪，後二項罪名為非自願性殺人。

(2)一級謀殺(First Degree murder)：若犯罪是有預謀及故意，如明知或故意殺人，則罪名有一級與二級程度之分；重罪中因強姦罪(rape)、強盜罪(robbery)、縱火罪(arson)、綁架罪(kidnap)或夜間侵入住宅罪(burglary)，而意外造成死亡結果，均屬一級謀殺罪。

(3)過失殺人罪：自願 v. 非自願 (Manslaughter)

①若殺人因情緒激動而造成憤怒之際殺人，無冷卻思考期間，該殺人結果，一般稱為自願性過失殺人(voluntary manslaughter)。

②若對人之生命漠不關心(indifference to the value of human beings)，而導致死亡結果，雖然對造成死亡的危險性較小，但因輕率從事該魯莽之行為，經常構成非自願性殺人(involuntary manslaughter)。 有些州稱為輕罪殺人罪(misdemeanor manslaughter)。

2.客觀犯意(Objective Mens Rea)

客觀犯意通常指過失。根據刑法學者Holmes的理論，客觀責任可能是獨立於客觀過失之外。危險即是過失。並沒有企圖選擇危險傷害的人，亦可能會受到刑法制裁，根據刑法學者Hart的理論，過失本身即是受處罰可歸責的主觀意識狀態。

3.一般犯意(General Intent)

一般犯意需視刑法的規定。有些州把一般犯意定義為重大過失(gross negligence)。有些州則稱一般犯意，乃主觀意識不合理的危險(subjective awareness of grossly unreasonable risk taken)。

4.特別犯意(Specific Intent)

特別犯意指故意或有目的之犯意。通常指為了某種目的，進行計劃中之一種行為。例如，在攻擊行為裡具有特別犯意去強姦。這個目的是去實現一般犯意可能造成的結果。例如，企圖去殺人，但計畫沒有成功，即有意圖的殺人未遂(attempted murder or attempt to murder)。　在犯意裡，犯罪故意(purpose)和明知(knowledge)，常被法院用來衡量特別犯意；　輕率魯莽(reckless)和過失(Negligence)，則被用來判斷一般犯意之構成要件。

5.模範刑法典(Model Penal Code, M.P.C.)

在1962年，全美之刑法專家、學者、法官、律師等專業人士，制定了一套有系統的模範刑法典。其中規範了有責性的種類，例如在行為裡，區分了行為(conduct)，情況(circumstances)和結果(result)。　每一罪名均有其特別的構成要件(elements of a particular crime)。茲就犯意種類細分如下：

(1)故意目的(purpose)：在普通法裡通常是特別犯意的化身。MPC的定義為有意識的目標(conscious object)。

(2)明知(Knowledge or Knowingly)：認知在普通法通常指明知(knowingly)。而且是主觀的明知(參見MPC § 2.02 (7)和 § 2.02 (b))。

(3)輕率魯莽(Reckless)：在普通法的原則下，任何守法之人(law-abiding persons)應知道或能知道(know or should have known)，而確信不會發生，並漠視高度危險結果的行為。在

MPC 的規定，以主觀和客觀標準判斷是否輕率草莽　（參見 MPC § 2.02 (2) (c)），重大歧異於一般守法之人的行為，如是謂之輕率魯莽(Gross deviation from law-abiding principles)。常見的罪例如reckless to do serious bodily harm, battery, arson, manslaughter, depraved heart murder。

(4)過失(Negligence)：在普通法，指不合理的行為。在MPC，指一般正常合理人(reasonable men)未能認知該危險。MPC採主觀和客觀的標準衡量過失。重大歧異於一般正常合理人的行為，謂之過失(Gross deviation from reasonableness)。另有嚴格責任(strict liability)，即不問是否過失，均科以刑責，例如超速，準強姦罪(statutory rape)。

(三)競　合(Concurrence)

有時候，行為(actus rea)和犯意(mens rea)會同時存在或相關，而發生競合相連的現象。大部分刑法之罪均發生競合現象。

(四)因果關係(Causation)

其分類如下：

1.一般的因果關係可分為：

(1)事實原因的因果關係(cause in fact)：通常指發生原因和結果有直接的關聯，若非其行為之介入，其結果可能會和不介入時不相同(But for test)。另原因和結果有二個以上的外力或人介入時，若無法分辨究竟是誰造成的，法院會採取實質造成結果的人或因素說(substantial factor test)。刑法的因果關係和侵權之因果關係相類似，但刑法之因果關係，則採較直接之因果關係說，不採一般侵權因果關係。

(2)間接或法律原因之因果關係：外力以人之介入時，可分替代的介入原因(superseding cause)和不可替代的介入原因(non-superseding cause)。 通說以是否預見來判斷(foreseeability test)，但在實務上因果關係之運用，常依立法政策考量公平正義，來解說這複雜的關係。

原則上第三人之不法行為(criminal activity)、天災或上帝的傑作(act of God)，或故意侵權行為(intentional tort)為替代性的介入原因，可切斷原來第一個歸究的原因，即這些行為吸收取代了第一個原因的行為。

但是有些行為若可預見，即使不能預見其特別結果，但可預見一般的結果，則這些原因稱之不可替代的可預見的原因，此時原來第一個被告的行為並未被後來介入之人或行為所吸收或取代，亦即原來第一個被告對其所造成的傷害或死亡結果仍需負責。

常見的有因傷痛苦而自殺(commit suicide)，旁人過失的解救而導致死亡(rescuer's negligence)，車禍後所受傷勢加重前傷而導致死亡結果(post-accident injury or post-accident aggravation of wound)，高度危險之行為(highly dangerous act)等。醫生誤診(medical malpratice or wrong medicine given)，則較眾說紛紜(split)。有些州認為誤診致死行為並不能替代切斷原來第一個侵害人的行為。有些州認為醫生誤診為一替代性法律原因，切斷原先犯罪人的行為或原因。受害人可分別起訴侵害人和醫生，或起訴二者為共同被告。多數州認為，若傷口之發炎導致死亡結果，並非醫生之誤診或藥物因素，基於立法理由，法院傾向不切斷原來侵害他人之因果關係。醫療誤診學說上近年以「疫學因果關係」判斷醫療之過失問題，即引進新過失理論注重結果迴避義務，如結果發生之預見可能性雖存在，但成立過失犯之條件仍不足時，必須從

事醫療工作人員未盡防止結果發生之義務，始能成立過失犯。此學說可避免醫療機構工作者動輒觸法之機會，故此與第三人之不法行為（刑法或侵權行為）之因果關係認定有所區別，第三人之不法行為雖無法預期特定之損害結果,但如能預見一般損害結果,即可認定因果關係之存在，醫療之疫學因果關係可謂以立法政策考量，藉此理論彌補刑法相當因果關係適用之不足。㉑

2. 因果關係(Causation)之分類：

　(1)Cause in Fact (actual cause) [事實原因]

　　　A. But for test [若非]

　　　B. Substantial factor test [實質因素]

　(2) Proximate cause (legal cause) [法律原因]

　　　A. Direct cause [直接原因]

　　　B. Indirect cause [間接原因]

　　　　①superseding intervening cause [替代介入原因]

　　　　②non-superseding intervening cause [非替代介入原因]

3. 綜上，死者受傷後本身的行為(例如被送入醫院後，自己把插管拔除，而導致死亡或死者受到性攻擊，雖未至強姦地步，但飲毒藥自殺)，若在行為後和死亡或受傷結果前，不可能有外力或第三種替代行為或第三人之行為原因，則第一個侵害人仍依「可預見理論」，應受刑法制裁。若後來被害人的原因行為，可歸責於其他原因行為，而產生自然和可能的結果(Natural and probable of the result within chain of causation)，則由其他原因負責。刑法所要求的法律原因比侵權行為(tort)的法律原因還要嚴格，

㉑　曾淑瑜《醫療過失與因果關係》，翰蘆出版，民國八十七年，頁485–552。

即要求更多直接的原因(more direct causation)。刑法要求州政府必需在無合理的證據力下(beyond a reasonable doubt)，證明被告合乎每一構成要件之罪名。(另參見前侵權行為之舉例說明)

㈤結　果(Result)

結果指在犯意和行為結合下的產物，例如，死亡即結果。若非某一行為或事件，結果可能因為沒有該行為或事件之分辨而有不同。

㈥伴隨狀況(Attending Circumstance)

一般指時間地點附隨於行為時一切之客觀事實，例如，夜間侵入住宅罪，其附隨情況，即指夜間(in the night time)之構成要件，伴隨狀況和犯意沒有任何關聯。

三、對人之罪(OFFENSES AGAINST PERSONS)

㈠殺人罪(Homicide)

殺人罪(homicide)涵蓋了一級謀殺(murder in the first degree)、二級謀殺(murder in the second degree)、自願過失殺人(voluntary manslaughter)和非自願過失殺人(involuntary manslaughter)。

有些州稱有預謀的蓄意殺人為一級謀殺(with malice afore-thought)。有些州稱故意造成人身傷害致死為二級謀殺(inflicting serious bodily harm)或稱自願性過失殺人(voluntary manslaughter)。有些州則稱漠視人命的冷血殺人為二級謀殺或非自願性過失殺人(involuntary manslaughter)。重罪殺人罪(felony murder)，則指在犯重罪之際，意外產生了受害人死亡結果。大部分的重罪指謀殺(murder)、強姦(rape)、重傷害(mayhem)、強盜(robbery)、竊盜(larce-ny)、縱火(arson)、過失致人於死(manslaughter)、夜間侵入住宅罪

(burglary)等。

(二)威脅攻擊和毆擊罪(Assault and Battery)

威脅攻擊(Assault)，指意圖使人蒙受毆擊之恐懼，威脅將實施身體直接之侵害(one in apprehension of imminent bodily harm or contact)。在紐約州稱為威脅(extortion)，有些州則稱為Blackmail，有學者稱Assault為毆擊未遂(attempt to battery)。威脅攻擊在大部分的州，只是輕罪(misdemeanor)之一種。

毆擊(Battery)則指行為人使用武力或力量，直接或間接接觸或侵害他人之身體。例如，叫狗去咬人，則構成毆擊他人。請注意，在侵權(tort)的毆擊罪，其定義和刑法非常類似，只不過很多州把侵權的毆擊罪，只視為刑法之攻擊罪。故有人稱刑法之毆擊罪，為攻擊之既遂(completed assault)，在紐約，毆擊罪則需更嚴格之限制，另有加重毆擊罪(aggravated Battery)，例如，使用致命武器，攻擊小孩、婦女或警察。

(三)其他對人侵害之罪(Other Offenses)

1.綁 架(Kidnap or Abduction)

美國習慣法把綁架視為輕罪之一種，但是最近的刑法典，則把綁架列入重罪之內。通常綁架之構成要件，必需把限制受害人行動侷限於一隱密之地方(secret place)，且把被害人移動至某些範圍(usportation of the victim)。

加重綁架罪常包括為了贖金而綁架(for ransom)、為了實施其他罪而進行綁架(for commission of other crimes)、為了其他非法目的而綁架(for offensive purpose)與綁架小孩(又稱child stealing)。

2.墮胎罪(Abortion)

這項罪名常被憲法所挑戰。最近的一個案件Roe v. Wade，❷

美國聯邦最高法院認為德州刑法墮胎之限制違憲。德州有關墮胎之刑法規定，第一期(前三個月)墮胎之決定，必需受制於醫生的醫學決定，　第二期(三個月後)之墮胎決定，　州若有強有力之利益(compelling interest)，可以制定必要程序來保障管理婦女之健康，最後一期(六月後)的決定，州可制定(regulate)法令禁止(proscribe)墮胎，例如此墮胎在保障母親生命和健康之正常理由。聯邦最高法院以個人隱私權(right of privacy)來跳越刑法所強制之決定程序而宣布該法違憲。O'conor大法官指出，該州之立法不合理地使婦女負擔其受憲法保障隱私權，則該州刑法違反美國聯邦憲法(Thornburgh v. Amer. College of obstetricians & Gynecologists)(1986)。

刑法若規定未成年人之墮胎，必需父母親之同意，常因缺乏最佳未成年人利益之證明，被解釋為違憲，Hartigan v. Zbaraz(1987)，最高法院認為縱未成年人也有隱私權之權利。在Conn v. Conn，㉓判決父親不得禁止其女兒墮胎之決定。惟此種墮胎法令，仍是燙手山芋(hot potato)。有些州禁止墮胎，有些州則允許部分範圍之墮胎。很多婦女在這州不能墮胎，常跑去他州合法墮胎，故很難正確計算真正墮胎人數，美國人喜歡一夜風流(one night stand)，屢見不鮮，如何平衡憲法的個人隱私權及刑法保障嬰兒之生命法益，有待時代潮流之演進而作修改。

3.強　　姦(Rape)

通常強姦的客體是非配偶的女性，但在美國加州或紐約州，先生均有可能被控強姦太太之罪名。和性有關係的罪名，在刑法

㉒　　410 U.S. 113 (1993).

㉓　　525 N.E. 2d 612 (Ind. App 1988).

尚有性攻擊。另外在1964年民權法案(Civil Right Act of 1964)亦對性騷擾(sexual harassment)有擴充適用之解釋。準強姦罪(statutory rape)適用在行為人與未成年少女之性行為，不論該女孩看起來多成熟，例如，看起來二十八歲，但實際只有十六歲或未達法定年齡女孩，在法律上仍以準強姦罪論。雖然仍有少數州認為強姦的客體必需是非配偶之女性，但若先生通謀他人使他人和自己的太太從事強暴性強姦，則該先生亦構成強姦自己太太之罪名。❷⁴

4. 非法監禁(False Imprisonment)

非法監禁在習慣法係輕罪之一種。其構成要件常包括未經同意非法限制監禁他人。此同意非由脅迫、詐欺或利誘所引導，同意必需是自願且自主性(voluntariness and free will)。只要有任何威脅、武力或以武力威脅，讓對方侷限於一定區域內，不敢或不能行動，而致失其自由即屬本罪。非法監禁屬特別犯意之一種罪名。

5. 重傷害罪(Mayhem)

重傷害在習慣法指傷害或分解某部身體器官或分屍。但最近的法律擴充其範圍至永久性的毀損身體，例如，嚴重損害他人身體或毀容。我國之重傷罪之成立，必須行為人原具有使人重傷之故意，毀人一目或一耳等，這和普通傷害不同。

6. 私下決鬥(Dueling)

這在習慣法也是輕罪之一種。雖然二人相約私下決鬥，均有暗示對方，同意(consent)傷害彼此身體或生命之法益，惟法律仍不得以其同意為抗辯，仍視其為非法行為(unlawful act)。故一方致他方於死者，則可能觸犯了非法過失致人於死罪(involuntary man-slaughter)。

---

❷⁴　See N.J. stat. Ann ch. 95 § 2C: 14–2.

四、對住所之侵害罪名(Offense against Habitation)

　　早期普通法認為打破門窗或進入他人居住目的之處所，且意圖去犯重罪，則稱為夜間侵入住宅。惟現行法律，大多數州已把侵入住宅罪範圍，不限於重罪而擴充到任何罪，且不限於夜間。此處的進入包括推定進入(constructive entering or breaking)，例如，以詐術進入或門根本沒鎖，或以鎖匙開門，但卻在沒有授權之情況中，進入或闖入該住處。

五、侵害財產之罪名(Offenses against Property)

㈠竊盜罪(Larceny)

　　一般所謂的偷(stealing)，即我們常聽到的竊盜(Larceny)。若偷竊行為利用詐術，剝奪他人對動產之佔有，則犯了詐術竊盜(obtain by trick)；若以謊言企圖剝奪他人動產之所有權(title)，則犯了詐欺竊盜(Obsession by false pretense)。另外，若以現有合法佔有他人之動產之際，移轉成自己的財產，則此不法行為，稱為侵占罪(Embezzlement)。

㈡強盜罪(Robbery)

　　強盜罪之構成要件通常指在他人面前以武力或告知以武力威脅，使他人交付其財產，企圖永久性剝奪他人之動產。(The elements of robbery are theft from person or presence by force or threat of force.)強盜罪等於竊盜(larceny)加上武力或威脅恐嚇(force or fear)，通常其侵害的客體必需是人類，但即強盜死人，亦可構成強盜罪。加重強盜罪(aggravated Robbery)，指以致命或危險之武器，強奪他人財物。

(三)侵占罪(Conversion or Embezzlement)

習慣法依侵害財產之價值，分為加重侵占罪(Grand embezzlement)與輕微侵占罪(petit embezzlement)。前者係重罪，後者係輕罪。基本上侵害人意圖在其合法佔有他人財產時，以詐欺手段非法侵占他人財產，即構成侵占罪。公務上或因公持有之物，意圖自己或第三人不法之所有而侵害者，得構成業務侵占罪。

(四)詐欺竊盜(False Pretense)

美國習慣法把詐欺竊盜罪分成加重詐欺罪(Grand false pretense)和輕微詐欺罪(Petit false pretense)，前者為重罪、後者為輕罪。其構成要件常指以詐欺謊言(claim)或虛偽不實陳述(misrepresentation)，意圖故意詐欺他人並剝奪他人財產之所有權。(Obtaining title to the property of another by false pretense or claim with intent to defraud the other.)

(五)詐術竊盜(Larceny by Trick)

竊盜人若施以詐術，意圖剝奪占有(Obtain)他人合法占有之動產，則稱為以詐術竊盜(deprivation of possession)。這和詐欺竊盜(obtain by false pretense)，以剝奪他人所有權(title)不同。

(六)收受贓物罪(Receiving or Concealing Stolen Property)

習慣法把收受贓物罪列為輕罪。其構成要件為接受並控制占有可能係贓物之他人動產，意圖永久剝奪所有人對該財產之所有權。紐約州推定占有贓物之人，即有意圖收受贓物，除非提出反證，證明自己沒有該意圖。

(七)惡意毀損罪(Malicious Mischief)

習慣法所稱之惡意毀損罪，指惡意對他人財產毀損(malicious destruction or damage to property of another)，只要部分損壞並使其

價值減少，即足構成惡意毀損罪。(參見MPC §220.3)

⑧偽造文書罪(Forgery and uttering a forged Instrument)

習慣法之偽造文書罪，通常包括意圖變造或偽造文書，並企圖詐欺他人(marking or altering of a false writing with intent to defraud)。

⑨恐嚇罪(Extortion or Blackmail)

習慣法的恐嚇罪，通常以口頭或表面收取非法金錢或財物，而恐嚇威脅他人。恐嚇(又稱threat)不必真正涉及直接的傷害接觸，令其心生恐懼之感即為已足。

六、預備階段罪名(Inchoate Crimes)

㈠未遂罪(Attempt)

1.預備階段

預備階段罪名有未遂(attempt)、共謀(conspiracy)及教唆(solicitation)罪名。

未遂為有特別犯意之一種罪名。被告之犯罪責任與侵權能力，必需逾越準備階段(beyond mere preparation)。公然明顯之行為(overt act)必需伴隨。有部分的州採習慣法(common law)，大部分州採模範刑法典(MPC)。對於認定究竟犯罪行為(sufficient act)到什麼的地步才構成未遂，莫衷一是。在早期的習慣法，以若非警察或第三人之及時介入，其危險之犯罪已經成功既遂，為判斷之標準(dangerous proximity to the success of crimes)；但MPC則改以更進一步要求未遂犯之行為，必需構成實質地步或接近犯罪成功既遂(Substantial step test)為判斷標準。另外尚有少數州以最後地步(final step)為判斷時刻並以行為確切之犯意為標準(equivocal in-

tent to commit the crime)。目前多數州仍以MPC為主。

2.抗辯事由(Defense)：不能犯(impossibility)

傳統的普通法(common law)不承認事實不可能為一有效的抗辯，惟有法律上之不可能方能成為有效抗辯事由。但在模範刑法典(model Penal code)均不承認事實和法律不可能為有效之抗辯事由，除非該不可能係在方法上相當明顯不可能(inherent impossible)。例如施法於布娃娃，欲使他人發生死亡之結果(voodoo)。惟請注意事實不能與事實錯誤不同，法律不能亦與法律錯誤不同。事實錯誤得推翻犯罪人之主觀一般犯意，只要該事實錯誤係合理的；對於特別犯意之罪，只要是主觀誠實的錯誤(honest mistake)，即得推翻特別犯意之構成要件，不以合理錯誤(reasonable mistake)為必要。法律錯誤基本上沒有抗辯事由，即使是合理的法律錯誤亦同，但若有罪名以求故意(明知或knowledge)為構成要件之一時，則行為人可用來推翻無該特別犯意而要求減輕或免除其刑。

未遂之中止，必需有內心自願性的放棄其目的(internal and voluntary renunciation of purpose under MPC section 5.01 (4))。

教唆(solicitation)之中止，只需要及時有效的通知且勸告被教唆者不要去犯原教唆行為。對於共謀(conspiracy)之中止(renunciation)，則大部分的州，要求非但共謀者內心有中止之意思(internal renunciation)，並且必須有一行為企圖阻止既遂之完成(thwart the success of the completed crime)。有些州規定至少打電話報警。

例如共犯搶銀行，在外把風之共犯心生恐懼，默默不語自行逃離現場，仍不能以中止犯來減輕或免除其共犯之刑責。

我刑法第二十七條規定：「已著手於犯罪行為之實行，而因己意中止或防止其結果之發生者，減輕或免除其刑。」

㈡教 唆(Solicitation)

教唆在習慣法指教唆、鼓勵或刺激、勸引、命令他人去犯非法之罪，即構成教唆罪。該罪名在教唆行為成立完成時，即成立教唆罪，事實或法律不可能不是一種抗辯事由。教唆犯得視教唆行動之多寡，而變為共犯或未遂犯。但有些州規定教唆未遂不是一項罪名，若該州刑法典並不處罰該未遂罪。基本上，教唆行為一旦成立，不可能發生中止問題，惟若該刑法立法並不處罰該教唆未遂罪名，則教唆人應有中止犯之抗辯事由，得要求減輕或免除刑責。

㈢共謀罪(Conspiracy)

共犯之構成要件在習慣法通常有下列（共謀）：

⑴共同之同意計劃(Agreement)或公然顯明之行為(overt act)，去實施共犯共謀之意思表示或計劃。

⑵特別犯意(Specific intent)：有計劃實施一般犯意之行為。

⑶人數為複數(Plurality or Wharton rule)。但紐約州容許單方共犯之共謀罪成立(Unilateral conspiracy)，常發生的為警員為求早日破案，夥同共犯之一進行合作非法行為，嗣後再舉發或進行逮捕該共犯。按複數說，一人不可能成立共犯之共謀罪，但基於保護社會法益和立法理由，有些州則仍有處罰規定。又例如Mann Act，處罰一男子運送一女子至他州，從事非法不道德交易，雖女方自願去賣春，並無共謀一起去賣春，但仍然可以單方共謀共犯起訴該男子。若有一方為法律所保護之對象(protected class)，則即使其同意犯罪，他方仍會單方擔刑責。例如與未達法定年齡之少女有性行為，則不論有否有其同意，此仍成立準強姦罪。 共犯對於其他共犯(accom-

plice)之行為負共同罪名，只要該罪係在實施促進共犯之目標(in furtherance of objective of conspiracy)且該罪係自然且可能是共謀之因果關係(natural and probable consequence of the conspiracy i.e., foreseeable)。中止與不能犯原則上不是共犯的抗辯事由之一，但有些州仍容許其為減輕或免除抗辯事由。但要求內心之放棄應為自願性，且行為至少必需企圖阻擾破壞將實施既遂目的之地步。

㈣吸收關係(Merger)

一般的未遂行為(attempt)會被既遂的罪所吸收，教唆(solicitation)會被共謀(conspiracy)與既遂之罪吸收(有些州對教唆未遂，仍以未遂犯處罪之)。 然而共謀罪(conspiracy)為了處罰共謀人之陰謀，特設另一刑罰規範，故共謀罪乃單獨分離於既遂罪之外，故不適用吸收關係，不會被既遂罪吸收。

美國憲法第五修正案(fifth amendment)亦提及人民不可受到雙重或二次危險(double jeopardy)。 但共謀與既遂之罪(例如強盜罪)為分別獨立，各自有其刑法罪名之獨立構成要件，故同時處罰既遂之罪與共謀罪，並沒有違憲。

七、責任：犯罪能力之限制(Limitation on Criminal Capacity)

㈠未成年人(Infancy or Minor)

早期普通法認為，七歲以下之人為無行為能力，七歲以上十四歲以下為限制行為能力人，十四歲以上為有行為能力人。今日美國大多數的州以十四歲以下之人為未成年人，專屬於少年法庭之管轄。十四歲以上十八歲以下，檢察官可依職權決定是否移送少年法庭，十八歲以上則係成年人具有行為責任能力。

㈡心神喪失及精神異常(Insanity or Incapacity)

有些人沒有能力去辨別是非(M'naghten Rule)，甚至不知其行為乃法律所禁止之規定。有些人是一時衝動沒有辦法控制情緒，一時失去理智(irresistible impulse rule)；有人則認為精神不正常，是身體或心理疾病所造成(Durham rule)。 現在模範刑法典(MPC)則以該人是否有實質能力去判別違法之行為(substantial capacity to appreciate criminality)，作為是否心神喪失等之標準。

若一個被告以為拿槍打人，如同在開罐頭一樣，在刑法的主觀犯意裡，他是沒有犯意的。我們常搞不清什麼是動機(motive)，什麼是犯意(intent)，簡單來說，犯意指一個人要作什麼(what one intends to do)，而犯意則指為什麼他要這樣作(Why one intends to do)。因此我們在分辨正常人與精神異常之人，需觀察二者之心態，來判別是否精神正常或異常。

㈢酗　酒(Intoxication)

自願性酗酒(voluntary intoxication)不是一種抗辯事由，若被告係一正常人，根據他的經驗，酒精成份達到一定程度，即會有酒醉之情形，即屬自願性酗酒。雖然一般的輕率魯莽(reckless)不致構成特別犯意(specific intent)之罪名，但若知悉過去其有酗酒之記錄且傾向仍不加理會，讓其發生酗酒現象，則法律認定該被告有特別犯意，故意從事自願性酗酒。因此自願性之酗酒情形，美國法律通說仍採「一般合理清醒人」標準(reasonable sober person test)決定其刑責。

非自願性之酗酒(involuntary intoxication)則可否定特別犯意之構成要件，因該人並無企圖和犯意。酗酒可能係由他人或外物

造成酒醉之結果。例如被醫生注射藥物而導致非自願之酗酒。因此非自願性之酗酒，美國法律通說採客觀情況，作為判斷是否為抗辯事由，若依當時情形，被人施以注射酒精且並無過失，則陪審員可裁量為正當抗辯事由，用以阻卻違法。

被告若欲抗辯其犯罪之當時，已因醉酒而無法實施形成要求的犯意行為，則被告需負舉證責任，得以優勢證據(evidence of preponderance)或清晰可信證據(clear and convincing)來反駁其控訴之名。例如，醉得根本手舉不起來。

另外一種以行為能力減低主張阻卻違法事由，係當事人沒有能力對較重之罪，來構成其必要之特別犯意 (diminished capacity)，但這種抗辯僅屬部分的抗辯(partial defense)，只能減輕刑責，不能用來免除其刑責。常見的案子發生在蓄意殺人而以行為能力減低作為抗辯。

八、阻卻違法事由(Defenses)

㈠公權力(Public Authority)

美國聯邦並無所謂的司法警察權(police power)，司法警察權屬於州的權限，主要在提昇公共安全道德、福利和健康等權益。因此若司法警察為了上述目的執行公權力，常有阻卻違法的正當理由。例如逮捕現行犯、脫逃犯等。

㈡預防犯罪(Prevention of Crime)

預防犯罪是正當阻卻違法之正當事由之一。（參見MPC 3.07(D)）

㈢自我正當防衛(Self-Defense)

阻卻違法事由之一。（參見MPC 3.04）

The elements of self-defense rest on reasonable appreciation of imminent bodily harm from unlawful force. However, one may defend with reasonable necessary force. Excessive force is not allowed.

正當防衛必需防衛不法之即時侵害，不得防衛過當，需使用合理之力量反擊，除非無法安全逃脫，否則不得輕易使用致命武器。

㈣防衛他人(Defense of Others)

防衛他人必需以合理之力量，不得使用致命武器。

㈤防衛住宅(Defense of Habitation)

防衛自己的住宅可使用致命的武器；防衛他人的住宅或不動產不得使用致命的武器，但得使用合理的武器或武力。

㈥防衛財產(Defense of Property)

防衛他人動產亦必需合理且不得使用致命武器。

第八節　刑事訴訟法(Criminal Procedure)

一、美國刑事訴訟法簡介(Criminal Procedure)

㈠美國刑事訴訟法之由來

1.簡　介

美國因有聯邦和州之雙軌系統，故其刑事訴訟法亦有雙軌之分。刑事訴訟法的很多規定直接和美國憲法互有關係。例如美國憲法第一修正案至第十四修正案，均與刑事訴訟法息息相關。聯邦系統可分：⑴地方法院(District Court)；　⑵上訴法院(Court of Appeal for Circuit court)；和⑶聯邦最高法院(U.S. Supreme Court)。

各州的系統較為繁亂，基本上可分：⑴初級法院或地方法院(Trial court)；⑵上訴法院(Intermediate Appellate Court)；和⑶州最高法院(Supreme court)。但在初級法院常有治安法庭 (Peace court) 或小額訴訟法院(Small claim court)，有些州稱為Superior court，如加州；上訴法院名稱亦不盡相同，例如紐約州之中級法院Supreme court/Appellate Division，其最高法院稱為Court of Appeal。有些州(例如Wyoming)並無中級法院。大多數的州最高法院則以Supreme court居多。另有交通法院(Traffic court)、少年法庭(Juvenile court)或遺囑認證法院(Probate Court)。

美國聯邦法院管轄的範圍如下：⑴根據憲法制定之美國法律、外國與美國所訂或將訂條約而發生之一切案件。⑵關於大使，和領事之案件。⑶涉及海商及海事管轄之案件。⑷以美國(United States)為被告之訴訟。⑸州與州間之訴訟。⑹不同州公民間訴訟(diversity of citizenship)。⑺同一州公民與他州公民買賣或讓與土地爭執之訴訟標的。⑻美國公民與外國人之訴訟。 ㉕另反托拉斯法、商標、專利、著作權、破產等案件均受聯邦之管轄。

刑事訴訟法的規定不得抵觸最高指導原則之憲法規定，任何抵觸之條文，皆被解為違憲(unconstitutional)。

2.刑事訴訟之流程

美國刑事訴訟的程序大致如下：

⑴受害人提出告訴：受害人得向司法警察提出告訴。

⑵司法警察或檢察官進行逮捕(arrest or book or apprehend)。

⑶移送告訴案件至檢察官(prosecutor)。

⑷檢察官決定是否移送少年法庭(juvenile court)。

㉕ 美憲法第一條第八節第十八項。

⑸若提起刑事告訴則依所犯罪名(file charge)。

⑹告訴罪名大多經由舉發之自白(affidavit)或檢察官提起告訴(information)或依大陪審團(grand jury)之起訴程序(indictment)而移送法院。

⑺地方法院法官審查該案件是否具有可能之原因(probable cause)。

⑻若有可能之原因，則可發出搜索狀或逮捕狀(票)。

⑼傳喚第一次出庭並分別告知修正案之第五條及第六條之權利。

⑽接下來第一次正式出庭，法院視被告是否無力(Indigent defendant)僱請律師而指定公設辯護人。

⑾進入預審聽證或決定預審會議，例如保釋金之多寡，提出排除證據或發見證據之異議。

⑿質詢證人(deposition or interrogation)。

⒀認罪之協議(plea bargain)：此協議除非有正當原因，法官不得介入，只存在檢察官和被告間之協議，故此認罪之協議，是檢察官或被告律師暗示性相互間讓步，以求事件早日結案或早日破案。被告因陳述承認某些事實，則可減輕其刑。但此建議法官減輕被告其刑，只是檢察官基於公法契約之建議權，若法官不買帳，被告仍可撤回認罪之協議，其先前依協議所陳述之自白，不得在庭上作為控告自己不利之證據。

⒁審判(trial)：由陪審團或法官(若自願性放棄陪審)評決或判決被告有罪或無罪。在刑法通常以People (NY), Commonwealth (Penn)或State代表人民，對被告提起告訴。

⒂判決徒刑之預先報告(pre-sentence report)。

(16)正式判刑(sentencing)： 決定是否入獄(prison or jail)或緩刑(probation)。

(17)執行被告所犯之罪於各個犯罪防治中心(Department of Correction)。

(18)被告若有不服，得提起上訴。但上訴並非憲法保障之權利。

3.個人受憲法保障之權利

　　基本上刑事訴訟法，係站在政府公法上之考量，例如整個社會的法益(general welfare)。在州方面則有警察權(police power)的考量，如提昇公共健康道德及公平正義，這些考量必需和憲法所保障之基本權益，即個人私法之期待權(right of expectation)。例如未經法律正當程序，在沒有可能原因(probable cause)，不得逕自逮捕人民；人民有受律師有效幫助和保持緘默之權。若有程序違法，大部分的州採用「證據排除」原則(exclusionary rule)，對被告未經正常法律程序而為之自白或認罪，該證詞不得採信。故憲法的相關法條常被視為被告之護身符， 在講究無合理懷疑之證據標準(Beyond reasonable doubt)下， 足見美國對被告之保護相當周全。O. J. Simpson的無罪開釋，可略見一二。

㈡O. J. Simpson案例探討

　　刑法和刑事訴訟法為一體之兩面，從O. J. Simpson的案例，我們可看出現今的法院在處理刑事案件之流程，已融合了電腦、科技和法律。法院重視正當程序，替代了辯才無礙的律師，法院一切講究證據，若無合理懷疑或超越合理懷疑(beyond a reasonable doubt)之證據能力，被告絕對會被諭知無罪。

　　自從辛普森(O. J. Simpson)的案件結束後，全世界舉目所見盡是科技與法律結合畫面，CNN媒體不時追蹤美國法院和評論司法制度之畫面。美國第一夫人希拉蕊之白水(White Water)案件，與柯林頓之醜聞案件亦曝露了大陪審團之調查經過與特別檢察官(Special Prosecutor)制度。英美法之所以異於大陸法系國家，主要在於刑事制度和程序與大陸法大異其趣。舉凡大陪審團、小陪審團、認罪協議、保持緘默權等均與我司法制度不同。本書拋磚引玉，摘錄濃縮美國法院判決公文書，並將筆者於美國密西根市法院與Judge Steven實習所獲經驗，分享給英美法學習者。

二、第四修正案：搜索和扣押(Search and Seizure)

㈠警察實務(Police Practice)

證據法之證據排除原則(exclusionary rule)，指若有違反正當法律程序所扣押的證據，因程序違法而導致整個實體證據，不得作為判決之依據。

警察於從事逮捕之前，若無非常迫切之緊急情況，非於判斷被告具有合理可能原因(probable cause)犯罪，不得向法院聲請拘票或搜索票逮捕之。

實務上，如警察依據其服務之年限與經驗，合理懷疑判斷被告可能攜帶危險武器(reasonable suspicion of carrying dangerous weapon)，得不依可能原因(probable cause)之標準，逕行對被告命令其勿動並進行摸索其外部的衣物(pat down outward)。所謂可能原因，即被告可能犯罪的機率大於不可能犯罪(more probable or likely than not)，但為了保障警察伸張正義，打擊犯罪，法律認為警察得不必等到具有可能之原因標準，只要依客觀事實與平日經驗論理原則，只要有合理懷疑對方可能攜帶危險武器，即可對其命令勿動(stop)並搜查(frisk)其外部的衣物。這是上述所謂正常情

況之例外之一(見Terry v. Ohio)。❷不用判斷可能原因之例外情形如下：

(1)Stop and Frisk(勿動並接受外部搜身)： 只要有合理之懷疑即 (reasonable suspicion)為之。

(2)consent(同意搜查)。

(3)plain view(視線所及之處若看見違禁物，均可逕行逮捕)。

(4)hot pursuit(逮捕現行犯)。

(5)Inventory search(存貨檢查)。

(6)school search(學校行政上之檢查)： 只要求合理懷疑即可(reasonable suspicion)。

(7)border search(邊界搜索)。

(8)automobile search(汽車搜索)。

(9)exigent circumstance(緊急情況)。

(10)search incident to lawful arrest (合法逮捕後之搜查)。

上述皆為立法之考量，為了避免證據之流失，允許這些情況，得不必聲請可能原因之搜索或逮捕狀，警方得直接向被告施以羈押。

因此，對人的搜索和扣押常常剝奪了人對隱私權之期待。故如何找出其平衡點，則為刑事法學研究之重要課題。原則上，檢警單位從嫌犯(suspect)簽名、談話錄音、查詢其銀行存款提款資料、私人訪問、例行定點盤檢、或利用訓練警犬從事對嫌犯之偵察工作，多為實務上接受。惟整個情事若侵犯嫌犯應有的隱私權，無合理懷疑或可能原因下，逕行從事違法之搜索或扣押，則應屬為違憲。

---

❷　Terry v. Ohio, 392 U.S. 1, 20 L.Ed. 2d 889, 88 S.Ct. 1868 (1968).

惟何謂可能的原因，一般指高於50%可能性，即強烈懷疑嫌犯或被告犯罪之機率高於50%(strong suspicion of guilt)。

㈡檢察官職權(Prosecutor's Discretion)和大陪審團之公訴 (Grand Jury Indictment)

檢察官(Prosecutor or District attorney or D.A.)是負責偵查階段的執法人員。重大刑案涉及死刑或不名譽之罪時，須由大陪審團提起公訴。故檢察官之職權，不若臺灣之「檢座」，擁有極大權限，因為遇有重大刑案，需要雙方互相配合，由大陪審團幫助檢察官，共同偵察犯罪事實，以決定是否提起公訴或移送法辦。

一般起訴方式有三：⑴由人民以宣誓書(affidavit)舉發告訴；⑵由檢察官之起訴書(Information)起訴；⑶由大陪審團提起公訴(Indictment)。大部分的州仍以檢察官起訴書起訴居多。聯邦憲法第五修正案規定，人民非經大陪審團起訴，不受死罪或其他不名譽罪之審判。檢察官之羈押權，如我刑訴法第416條規定，仍需受制於法院之事後審查。故在偵察階段檢察官和大陪審團（死刑或不名譽罪）共同監督起訴，另法院審判階段中有12位（或6位）陪審員及法官（又稱第13個陪審員）組成，故共十三人同時監督互為審理事實真象。

最近我國欲擴大檢方職權不起訴範圍，減低第一、二審法官之辦案壓力和數量。限制上訴第三審案件範圍擴大(刑訴§376)，除最重本刑為3年以下有期徒刑外，增列竊盜罪、侵占罪、詐欺、背信、恐嚇、贓物罪等，均不得上訴第三審法院。很多人不信任二審法官的判決原因，不外我國採事實二次審。一審和二審均可為事實審，自由心證又不得不引用情況下，其結果可能犧牲了人民三級三審的權利。若太注重法官的辦案數量，卻剝奪人民受審

之公正裁判品質之權益，如何提昇司法公信，難自圓其說。如回歸在第一審採事實一次審，避免二審事實審之再現，方是提昇司法改革之重點。另羈押權究歸檢察官或法官也是一般人較易混淆的地方，英美法之國家，羈押權屬於法院，英國可由警察機關向法官對嫌犯聲請羈押。檢察官並沒有簽發拘票或押票的權利，搜索票必須向法院行政官(magistrate)聲請，若沒有符合緊急不需搜索罪之例外情形時，則所採擷之證據為非法取得，若當時情況緊急，符合例外情事之事由，則需有預備公聽會(preliminary hearing)，於72小時或48小時內，決定該沒有搜索票之逮捕羈押是否合法，即是否具有可能之原因(probable cause)。臺灣目前規定，檢察官仍存強制羈押權，犯罪嫌疑人移送至法院檢察署後，檢察官方能進行偵察，再依偵察作出起訴或不起訴處分，檢察官在決定羈押後，在24小時內連同卷宗、證物需立即移送法官，法官在48小時內馬上審查裁定，即所謂事後立即審查制。檢察官得於24小時內抗告，抗告應於48小時內裁定後向法院抗告。羈押人犯後，應即告訴本人及親友，落實羈押人犯的通知義務。在美國，事前需向法院請求押票，可防止檢方私下用刑逼供，檢警機關必須先蒐集相當充足之證據，以能徵信於法官，而非以嚴刑拷問，逼供取得被告之自白。

檢察官的另一職權，即與被告作認罪之協議(plea bargain)，再把協議書呈給法官，作為減刑之建議。認罪之協議為眾多國家所攻擊，主要原因即被告得施加壓力於檢察官，要求刑期減少交換檢察官之早日破案。雖然實務上提早破案，提昇司法之效率，但卻助長賄賂討價還價之困擾。美國還有一種特別檢察官(Independent or Special prosecutor)，即司法部可基於國會之要求，聲請華盛頓特區之聯邦上訴法院，指定一獨立特別檢察官，調查高階行政部門官員之犯行。例如水門事件之特別檢察官與調查柯林頓之特別檢察官。

通常之起訴以檢察官之起訴書(Information)即可。但依據美聯邦憲法第五修正案，任何死罪或不名譽之罪之起訴，需經大陪審團(Grand jury)來提起公訴(Indictment)。大陪審團由16～23位非法律專業人員所組成，主要目的在幫助檢察官調查事實。其評決方式只要過半數同意即可(majority vote)。接受大陪審團審判並非憲法保障之基本權利。大陪審團得依非法取得之證據或傳聞證據，起訴被告。因此在偵察階段有大陪審團制衡檢察官之職權起訴，猶如審判訴訟中有一般陪審團牽制法官之判決一樣，充份表現美國司法制度中相互制衡的一面。

大陪審團得單方秘密進行(secret & ex parte)，調查事實。有些州並不以大陪審團來提起告訴，而以檢察官起訴居多。但在聯邦對於不名譽之罪，人民有權要求受大陪審團負責起訴之權利，基本上大陪審團制度對原告（檢察官）較有利，但預審公聽會或預審(preliminary hearing)則對被告較有利。

三、逮　捕(Arrest)

㈠搜索票(Warrant)

搜索票(Warrant)之執行通常在警員執行任務時，因具合理可能原因(probable cause)確信而向法院聲請搜索票後，方能遂行搜索或逮捕。倘無合理可能之原因，則屬程序上之違法。警察執行勤務時發現非常緊危情事，來不及向法院聲請搜索或逮捕狀時，根據其經驗論理客觀因素，若非即時扣押，則該嫌疑犯可能逃之

夭夭，證據之保持不易時，可在沒有搜索票之情況下，逕行搜索或逮捕嫌疑犯。❷根據美國聯邦憲法第四修正案，對人民之身體、住家、文件及個人之物，非經法律正當程序，聲請搜索票後，不得逕行逮捕與扣押。法律正當程序(Due process of law)要求警方舉證合理可能原因(probable cause)，並需於搜索票載明搜索地點、欲搜索之事物。

㈡搜索之例外

不用搜索票例外情事，已於警察實務敘明。茲摘要敘述例外情形如下：

1.搜　身(Stop & frisk)

警員於執行勤務時，遇見可疑人等，對於嫌疑犯可能攜帶致命危險武器(deadly weapon)時，且逾合理懷疑(reasonable suspicion)階段，警察可逕行命令其停止行動，並由衣服外部(outer cloth)拍向內部衣服，檢查該嫌疑犯是否攜帶任何危險武器。該由上而下拍衣服(pat down)之行為，不得直接向衣服內部搜索，其目的只針對搜查衣服內部危險武器(dangerous arms)，而不可為其他之目的。一般不需搜索票之例外，所要求之證據多為可能原因(probable cause)，而非合理懷疑(reasonable suspicion)之地步。

2.嫌犯或第三人同意警察搜查(Consent's search)

若嫌犯同意警察於無搜索狀情況下搜查，表示嫌犯同意其搜索，警方並不會因為缺少搜索狀，而所採之證據被視為程序不合法而失其證據能力。同意人若為嫌犯之家屬(family)，實務上認為嫌犯家屬之同意，等於嫌犯之同意，嫌犯不得提出異議主張湮滅

❷　Giordenello v. United States, 357 U.S. 480, 2 L.Ed. 2d 1503, 78 S.Ct. 1245 (1958).

證據(motion to suppress evidence)。因此，只要嫌犯之同意被搜查是自願性的，即屬合法。但房東同意警員入內搜索房客(嫌犯)之房間，褓姆同意警員入內搜查嫌犯房間，旅社主人或僱主同意警察入內搜查嫌犯之房間時，不等於嫌犯自願之同意。即使嫌犯之同居人或家屬同意警員入內搜索，但僅能搜索公開未上鎖之空間部分，對於已上鎖之個人隱私部分，仍不得為之。

3.視線所及之搜索(plain view)

對於警察視線所及之公開搜索(open field investigation)，並不須搜索狀，因此，警員利用放大鏡，從事合法之搜索，亦屬合法。例如，警員於道路之一側，以望遠鏡眺看屋內之動靜。警員於搜索汽車時，視野掃描到後座之槍枝，警員得不須再回法院聲請搜索狀，而得逕行沒收扣押該物並採為證據。

4.逮捕現行犯(Hot pursuit)

對於現行犯之逮捕，因情事緊急，若非即時現時逮捕，對於證物、嫌犯可能流失或逃匿。因此特開例外，不用聲請搜索票。但該現行之急迫必須是非常緊急(Very hot)。

5.存貨檢查(Inventory search)

對於任何有存貨之地方，警方得逕行要求檢查。例如汽車之行李，貨車之貨櫃。

6.行政或學校之檢查(Administrative or school search)

行政或學校之檢查須符合合理懷疑地步，而不須如較高的可能原因(probable cause)標準。例如學校校長主觀上認為有合理懷疑，該學生可能攜帶黃色書刊，得檢查其書包。因行政或學校之檢查不若司法警察之檢查，故所要求的標準降低，這與搜身扣押(stop and frisk)所要求的程度相當，即合理懷疑標準(reasonable

suspicion)即可。

7.邊界搜索(Border search)

　　本例外情形乃針對逃犯可能企圖逃往邊界，而賦予警方人員不需搜索票之逮捕和搜索。

8.汽車搜查(auto search)

　　汽車之搜查以視線所及之處(plain view)為主。　❷但若無可能之原因，例如無超速或其他可疑之處，警察不得隨意阻擋來往行車(random stop)，除非該車輛檢查是例行公事(routine check)或定點道路臨檢(roadblock check)，如酒醉程度(sobriety)測試。大部分州只允許警員檢查前座和後座的空間，有些州允許檢查前座置物廂(glove box)，有些州則不允許；有些州更允許可檢查後車子行李箱(trunk)，若該合法程序已具備，但有些州仍不允許。一般而言，在高速公路上，奔馳之車輛不得主張警方之檢查其車輛違反人民隱私權。但若使用監聽汽車之方式，則需依法定規定，不得對被告任意監聽。

9.緊急搜索(exigent search)

　　任何合於緊急情狀，具有正當理由，得在沒有搜索票之情狀下，逕行搜索。例如由可靠消息(reliable information)獲知犯人或被告正搭機潛逃。

10.合法逮捕後附帶搜索(search incident to lawful arrest)

　　若警方進行合法之逮捕後，另行於搜索時發現其他非法證據，則該證據亦可成為日後庭上控告被告或嫌犯之證據。該合法逮捕後附帶搜索，並不需聲請搜索票。反之若於不合法逮捕後，發現

---

❷　United States v. Rabinowitz, 339 U.S. 56, 94 L.Ed. 653, 70 S.Ct. 430 (1950).

其他非法之證據，則該證據不得使用，除非符合善意取得原則。㉙

　　但基於防止證據取得之流失，有些雖犧牲了人民的隱私權，有限度搜索仍是合法的。因聯邦憲法第四修正案禁止非法之搜索和扣押，而非禁止合理之搜索。各州視為合法之搜索，人民必需犧牲隱私權，以換取提昇公共道德、健康和安全等公共利益考量，例如法庭或警察局內之照相行為、命令書狀簽名、錄嫌犯之聲音、查嫌犯或被告銀行存款、在嫌犯或被告廢棄房屋找尋到之財產、警犬嗅出被告之違禁物、定點臨檢酒醉程度、公立學校檢查學生在校的個人財產、任何在公開場合警察所檢查之事項或任何私人和嫌犯之對話，這些搜索或接觸，並非第四修正案所稱「非法之搜索」。

四、證　據(Evidence)

㈠證據排除法則(Exclusionary evidence)

　　檢警單位若沒有合理懷疑，對人搜身檢查是否攜帶危險武器或於沒有可能原因或沒有搜索票情況下，逕自搜索和扣押人民身體或財產，違法搜索扣押期間，所獲得的證據，均不得於日後在庭上作為控告被告的證據。此一原則又稱「**壽樹果實原理**」(fruit of poisonous tree)，即由壽樹所採摘的果實，係不可食的！故非由法定程序所取得的證據，法院不得採用。但有些州卻仍容許一些違反法定程序(Due process of law)所取得的證據，只要該證據之取得在「**善意原則**」下獲得(good faith exception)。早期聯邦的案件，任何違反法定程序所取得的證據，皆不可採。但目前已有判例援

㉙　Katz v. United States, 389 U.S. 347, 19 L.Ed. 2d 576, 88 S.Ct. 507 (1967).

用雖於事後發現搜索狀格式或記載項目稍有瑕疵，但對所採到之證據或證物，仍不排除其證據能力。❸

(二)傳聞證據(Hearsay)及證據能力

刑法所要求的證據能力為無(或超越)合理懷疑證據力(beyond reasonable doubt)，不若民法要求之優勢證據(evidence of preponderance)，只要求50%以上之證據力程度即可。無合理懷疑證據力指為證明被告犯罪，州必須證明每一犯罪構成要件符合犯罪事實，只要有一項或一點具有合理懷疑，被告應被判無罪。推定被告無罪(presumption of innocence)乃刑法之基本原則。近年民刑事，有些州已要求清晰具說服力之證據程度(clear and convincing evidence)，此證據能力，介於優勢和無合理懷疑證據能力之間。

傳聞證據(Hearsay)是一種在法庭外第三人所說的話。是否傳聞證據具有證據能力，需視該傳聞是否具有可信性。所謂具有「證據能力」(competent evidence)，指該證據實質上很重要，在邏輯上和法律上相關，足以採信。原則上，責任保險、事後之補救措施、和解協議、類似之行為、人格證據，不具證據能力，除非它是直接根據或情況證據，最好是原始證據。口頭證據(parol evidence)亦為有效之證據；專家證詞亦具有證據力；臨死之人所講之詞，通常在刑事案件，具有證據能力。一般眾所皆知，由政府公告的事實，亦不需查證，即屬具有採信之證據能力。

由某人於法院外所得知傳聞之詞，不得為證據法之證據能力，除非該言詞係用來證明情況證據之心理感受、認知等證明合理聽眾者於聽後之感想與法律上重要之事實。另傳聞證據於下列例外中，亦屬有效，即使講傳聞之人不知其下落(Hearsay exception:

---

❸　U.S. v. Leon, 468 U.S. 897 (1984).

availability of declarant is immaterial)：⑴證明目前感受印象：即描述或說明現在或之後所觀察之印象(Present sense impression)；⑵受刺激而發之語，在沮喪或震驚下所講的話(Excited utterance)；⑶當時存在心智上、情感上或身體上之情緒反應(Then existing mental, emotional, or physical emotion)；⑷為醫學治療目的而說之話(Statement made for medical treatment)；⑸曾經記錄的筆錄(Recorded recollection)；⑹商業記錄(Business record)；⑺公共記錄和報告(Public record and report)；⑻出生日期、死亡日期及結婚日期之記錄(Record of birth, death, or marriage)；⑼任何影響財產利益文件上之言詞(Statements in document affecting interest in property)；⑽早期古老文件(Ancient documents)：指超過20年之文件；⑾市場報告、商業上出版報告(Market reports, commercial publications)；⑿具有學術性知名論文(Learned treatises)；⒀人格名譽(Reputation as to character)；⒁昔日犯罪判決(Judgment of previous conviction)；⒂其他公平利益之情形。

　　另外一組例外情事，必須以講傳聞之人(declarant)已下落不明或無從出現(declarant must be unavailable)為前提方具證據能力：⑴先前證詞(Former testimony)；⑵因預見且相信死亡將發生所說之詞(Statement made under belief of impending death)；⑶任何在民法或刑法上之所說對自己不利益之言詞(Statement made against interest)，若為刑法上之不利益(penal interest)，必須經過證實(corroboration)否則不具證據能力；⑷對個人或家庭歷史之所說之言詞(Statement of personal or family history/family pedigree)；⑸其他依公平利益之例外(other exception in the interest of justice)。另外有一種「例外之例外」，即「傳聞中之傳聞」(Hearsay within hearsay)，

該二組或二組以上之傳聞均應符合傳聞證據之例外情形，其證據方具有證據能力。

(三)預備公聽會(preliminary Hearing)

預備會議，係行政或治安法官(magistrate)對沒有搜索票情況下之逮捕或搜索時，進行決定逮捕過程是否具有可能原因(probable cause)。這是多一層保護被告之權益。預備公聽會是公開舉行討論可能原因。證據排除原則、緘默權與接受律師權利，均適用於預備公聽會。但接受預備公聽會審判，並不是一種憲法所保障之權利，此種公聽會對被告而言，仍較有保障。

若被控罪名係輕罪(misdemeanor)時，不得要求預備公聽會。當被告放棄大陪審團會審判時，亦視為放棄預備公聽會。當大陪審團已提起公訴時，被告無權要求陪審。預備公聽會之舉行方式，得公開或單方秘密(ex parte)進行。其目的在縮小調查之範圍。律師得於預備公聽會出席，為被告主張犯罪可能原因之不存在。

(四)傳票提出文件證據(subpoena duces tecum)

若訴訟之一方知悉有利自己之證據，但無法獲得時，得聲請法院透過傳票方式(Subpoena)，要求相關人員提出一些文件(Subpoena duces tecum)。

民事訴訟法有些規定，亦適用於刑事訴訟法。例如開證制度(Discovery)中，有關證據採擷之規定；例如對人管轄、當事人辯論主義等。

五、保釋制度(Bond)

保釋權利並非憲法第八修正案所保障的基本權利，第八修正案只規定法院不得科以過高之保釋金。對於實質保障，法院不得科以過高之罰金(bond)或命令繳交數額過高之保釋金，但並不是每一個人均得要求保釋。　保釋制度只適用於非死刑之罪(non-capital offenses)。保釋制度在確保被告如期到庭應訊、預防嫌犯脫逃與確保社區安全。若在沒有保釋金之選擇時，被告得依違反實質之法律正常程序作攻擊防禦的答辯。法院依據嫌犯之背景、所犯罪名、過去所犯罪名、動機等作出保釋金之金額。因此保釋金因人而異。若在第一次聲請保釋被拒，仍得上訴繼續聲請。此時上級法院必須嚴格審核下級法院，決定下級法院是否可能犯嚴重之錯誤(Reversible error)，　嫌犯或被告是否有逃亡之虞(risk of flight)及嫌犯或被告對社區之危險性(danger of defendant)。

六、保持緘默權(Right to Remain Silent)

當嫌犯或被告被監禁或拘提時，而且被警察詢問對自己不利之問題時，憲法第五修正案賦予人民不得被迫自證其罪，被告有權要求告知被控告之罪名。此即Miranda Warning。在警察從事上述行為時，必先⑴告知被告有權保持緘默；⑵任何自願對自己不利之證詞可用在將來庭上成為控告自己之證據（呈堂證供）；⑶告知被告有權請律師協助；⑷若被告貧窮無力僱請律師時，政府必須提供辯護律師或公設辯護人。❸ 因此，倘警察沒有告知被告上述權利時，即違反法定程序後，被告所說之詞，不得採為對被告不利之證據，除非警察或州能證明，被告係在有意識下，自願性明知放棄第五修正案之緘默權。"I take fifth." 表示被告欲主張緘默權(我要主張第五修正案權利)，警察於告知Miranda權利後，變成

---

❸　Miranda v. Arizona, 384 U.S. 436, 16 L.Ed. 2d 694, 86 S.Ct. 1602 (1966).

沉默之一方。之所以稱為Miranda警告，乃因Miranda v. Arizona的案例，使以後Miranda warning適用上述被告四項權利。第五修正案之緘默權僅適用於刑法，民法不適用之。

七、受律師幫助之權利(Right to Counsel)：第六修正案

接受律師幫助權利為憲法第六修正案中，賦予美國人接受有效之律師幫助(effective assistance by counsel)。只要律師公平公正盡力替客戶辯護且無過失，即使敗訴，客戶不得主張無效之律師幫助而主張違憲。因此律師之無經驗、缺乏時間投入案情、無法覓得主要證人、或重大複雜案件，因而打輸官司，不得遽以認定第六修正案中，接受律師有效幫助之權利被剝奪，以下階段均視為重要階段(critical stages)，被告得要求律師必須在場：⑴公訴後之嫌犯排列供人指認；⑵審判後之被告排列(line up)供人指認；⑶預備公聽會；⑷認罪之協議；⑸宣判徒刑；⑹提審(arraignment)；⑺上訴；⑻輕罪起訴，但最後被處以重罪。但下列情況則非重要階段，律師不須在場：⑴警察調查階段；⑵行政上之程序；⑶任意之上訴；⑷預備嫌犯身分指認；⑸未提起公訴前之嫌犯排列供人指認；⑹一造非雙方辯論審判；⑺人身自由保護提審(Habeas corpus)；⑻大陪審團公訴(Grand Jury indictment)；⑼照相。通常被告律師有訴訟策略之選擇權，如需採被告所建議方案或說詞，被告不得以未受律師有效幫助，而抗辯第六修正案權利受損。

另在美國，被告亦得自訴(self-representation)，但這非憲法所賦予之權利，被告得選候補律師(Standby counsel)，向其諮詢，但一切程序需由被告主導訴訟，候補律師不得過份影響被告之訴訟抉擇。要證明律師有法律誤診或缺乏效率，被告必須舉證律師的

表現欠妥，而且若非該律師之缺失表現，❷被告之權益應不會被剝奪(reasonable probability test)。

八、罪狀認否程序(Arraignment)

㈠答 辯(Plea)

1.有 罪(guilty)

百分之九十以上的案例，均於被告之自白(confession)中承認有罪而結案。但自白需出自於自願，不得受脅迫或違反法定程序。

2.無 罪(not guilty)

若被告於答辯中堅稱無罪，州必須證明被告無合理懷疑，已犯下該罪(beyond reasonable doubt)。 被告係被推定為無罪(presumption of innocence)，故不得恣意推斷被告有罪，美國是一個採取法定證據的國家。第一審由陪審團組成，在法官之陪審指示書(Jury Charge)下， 共同參與評議(deliberation)後， 而下評決(Verdict)。

3.不願辯護但不承認有罪(nolo contendre plea)

有時候被告不願辯護但不承認有罪，也不否認該訴訟，造成法院以後不可以一事不再理(Res judicata or issue preclusion)否決以後被告再次提起原案,因為爭端或案件並非依法得到最終判決,因此很多民事上，自然人或公司利用此種答辯方式，企圖製造日後翻案之機會。

㈡認罪協議(Plea Bargain)

認罪之協議通常由檢察官(prosecutor)與被告間協議，而非法

---

❷ Strickland v. Washington, 466 U.S. 668, 80 L.Ed. 2d 674, 104 S.Ct. 2052 (1984).

官和被告協議。除非法官有「**正當理由**」(good cause)，得禁止被告與檢察官作認罪協議，否則法官不得介入。

認罪之協議是一種公法之契約，即檢察官把與被告達成了認罪協議書寫成公法上之契約，將它呈給法官並作成求刑之建議，法官沒有絕對義務接受該協議。因此，法官若不接受，該協議視為原始撤回，不生任何效力，惟此時「**心理效果**」(psychological effect)已形成，對被告有某程度之不利。因此法官以不利於被告之證詞起訴，會違反第五修正案之二次危害(double jeopardy)原則。有關私法契約法之原則，例如禁止反言(promissory estoppel)或特別履行(specific performance)等原則，均不得適用於檢方與被告間認罪協議之公法契約。

九、審　判(Trial)

㈠律師在場(Right to Counsel)

在審判階段，律師必須在場辯論，因這是一項重要階段。由開始辯論(opening statement)、經直接質詢(direct examination)、交互質詢(cross examination)、再直接質詢(redirect examination)、反駁質詢(rebuttal examination)至結束辯論(closing statement)，律師依第六修正案均需在場。

㈡公開迅速之審判(Public Speedy Trial)

1. 公開審判

審判必須公開，除非法院認有正當理由，得秘密隔離某部分人，以免曝光。例如被強姦未成年少女，於審問時，得限制聽眾聆聽等。美國甚至得允許電視進入審判。但若該電視播放不該播的部分，法院可禁止之。例如鏡頭照到O. J. Simpson之陪審員時，即屬不當。

2.公平審判(Impartial Jury)

審判必須秉持公平原則。對雙造當事人，對社會國家負責，以維司法公信力。因此，陪審團員之選任，扮演著重要的角色。在O. J. Simpson的案件裡，被告(黑人)由多名黑人，二名白人和一位黃種人組成之陪審團接受審判。即秉持每一社區中不同地域的不同族裔代表人民，組織一無種族偏見、無男女歧視、無宗教歧視之陪審團，作出評決。若無陪審團的案件，法官必須依客觀公平的論理與衡平原則下，力求伸張司法正義。

3.迅速審判(Speedy Trial)

當被告被逮捕或起訴時，被告有權要求接受迅速審判。但迅速審判必須視案件之複雜性，承辦司法人員之身體狀況或生病而延展之。根據The Speedy Trial Act規定，被告應於第一次詢問後70日內指定審判日。檢察官是否有過失常是判斷迅速審判之依據。下列因素為判斷迅速審判之原因：⑴遲延之期間(Length of delay)；⑵被告利用答辯機會拖延訴訟(Assertion of Defendant's right)；⑶是否偏見(prejudice)；⑷遲延之原因(reason of delay)，例如法官生病，懸而不決之評決(hung jury)因而需要重審(retrial)，造成社會動盪。Rodney King的評決中四名白人警察被判無罪後，造成洛城黑人大暴動，因而重審。(但有些專家認為重審，違反了憲法第五修正案有關禁止二次危害之原則。)

㈢陪審團評決(Jury Trial: Verdict)

陪審團之組成通常由12人組成，亦有6人組成之小陪審團(petit jury)，但後者其評決需全體一致通過。刑事案件中之微罪(petty offense)不得要求陪審，縱美國憲法第六修正案規定，任何

人得要求受陪審團審判之權利，被告亦可放棄接受陪審權利，但該放棄必須自願性、有意識的、明知的情況下。我國早期亦有陪審，但經國家動盪，只實施幾年因而作罷。民國38年後，在立法院民刑商法委員會(即司法委員會)決議不採。美聯邦司法案件要求需12人全體一致同意通過審判，大部分的州亦採12人之陪審團，其表決方式也是需要全體一致通過。惟現行已有11:1或10:2或甚至9:3之評決(verdict)出現。這12人均非法律專業人員，而是由平民百姓所組成，即社區之成員代表(fair cross section of community)，其任務首在第一審，發現事實真相(fact finder)，法官只於第二、三審，依法律審適用法律，不得於第一審調查事實。律師於選擇陪審員時，得利用聲請強制迴避(peremptory challenge)來拒卻某一陪審員，但不需說明原因，大致上可利用此權利次數民刑事有上限之規定，因為具原因之說明拒持時，會使對造律師知悉其訴訟上之策略(work product of strategy)，因此只需提供中立之解釋(neutral explanation)，均可順利排除該陪審員，例如種族歧視，高度偏見(bias)等。充任陪審員是國民之義務，若被選上卻又遭律師們聲請強制迴避拒持，心中難免有所不服，因此愈來愈多的人於被聲請迴避，不得充任陪審員後，立即以違反憲法平等保障(equal protection)原則，抗辯違憲。但只限於重罪之起訴，輕罪之案件，不得以平等保障抗辯違憲。

雖然放棄陪審是一種權利，但這種放棄必須是自願明知或有意識，有時檢察官會依職權調查後方同意被告放棄。陪審團於二造律師結束辯論後(closing argument)，進入評議(deliberation)階段。O. J. Simpson的案子，雖歷經約一年，但陪審團只花了四小時評議，就作成無罪之評決(Verdict)。

在紐約州，警察、律師、消防人員、醫生、物理治療師、神職人員、裝義肢之人員、逾70歲之老年人、照顧小孩之母親、小企業僱用三人以下的公司人員，均得不必充任陪審員。

㈣對質權利(Confrontation)

被告有權要求知悉被控之罪名及理由。被告有權依第六修正案，要求與不利於己之證人對質(right of confrontation)，並要求法院以強制方式傳喚證人，如要求有利於己之證人，到庭作證(subpoena favorable witness to testify in court)。

㈤強制迴避或拒卻(Peremptory Challenge)

兩造律師與檢察官得利用聲請強制迴避來選擇自己喜愛之陪審員。這是一種訴訟策略(trial strategy)，且不必具體說明原因，便可直接排除某陪審員(juror)，但拒卻次數不得使用太多，例如有些州刑事三次(或六次)以上，法院則要求說明正當原因。這種制度近年來倍受攻擊為違憲，原因不外乎違反平等保障原則，加州和其他少數州甚至允許法官於正常理由下(good cause)，亦可替換任何不合作陪審員。在白人Dennis beating的案件和黑人O. J. Simpson案例中，法官均曾替換了諸名不合作或言論偏激的陪審員。

十、雙重危險(Double Jeopardy)

一事不再理(Res Judicata or issue preclusion)建立在美聯邦憲法第五修正案規定之二次危險之禁止(double jeopardy)。 像O. J. Simpson的案件，一旦O.J.被當庭開釋無罪，則不得就相同事實，以另一刑事訴訟再行起訴，因美國的事實審只有一次，二三審均為法律審。 二次的危險即雙重危險(Successive prosecution for the same offense)，如不知什麼時候屆至，必會對被告造成壓力。但有

些大陸法國家，因容許二次事實審，認為被告於同一案件中經歷多次控訴，自始至終，方為整個流程之繼續，焉有雙重或二次危險之虞？故應只有一次危險而已。惟英美法採用禁止雙重危險規定，禁止連續起訴相同罪名，被告似乎較保障。

雙重危險之禁止於被告在有陪審團宣誓時或於沒有陪審團時證人(Witness)宣誓時，即可主張。雙重危險僅適用於刑法和少年法庭，但不適用於民法。因此O.J.的案外案，即好幾個控告O.J.民事訴訟接踵而至，不因刑事之獲諭無罪，而採一事不再理。通常依公共利益、檢察官惡意起訴、經查具有偏見、程序瑕疵等，或造成社會暴動，該案均得要求重審(retrial)，常見的重審原因如下：⑴懸而不決之評決(hung jury)；⑵誤判(mistrial)；⑶證人失蹤(missing witness)；⑷偏見(prejudice or bias)；⑸檢察官惡意起訴(prosecutor vindictiveness)；⑹嚴重證據上錯誤(reversible error)；⑺新證據之發見(new evidence)；⑻起訴前之遲延(preindictment delay)；⑼不同民刑事要件罪名之起訴；⑽違反認罪之協議；⑾法定上訴；⑿雙重管轄(dual sovereign)：　例如民刑事管轄或聯邦與州之不同管轄競合；⒀被告不當行為造成誤判(defendant's misconduct)等。

但下列情況通常非憲法所保障雙重危險之禁止之列，即不得要求重審：⑴檢方故意至陪審宣誓後方揭示程序或實質瑕疵；⑵被告已判無罪(acquittal)；⑶另行起訴較重罪名(greater offense)；⑷檢方故意錯誤而獲敗訴；⑸證據不足。

十一、審判後救濟(Post-trial Remedy)

㈠州法律救濟(State)

州初級法院若對被告有不利之判決時，得上訴中級（高等法院(Appellate intermediate courts)。 但上訴時需注意是否該案件(claim)或爭議點(issue)已在實質面判決過。若實質上前一次的判決 (評決)，已達最後且為有效判決時，第二次審判如對相同的事實再作一討論，證據已經充份討論過和作成決定，攻擊防禦之人亦已有充足和公平機會言詞辯論，根據「一事不再理」中爭議點禁止重覆提起原理(issue preclusion)，不得再為上訴之標的。同樣，若先前判決已終結且實質上有效判決後，第二次的當事人或因相同契因(privity)之當事人與第一次相同，而且訴訟之案件範圍和第一次相同，根據一事不再理之重覆案件禁止原理(Res Judicata)，亦不得成為上訴之標的。惟上訴並非憲法所稱之基本權利，有些案件得禁止上訴。

(二)人身自由保護(Writ of Habeas Corpus)

當州受刑人已被羈押(custody)或提審中，於判決時，仍有權向聯邦法院主張於提審階段中其人身自由權受侵害。惟被告不得故意越級，尋求聯邦人身自由保護規定(deliberate bypass)，當州已提供足夠之救濟(state available remedy)， 足使被告有機會申訴公平之管道。人身自由之主張，雖不得主張第四修正案之違反，但得主張第六修正案之違反。被告需於指定時間內(通常20日內)，得提出證明人身自由權之違反，例如遭毆打，逼供，刑求。這是一種重新之審判(de novo trial)。 州的監獄受刑人必須先證明州法律違反該保護規定， 否則越級(by pass)視為程序違反(procedural default)。

聯邦對人身自由亦有管轄權，聯邦法院於接到州受刑人主張人身自由違反，會先看州之人身自由聲請狀，是否違反公平正義原則(miscarriage of justice)， 是否被告故意越級聲請救濟(deliber-

ate bypass)，若沒有上述情形，聯邦法院得重審該人身自由之是否違反。

十二、結　論(Conclusion)

　　我民事訴訟法第222條規定，法院為判決時，應斟酌全辯論意旨及調查證據之結果，依「自由心證」判斷事實之真偽。證據力之證明力，由法院自由判斷，雖然法官依論理和經驗法則，為自由心證，但反觀英美為防止法官專斷，採取法定證據主義，注重關連性、正常性及可信性證據，以無合理懷疑證據貫穿其刑法和刑事訴訟法。無證據或有合理懷疑時，不得推定被告犯罪之事實，美國憲法第四修正案中，保障人民不得受不合理之搜索、搜身及扣押；第五修正案中規定人民有接受大陪審團審判權利、保持緘默權、雙重危險之禁止、平等保障等法律正常程序；第六修正案中有接受陪審團評決之權及公開迅速公平審判權利、對質權利、接受律師幫助之權等；第八修正案有不得科以被告過重罰金或繳納過高保釋金等，足見美國對被告之保障比大陸法系國家，有過之而無不及。法律程序(Due process of law)之程序瑕疵或程序正義觀念，尤應建立，臺灣常常發生先抓人再詢問事實之實務，檢察官握有恣意羈押權、法官高高在上，恍如電視的包青天，人民對法律認識低落，社會犯罪與日俱增等。其實與刑法之預防宣導不足有關，倘能於中學甚至小學，灌輸孩童憲法及刑法觀念，以教育嚇阻方式齊頭並進，必能有效降低犯罪率；另教導從事司法警察人員合理搜索逮捕等法律常識，以期保障被告基本權益。我國欲邁向民主法治國家，應以司法優先(Judicial supremacy)之決策胸襟，而非一直以行政優先，製造一次又一次的官僚制度與君主專制。如此循次漸進改善司法，宣導法學教育，尊重實質正當法律程序，比較英美等其他先進國家法律，擇善從之。他山之石，可以攻錯，我想，必能於刑事訴訟法中，找到嫌犯之憲法基本人權與司法公信力之平衡點。

第三章　美國法律大綱(Legal Outline)

第一節　JUDICIAL PROCESS （司法程序）

I.GENERAL INFORMATION （以加州系統為主）

  A. California Courts System—not applicable to any other State or Federal Courts. （加州法院系統）

  B. Civil Lawsuits—Cases concerning personal injury, contracts, unlawful detainers and divorce. （民事訴訟）

  C. Procedure—It differs from substantive rules. （程序法）

  D. Federal Court System—See civil procedure outline. （聯邦制度）

II.THE STRUCTURE OF CALIFORNIA COURTS （法院結構）

  A. Preliminary Considerations

    1. Trier of Fact/Trier of Law (Jury/Judge) （事實／法律審）

      a. Trier of Fact—Jury listens to evidence presented and decides what actually occurred. （事實）

      b. Trier of Law—Applies the law to the facts and formulates

decision. （法律）

2. Original Jurisdiction/Judge Appellate Jurisdiction （最初管轄／上訴管轄）

  a. Original—Trial Courts （最初管轄）

  b. Appellate — Court of Appeals: intermediate appellant court （上訴管轄）

3. Jurisdiction （管轄）

  a. Subject Matter—basis of lawsuit, location of acts (cf: $50,000in federal) （標的事務管轄）

  b. Personal—place of residence, service of process （人之管轄）

  c. In rem （對物管轄）

  d. Quasi-in-rem （準對物管轄）

B. Trial Courts

1. Municipal Court （市政法院）

  a. Civil cases with damages less than certain amount （民事訴訟標的金額）

  b. Misdemeanor Crimes （輕罪）

  c. Infractions (Traffic Tickets, etc.) （交通違規）

  d. Unlawful (rent) Detainers （非法沒收：租金小於一定金額）

  e. Small Claims （小額訴訟）→represent on your own (attorney pro se)

2. Superior Court （上級法院）

  a. Divorce & Probate proceedings （離婚及遺囑認證程序）

　　　ｂ.Civil Lawsuits（民事訴訟標的金額）

　　　ｃ.Lawsuits involving Real Property (title of real estate)（不動產訴訟）

　　　ｄ.Unlawful Detainers（租金逾一定金額）（非法扣留押租金）

　　　ｅ.Felony Crimes（重罪）

　　　ｆ.Superior Court administered at County level （縣／郡法院）

Ｃ.Appellate Courts ＝ Intermediate Appellate Courts

　１.Court of Appeals（上訴法院）（中級法院）

　　　ａ.Appeals from Municipal & Superior Court decisions （由市政及上訴法院而來之案件）

　　　ｂ.Administered at District/Circuit level (NY: Appellate division)

　２.Supreme Court（最高法院）

　　　ａ.Appeals from Court of Appeals decisions (NY's Court of Appeals ＝ final court)

　　　ｂ.Appeals from some Superior Court decisions

　　　ｃ.Limited original jurisdiction

　　　ｄ.Administered at State level

　３.Superior Court (California): Appeals form small claims Judgment

　４.Limited Appellate Jurisdiction: Superior & Municipal Courts regarding own proceedings

Ⅲ. COURTROOM STRUCTURE（法庭結構）

A. Geography（位置）

1. Bench（法官席）

2. Bar（被告面對法官位置席；律師）

3. Counsel Table（律師席）

4. Witness Stand（證人席）

5. Jury box（陪審區）

B. Staff（人員）

1. Judge（法官）

2. Clerk（書記官／助理）

3. Bailiff（執行官）

4. Court Reporter（法院報導人）

5. Jury（陪審團）⟷Juror（陪審員）

Ⅳ. CIVIL LAWSUIT（民事訴訟）

A. Plaintiff/Petitioner (initiate)→Appellant（原告／上訴人）

B. Defendant/Respondent→Appellee（被告／被上訴人）

C. Complaint（起訴狀）

D. Summons（傳票；傳喚）

E. Answer/response (Reply)（答辯狀）

F. Legal Attacks（攻擊防衛）

1. Jurisdictional（管轄）

2. Sufficiency of Pleadings（訴狀之完整）

a. Demurrer（異議）

b. Motion to Strike（異議禁止）

G. Provisional Remedies (prior to Trial) [暫時救濟]

  1. Summary Judgment—No dispute for that of material Fact (discovery) [簡易判決]

  2. Judgment on Pleadings（訴狀判決）

  3. Provisional Attachment（假扣押）

H. Discovery—investigation（發見）

I. Judge/Jury—case at issue (Judge—law finder; Jury—fact finder) [法官／陪審團]

J. Trial Motions（異議之訴）

  1. Suppress（禁止）

  2. Amend（修正）

  3. Jury Instructions（陪審指示）

K. Trial（審判）

  1. Opening Statement（開始言詞辯論）

  2. Order of Presentation（順序）

  3. Trial & Objections（審判與異議）

  4. Prima Facie Case (rebuttable)（初步表面（證據）案件）

  5. Defenses（抗辯／答辯）

  6. Closing Argument（終結言詞辯論）

  7. Judgment（判決）

  8. Post Trial Motions（審判後異議）

  9. Appeal（上訴）

第二節　LEGAL　RESEARCH　（法律研究）

美國法律之浩瀚，在圖書館或電腦資料中，我們應學習如何找資料與引證出處，　以下資料簡述如何取得法律之引證處(citation)：

Ⅰ.GENERAL INFORMATION （一般資料）

　A.Common Law/Staturory Law/Case Law

　　1.Common Law─英國之遺產為大部分美國州之普通法

　　2.Statutory Law─立法制定訂立法律

　　3.Case Law─法院解釋與適用法條及先前判例之書面言論

　B.Doctrine of Stare Decisis （維持先前判決）

　　1."When a court has once laid down a principle of law as applicable to a certain state of facts, it will adhere to that principle, and apply it to all future cases where facts are substantially the same."

　　2."Stare Decisis" is the theory. （維持先前判例）

　C.Authority （法源）

　　The purpose of legal research is to find statutes and/or case law. These statutes or case law may be "cited" as the authority supporting a particular position.

　　1.Primary Authority （主要法源）

　　　a.Enactments of the Legislature (statutes) （法條）

　　　b.Written opinions of the Court (Case Law) （判例）

2. Secondary Authority（次要法源）

   a. All other Written Laws.（其他書面化法律文字）

   b. Scholar's publication（學者著書）

II. Research Sources—Primary Authority（主要法源）

  A. Statutes(codes)—法條（典）（例如Penal Code, Civil Code）

    1. California Codes—Statutory law of the State

    2. County Codes—Statutory law of the County

    3. Municipal Codes—Statutory law of the City

    4. U.S. Codes—Statutory law of the Federal Government

  B. Court Decisions (reporters)—依判決時間先後彙編之法院判決書冊，例如：

    1. California Reporter (Cal Rptr)

    2. California Appellate Reports (C.A.)

    3. California Reports (C)

    4. Pacific Reporter (Western States) (P)

    5. Lawyer Edition (L.Ed.)

    6. South Weatern (S.W.)

    7. North Eastern (N.E.)

III. RESEARCH SOURCES—SECONDARY AUTHORITY（次要法源）

  A. Books of Search—具有說明力之書籍

    1. Encyclopedia—百科全書，例如：

    California Jurisprudence (Cal Jur)

2. Summaries－彙編

3. Annotations－法條解釋文

4. Loose Leaf Service－最新更新活頁資料

B. Books of Index－書籍目錄

1. Dictionaries－definitions of legal words and phrases.（字典）

2. Digests－Contain a compiled index to Case Law.（摘要）

3. Form Books－格式化書籍（訴狀或契約等）

4. Citations－Contain information by which any reported case may be checked to determine if the rules of law（引證處）．例如：Shepard's

IV. CITATION（引證出處）

1. Case Law－All case law may be found in the Reporters.（案例）

2. Statutory Law－法條（制定法）

V. Basic Citation Form: Brief and memoranda（參見*A Uniform System of Litation*, the Harvard Law Review Ass'n）（引證格式示範）

A. cases:

1. P v. D, 348 F. Supp. 54, 56–58 (M.D. Pa., 1972), aff'd, 83 F. 2d 54 (3d Cir. 1973), aff'd, 41 U.S. 34 (1974)

2. W v. T, 800 P. 2d 107, 108 (Alaska 1979)

B. service:

1. P v. D, Fed. Sec. L. Rep. (CCH) 96, 509, at 93, 970 (N.D. Ind. May 22, 1978)

2. P v. D, No. 77-1205, slipop. At 3 (4th Cir. Aug. 3, 1978) (per curiam), aff'd, 44 U.S. 30 (1979)

C. constitutions: N.Y. Const. art. V., §9

D. statutes:

1. Civil Procedure Act §6.5 U.S.C. §666 (1988) 22 U.S.C. § 2567 (Supp. I 1983)

2. Department of Accounting Act. Pub. L. No. 89-670, §9, 80 Stat. 931 (1966)

E. legislative materials:

1. H.R. 305, 4th Cong., 3d Sess. §3, 12 Cong. Rec. 870 (1986)

2. Toxic Substances Control Act: Hearings on S. 77 Before the Subcomm. on the Environment of the Senate Comm. On Commerce, 94th Cong., 1st Sess. 43 (1976)

3. S. Rep. No. 10, 89th Cong., 1st Sess. 43 (1976)

F. books: Poll & F. Ma, The History of Law 1-14 (1895)

G. works not formally: H. Wech, Speech at the Meeting of the ABA printed the Supreme Court of the United States in Memory of Chief Justice White (Nov. 12, 1947)

H. periodicals:

1. Morris, Legislative Creativity, 78 Val. L. Rev. 587, 591-594 (1978)

2. Note, The Secession, 89 N.Y.U., L.J. 80, 80-120 (1980)

I. newspapers: *N.Y. Times*, Oct. 14, 1960, at 6, col. 1

J. treaties: G.S. Agreement, June 8-14, 1951, United States—Black Colony, art, IV, 2 U.S.T. 18, 1722 T.I.A.S. No. 23, at 8

*Blue book is a source for citations. See also *User's Guide to A Uniform System of Litton* (1988).

第三節 THE THIRTEEN FEDERAL JUDICIAL CIRCUITS（十三個聯邦巡迴上訴法院）

美國共有13個巡迴上訴法院如下：

第一巡迴區： Maine, N.H., Mass., Puerto Rico

第二巡迴區： N.Y., V.T., Conn.

第三巡迴區： P.A., N.J., Del, Virgin Island

第四巡迴區： V.A., West V.A., N. Carolina, S. Carolina

第五巡迴區： LA., TX, Mississippi

第六巡迴區： OH, KY, Tennessee

第七巡迴區： IN, IL, Wisconsin

第八巡迴區： N. Dakota, S. Dakota, Nebraska, Minnesota, Iowa, Missouri, Arkansas.

第九巡迴區： WA, Oregon, Idaho, Nevada, CA, Arizona

第十巡迴區： Wyoming, Colorado, Utah, New Mexico, Kansas, Oklahoma

第十一巡迴區： Alabama, Georgia, Florida

另二個獨立巡迴上訴法院如下：

*獨立巡迴區： Washington D.C.（和Federal各自獨立）

*獨立巡迴區： Federal Circuit（和D.C.各自獨立）

第四節　CONTRACT（契約法）

I.FORMATION（成立要件）

A.Offer — Offeror's proposal manifesting present intent to contract and creating a power of acceptance in offeree.（要約）

  1.More than intention to negotiate

  2.Definite and certain—parties, subject matter, time for performance, price are all essential (price can be implied) (price is a must in real estate contracts)

  3.Offer may be accepted until terminated by provision in offer, acts of the parties, or operation of law

B.Acceptance—Offeree exercises the power to create a contract which is properly communicated to offeror.（承諾）

  1.Must be unequivocal (unequivocal referable)（清晰對應）

  2.Must be communicated.（通知對方）

  3.Exceptions（例外）

    a.Waiver in offer（放棄）

    b.Act as acceptance（以行為承諾）

    c.Silence as acceptance: course of dealing or trade usage, receiving benefit（沉默＝承諾）

  4.Unilateral Contracts—performance of act as bargained for consideration (promise v. act)（單務契約）

  5.Bilateral Contracts—Offer requires the giving of a promise as bargained for promise or consideration (promise v.

promise)（雙務契約）

C. Consideration—a bargained for exchange of promises, acts or property by parties and resulting change in legal position by each（要約）

 1. Bargain—Each party incurring a legal liability in order to gain a legal right.（交易）

 2. Valuable Consideration—Consideration must have legal value. Adequate consideration is required. (sufficient consideration)（有價值之相當對價）

 3. Substitutes for Consideration（約因之替代物）

  a. Promissory estoppel（禁止反言）

  b. Promise in writing: e.g., marriage, real estate sale, answer debt for others, sale of goods over $500（書面）

  c. Promise supported by moral obligation（道德義務）

 4. Modification: good faith or unanticipated difficulties（修改）

Ⅱ. DEFENESES（抗辯事由）：Defenses to Formation

 1. Mistake（錯誤）

 2. Lack of Consideration（缺少約因）

 3. Fraud（詐欺）

 4. Illegal Contracts（不合法契約）

 5. Lack of Capacity（欠缺當事人能力）

 6. Failure to qualify for judicial enforcement（未符法定強制執行）

  a. Statute of Fraud (writing): marriage, real estate, etc.（防止

詐欺條例)

　　b. Unconscionable Contracts（不合理契約）

Ⅲ. RIGHTS AND OBLIGATIONS OF NON-PARTIES（非契約當事人之權利和義務）

　A. Beneficiary Contracts（第三人利益契約）

　　1. Performance directly to a third person

　　2. Beneficiary has direct right to seek remedy of a breach

　B. Assignment of Right and Delegation of Duties（債權讓與與債務承擔）

　　1. Party attempting transfer of rights is the "assignor" and designated recipient is the "assignee".

　　2. The party attempting the transfer of duties is the "delegator" and his nominee is the "delegate". (be aware not "delegatee")（債務承擔）

　　3. Parties may unilaterally assign or delegate, but cannot add or vary obligor's duty or the performance to which an obligee is entitled.（原則得單方讓與承擔）

　　4. Novation（債務免除）：第三人以書面表示債務免除

Ⅳ. PERFORMANCE OF CONTRACT（契約履行）

　A. Covenant—Terms which disclose what the parties promise to do or not to forbear form doing.（合同）；Failure to perform unconditional convenant is breach of contract.

　B. Conditions—Terms fixing the time or order of performance, or

circumstances under which duties become or cease to be present legal obligations. （條件）

1. Failure to satisfy a condition is not a breach, but discharges contract duties of the promisor whose conditional promise never mature.

2. Condition precedent—A contingency which must occur before a present duty matures. Until satisfied or excused, the promisor has no obligation to perform. （附停止條件）

3. Condition Concurrent—Contingency that must be satisfied at the same as performance is rendered. Occurs only in bilateral contracts and is usually constructive rather than express. （附同時履行條件）

4. Condition subsequent—Contingency which extinguishes a previous matured duty. Unless condition ripens, promisor remains liable on duty. If it occurs, further performance on duty is discharged. （附解除條件）

5. Excuse of Conditions—Duty to perform may arise without performance of condition. Arises when promisee indicates that he cannot or will not perform his conditional obligations and promisor agrees to perform anyway. Examples are:

  a. Waiver （放棄）

  b. Estoppel （禁止反言）

  c. Voluntary Disablement （自願性不能）

  d. Anticipatory Breach （事前違約）

C. Discharge of Matured Obligation （免除義務）

1. Operation of law（法律規定）

2. Impossibility — commercial impracticability, frustration of purpose（不可能）

3. Subsequent agreement of the parties（事後雙方同意）

   a. Mutual rescissions（雙方同意解約）

   b. Modification（修改）

   c. Novation（債務承擔）：writing & consent required

   d. Accord and satisfaction（和解清償）

4. Subsequent unilateral act of obligee（債權人事後單方行為）

   a. Cancellation（取消）

   b. Discharge（解除）

Ⅴ. BREACH OF CONTRACT（違反契約）

  A. Minor breach: does not excuse further performance（輕微違約）

  B. Material breach（嚴重的）

   1. Discharge is contract duty of aggrieved obligee（解約）

   2. Duty to mitigate damages（減輕責任）

Ⅵ. REMEDIES FOR BREACH（違約救濟）

  A. Monetary Damages（金錢賠償）

   1. Remedies restoring pre-contact status (status quo)（回復原狀）

    a. Restitution—It is measured by market value of benefit.（回復原狀賠償）

    b. Reimbursement—Costs are shifted to defaulting obligor

on estoppel theory even if no benefits have been conferred.（償還）

2. Damages for loss of benefit of bargain—Losses which are consequential, foreseeable, unavoidable and certain may be recovered in addition to out of pocket costs. (expectation)（所失利益）

3. Stipulated damages（約定賠償或逾期賠償）

4. Liquidated damages (damages are difficult to measure)（約定違約賠償）

5. Actual damages (out-of-pocket)（所受損失）

B. Specific Performance—Court order requiring breaching party to perform contract（特別強制履行或執行）

1. Real property is always considered to be unique.（不動產買賣契約）

2. Goods are so special.（特殊之物）

C. Injunction: When specific performance is not feasible.（禁止令）

第五節　TORTS（侵權行為法）

I. TORT—A private wrong. (1)duty imposed by general law (2) breach of such duty (3)causation (4)damages. Money damage is a remedy.（侵權行為）

II. INTENTIONAL TORT AGAINST THE PERSON（對人之故意侵權行為）

A. Battery—An act intentionally committed resulting in an immediate or harmful or offensive touching.（毆擊）

B. Assault—An act by defendant resulting in apprehension of immediate harmful or offensive touching/contact.（威脅攻擊）

C. False Imprisonment—Act with intent to confine victims in certain area.（非法監禁）

D. Intentional Infliction of Emotional Distress—Extreme and outrageous act by defendant intended to cause severe emotional distress.（故意造成精神耗弱／心神喪失）

E. Nesligent Infliction of Emotional Distress （過失造成精神耗弱／心神喪失）

III. INTENTIONAL TORTS—DEFENSES AND PRIVILEGES （抗辯事由與權利）

A. Consent—complete bar to liability （同意）

B. Self Defense—自我防衛

1. Reasonable belief of danger （合理相信危險）

2. Counter with reasonable force with necessity（必要時得以合理武力反擊）

C. Defense of Others—privilege only if person protected is actually privileged to use same amount of force （防衛他人：合理武力）

D. Defense of Property （防衛財產）

1. Reasonable fear（合理害怕）

2. Non-deadly force only（非致命武力）

E. Official Arrest—limited to lawful arrest（正式逮捕）

F. Discipline—i.e., parents or teachers（懲罰）

IV. NEGLIGENCE — An act (or omission to act) resulting in the breach of legal duty and which is the actual and proximate cause of injury and/or damage to the plaintiff.（過失）

A. Act or omission to act—A volitional (not intentional) act, including any wilful omission to act when under an affirmative duty to act.

B. Legal Duty（法律義務）

1. Duty of Due Care（注意義務）

a. Must act as a reasonable man would in same circumstances.

b. Applies to all adults regardless of mental disability

c. Children are held to the standard of a child of like age, intelligence, knowledge, experience, skill, and talent and education.

d. Person with special knowledge and skills held to higher standards: e.g., doctor's malpractice.

2. Special Duty（特殊義務）

a. Statutory duties—"negligence per se"（法定責任義務）

b. Owners & Occupiers of Land（場所主人責任）

(1) Trespasser—invader without privilege（非法入侵者）

⑵Attractive Nuisance—child or under age（具吸引力之危害）

⑶Licensee—social friends without monetary interest（被允許人）

⑷Invitee—customers with monetary interest（受邀請人）

C. Breach of Duty（違反注意義務）

　1. Res Ipsa Loquitur—"Thing speaks for itself."（不證自明）

　　a. Normally would not occur in absence of negligence

　　b. Instrumentality causing injuries under defendant's exclusive control

　　c. No contributory negligence by plaintiff

　2. Duty of Care

D. Actual Causation (cause in fact)（事實原因）

　1. But for rule—"But for A, the result would have been different."（若非原則）

　2. Substantial factor rule（實質因素）

E. Proximate Causation (legal cause)（法律原因）

　1. Superseding intervening cause—e.g., act of god, criminal activity, intentional tort (unforeseeable events)（替代介入原因）

　2. Non-superseding intervening cause — e.g., rescuer's negligence, postaccident injury, commit suicide, etc. (foreseeable damages in legal public policy)（非替代介入原因）

　3. Actual damages required（實際損害）

　4. Plaintiff must mitigate damages（減低損害）

輕鬆學習美國法律

5. Collateral source rule—recovery even if paid by insurance（附帶資源）

6. Respondeat superior—employer vicariously liable for acts of employee（雇用人責任）within scope of employment（主人免責）

7. Joint enterprise—same goal, purpose, control（共同事業：連帶責任）

8. Auto case（汽車案件）
  a. Family use rule（家人使用）
  b. Permissive use rule（允許使用）

V. NEGLIGENCE DEFENSES（過失之抗辯事由）
  A. Contributory Negligence: 1% bars recovery（與有過失）
  B. Comparative Negligence: NY/CA（相對過失）
  C. Assumption of Risk（風險承擔）

VI. STRICY LIABILITY（絕對責任）
  A. Animals（動物）
    1. Domestic animals: cat, dog （"one free dog-bite"）(N.Y. Statute)
      a. Known dangerous propensities（知悉危險傾向）
      b. Statutory strict liability（法定嚴格責任）
    2. Wild animals: lion, monkey（野生動物）
  B. Abnormally Dangerous Activities（極度危險行為）
  C. Proximate Cause（法律原因）

D. Defenses（抗辯事由）

  1. Assumption of risk（風險承擔）

  2. Comparative negligence（相對過失）

VII. PRODUCTS LIABILITY（產品責任）

A. Intentional Tort Theory（故意侵權理論）

B. Negligence Theory（過失理論）

C. Strict Liability Theory（絕對責任）

D. Implied Warranties—"fit for ordinary/intended purpose."（默示瑕疵擔保）

E. Express Warranties and Misrepresentations—"merchantability"（明示瑕疵擔保與不實陳述）

VIII. HARM TO PROPERTY（對財產之侵害）

A. Intentional Trespass to Land（不動產之侵權）

  1. Volitional act required（有意識的）

  2. Intent to go on land（犯意）

  3. Actual invasion of land（實際侵入）

  4. Direct or indirect causation（直接或間接原因）

  5. Damages（賠償）

  6. Actual possession or right to immediate possession（實際占有或有權直接占有）

B. Nuisance（公私害；危害）（騷擾）

  1. Possession or right to immediate possession（占有或有權直接占有）

2. Intentional, negligent or innocent conduct sufficient（故意過失無辜行為）

3. Substantial and unreasonable harm to property（對財產有實質不合理傷害）

4. Causation（因果關係）

C. Conversion—An intentional act by defendant which seriously invades a chattel (personal property) interest of plaintiff causing damages.（占有動產與侵害）

IX. HARM TO NON-PHYSICAL INTERESTS（對非身體權益之侵害）

A. Defamation—Publication to a third person by Defendant defaming plaintiff, causing damage to plaintiff's reputation（毀謗）

1. Libel—written or printed defamation（書面毀謗）

2. Slander—oral defamation（口頭毀謗）

3. Defenses（抗辯事由）

　a. Consent（同意）

　b. Truth（事實）

　c. Privilege（特權）

　(1)Private individuals: negligence/fault must be shown（私人）：證明事實不符＋過失即可

　(2)Public figures: actual malice must be shown（公眾人物）：惡意要件需證明

B. Invasion of Privacy—An act by Defendant which invades Plaintiff right to be left alone.（侵害隱私權）

1. Intrusion on physical or mental solitude（身體與心理之侵害）

2. Public disclosure of private facts（公開揭示私人事實）

3. False light（造成假象）

4. Appropriation of name or likeness（盜用姓名或相類似之姓名）

5. Defenses（抗辯）

   a. Consent（同意）

   b. Public interest: "newsworthy"（公共利益）

X. HARM TO RELIANCE INTEREST（信賴利益之侵害）

A. Misrepresentation（虛偽不實陳述）

1. Deceit—A false, material representation of fact, known to be false, made with the intent to induce plaintiff's reliance.（欺騙）

2. Negligence misrepresentation—negligent misrepresentation by defendant upon which plaintiff justifiably relies his representation（過失之虛偽不實陳述）

3. Defenses（抗辯）

   a. Contributory negligence（可歸責之過失）

   b. Assumption of Risk（承擔風險）

   c. Contractual waiver（契約之棄權）

B. Damages（損害賠償）：reliance damages（信賴所受之損害賠償）

XI. WRONGFUL DEATH（非法致人於死／意外致人於死）

  A. 普通法並無此罪名

  B. Measure of damages is services rendered and support beneficiaries would have received if victim had not died.（若被害人未死，受益人應得之勞務價值＝賠償）

XII. WRONGFUL LIFE（非法致人於身體缺陷生活）

第六節　CONSTITUTION LAW（憲法）

I. JUDICIAL POWER (U.S. SUPREME COURT)（司法權限）

  A. Power—The U.S. Supreme Court may review constitutionality of acts of other branches of the federal government.（最高法院得審閱其他聯邦部門行為是否違憲）

    1. Original jurisdiction (ambassadors, public ministers, counsel)（最初管轄）

    2. Appellate jurisdiction (certiorari, appeal)（上訴管轄）

    3. Review of federal court judgment（審閱聯邦法院判決）

  B. Limitation（限制）

    1. No advisory opinions（不得有意見之評論）

    2. Must be federal questions (diversity of citizenship) & subject matter over $50,000（必需是聯邦問題（跨州居民訴訟）與 $50,000 以上之訴訟標的）

    3. Ripeness (immediate threat of harm)（成熟性）

    4. Mootness (a real controversy)（爭議性）

5. Standing (legal qualification)（適格性）

6. Political question (<u>Goldwater</u> case)—executive branch（政治問題）

7. Abstention on unsettled state laws（對州未解決之法律應自制不予解釋）

8. Comity and federalism (pending state criminal or administrative cases)（互惠與保持聯邦原則）

Ⅱ. LEGISLATIVE POWER (CONGRESS)（立法權限）

A. Taxing: use tax, ad valorem taxes, franchise tax, licenses tax（稅收）

B. Spending power（預算）

C. Declare war（宣戰）：總統得製造戰爭(make war)

D. Investigation（調查）

E. Property power: taking v. just compensation/wild animals（徵收）

F. Postal power (P.O. Box)（郵局）

G. Naturalization/immigration/citizen (visa, F-1, E-1, etc.)（歸化／移民／公民）

H. Admiralty power (maritime)（海商法）

I. Commercial power (interstate commerce)（州際商業）

J. Currency/coin（錢幣）

Ⅲ. EXECUTIVE POWER (President)（行政權限）

A. Appoint all ambassadors, public ministers and counsels,

justices of the U.S. Supreme Court, officers of the U.S.（指派大使館人員、大法官及國家行政職員等）

B. Pardon（大赦）

C. Veto power (10 days to veto the disapproval by 2/3 votes of each house)（否決權）["fast track"]

D. Make war (commander in chief) [e.g., sent troops to Iraq]（製造戰爭）（非宣戰）

E. Foreign relations: e.g., MFN status on PRC（外國關係）

F. Treaty power（締約）

IV. INDIVIDUAL RIGHTS IN CONSTITUTION (Bill of Rights)（憲法賦與個人權利）

A. Due Process of Law（正當法律程序）

1. Procedural Due Process—"life, liberty, or property"（法律正當程序）

2. Substantive Due Process—"fundamental rights"（實質正當程序）

a. right to privacy: abortion, read *playboy*, marriage

b. right to domestic travel

B. Equal Protection（平等保障）

1. Strict scrutiny: race, alienage v. compelling state interest（嚴格審查標準）

2. Intermediate scrutiny: gender, illegitimacy v. important state interest（一般審查標準）

3. Rational basis/less scrutiny: wage, alien v. legitimate state in-

terest（合理審查標準）

V. FREEDOM OF SPEECH AND PRESS v. PRIOR RESTRAINT

(lst Amendment)（言論新聞自由 v. 事前限制）

A. Symbolic speech: "fuck the draft"（象徵性言論）

B. Fighting words v. clear and present danger（爭議言論）

C. Obscenity: national v. state v. community standard（淫穢：全國標準 v. 州標準 v. 地區標準）

VI. FREEDOM OF RELIGION（宗教自由）

A. Free Exercise: balancing test（自由行使權利）

B. Establishment Clause: secular purpose（宗教自由條款）

CONSTITUTION AMENDMENTS
(U.S.A.)

Preamble（序言）

We the people of the United States, in order to form a more perfect Union, established Justice, insure domestic Tranquillity, provide for the common defense, promote the general Welfare, and secure the Blessings of Liberty to ourselves and our Posterity, do ordain and establish this Constitution for the United States of America.（其餘修正案條文請參見第二章憲法一節）

第七節　CRIMINAL LAW（刑法）

I. CLASSIFICATION（分類）

　A. Felony（重罪）

　B. Misdemeanor（輕罪）

　　1. Malum in Se (evil in itself)（本身違法）

　　2. Malum Prohibitum（禁止）

　C. Degrees (Major Crimes Only)（級）

　D. Lesser Included Offenses（較輕之罪）

II. MATERIAL ELEMENTS（主要構成要件）

　A. Actus Reas—the act（行為）

　　1. Voluntary（自願）

　　2. Need not be inherently wrong（不一定是錯誤行為）

　　3. Omission to act（不作為）

　　　a. Statutory duties（法定義務）

　　　b. Contractual duties（契約義務）

　　　c. Undertaking（從事行為）：例如游泳

　　　d. Special relationship (e.g., co-inhabitant)（特殊關係：如同居人）

　　4. Acts of Others (Vicarious Liability)（他人行為：幫助與教唆）

　　　a. Agency（代理人）

　　　b. Accomplices—aiding & abetting（共犯：幫助與教唆）

5. Conspiracy（共犯；共謀）

B. Mens Rea—the mental element（犯意）

  1. Guilty Mind（犯罪之思想）

  2. Concurrence of Act & Intent（行為與犯意競合）

  3. Transferred Intent（轉移之犯意）

  4. Specific Intent Crimes—purpose & knowledge（特別犯意）：目的與明知

  5. General Intent Crimes—reckless & negligence（一般犯意）：草率鹵莽與過失

  6. Strict Liability—no mens rea requirement (e.g. speeding)（絕對責任）

C. Attendant Circumstance—specific elements peculiar to given offense（伴隨狀況）

Ⅲ. CAUSATION（因果關係）

A. Actual Cause (cause-in-fact)（事實原因）

  1. But for（若非）

  2. Substantial Factor（實質因素）

B. Proximate Cause（法律間接原因）

  1. Fairness—unusually unforeseeable events（公平原則）

  2. Intervening & Superseding Causes（介入及替代原因）

C. Anti–dumping cases:反傾銷案件之因果關係較偏政治面考量，常以其中之一或主要原因判定產業損害與低價傾銷具因果關係。

IV. DEFENSES (Excuse/Justification)（抗辯事由）

A. The Accused must assert defense（答辯）

1. Burden of Proof（舉證責任）

2. Affirmative Defenses（積極答辯）

B. Excuses—negate criminal responsibility（抗辯）

1. Age（年齡）

2. Mental Illness（心神喪失；精神異常）

a. Competency（行為能力）

b. Insanity（心神喪失或精神異常）

(1) M'naghten rule: "wrong or right" test（是非說）

(2) Irresistible impulse: "control" test（無法控制說）

(3) Durham rule: "product of mental illness" test（心神喪失產品說）

(4) Model penal code—substantial capacity to appreciate（缺乏實質辨識能力說）

3. Intoxication（酗醉）：非自願性(involuntary)

4. Mistake—fact v. law（錯誤）

5. Entrapment（誘陷）

6. Duress（脅迫）

C. Justification（阻卻違法事由）

1. Self Defense（自我防衛）

a. Amount of force（武力）：合理

b. Honest v. reasonable belief（主觀 v. 合理相信）

c. Imminent danger（直接危害）

2. Defenses of Others（防衛他人）：需以合理武力

3. Prevention of Crimes（預防犯罪）

4. Defenses of Personal Property v. Real Property（防衛動產 v. 不動產）：前者以合理武力保衛動產，後者得以致命武力保衛不動產

5. Necessity（必要）

6. Public Authority（公權力）

7. Consent（同意）

V. INCHOATE CRIMES (preparatory crimes)（預備階段罪名）

A. Attempt（未遂）：實質地步(Mpc) v. 危險地步(Common Law)

B. Solicitation（教唆）：複數＋同意＋犯意

C. Conspiracy（共犯；共謀）：獨立之構成要件

VI. CRIMES AGAINST PERSONS（對人侵害之罪）

A. Criminal Homicide（刑法之殺人罪）

1. Murder（殺人罪）

a. Malice aforethought（預謀）

b. Intent to kill（有犯意殺人）

c. Substantial bodily harm/injury（造成實質身體傷害）

d. Wanton reckless disregard for life（不顧他人生命法益）

e. Felony murder rule (felony cause unintended death result)（重罪謀殺）

f. Resisting arrest（拒捕）

2. Statutory Murder（法定殺人罪）

a. First degree（一級）

b. Second degree（二級）

3. Manslaughter（過失殺人）

a. Voluntary（自願）

b. Involuntary（非自願）

B. Assault & Battery（攻擊與毆擊）

C. Rape（強姦） v. statutory rape (under certain age)

D. Sodomy（略誘）

E. Kidnapping（綁架）

VII. THEFT OFFENSES（竊盜罪）

A. Trespassory Takings（侵占）

1. Larceny（竊盜）

2. Robbery ＝ larceny ＋ force（搶奪＝竊盜＋武力）

B. Fraudulent Takings（詐欺侵占）

1. Larceny by trick v. possession deprivation（詐術竊盜）

2. False pretenses (claim) v. title deprivation（詐欺竊盜）

C. Criminal Conversion（侵占）

1. Embezzlement（因公／業務侵占）

2. Larceny by conversion（竊盜侵占）

VIII. CRIMES AGAINST REAL PROPERTY

A. Burglary（夜間侵入住宅罪）：犯意為一般罪名為已足（目前夜間要件已取消）

B. Arson（縱火罪）

第八節 CRIMINAL PROCEDURE （刑事訴訟法）

I. CONSTITUTIONAL LIMITATION （憲法限制）

  A. Fourth Amendment—unreasonable arrest, searches and seizure （第四修正案）

  B. Fifth Amendment （第五修正案）

    1. Grand jury indictment (not applicable to states) （大陪審團）

    2. Double jeopardy （二次危險）

    3. Self-incrimination （自我控告）

    4. Due process of law （正當法律程序）

  C. Sixth Amendment （第六修正案）

    1. Speedy, public trial by jury （迅速、公開審判）

    2. Confrontation of witness （對質）

    3. Right to subpoena favorable witness（傳喚有利自己之證人）

    4. Right to counsel （律師在場及訴訟權利）

  D. Eighth Amendment （第八修正案）

    1. Excessive bail （鉅額保釋金）

    2. Cruel and unusual punishment （殘忍不尋常處罰）

II. SEARCH & SEIZURE （搜索和扣押）

  A. Reasonable Expectation of Privacy （合理隱私權期待）

  B. Areas Open to Examination （公開檢查區域）

  C. Plain View Doctrine （視線可及主義）

D. Stop & Frisk — reasonable suspicion of carrying dangerous weapon/arm（停止與外部搜身）

E. Search Warrant v. Exceptions（搜索狀 v. 例外情形）

  1. Probable cause（可能原因）

  2. Prevent loss of evidence, hot pursuit, border search, emergency, etc.（防止證據流失、逮捕現行犯、邊境搜索與緊急例外情形）

F. Search Incident to Lawful Arrest（附帶搜索）

G. Consent（同意）

H. Third Party Consent (family member v. baby-sitter)（第三人代為同意）

III. ARREST（逮捕）

A. Illegal Arrest—fruits of the poisonous tree（毒樹果實：非法逮捕）

B. Definition—significant deprivation of freedom（實質剝奪他人自由）

C. Warrantless Arrest（不需搜索狀之逮捕）

  1. Probable cause to believe felony has been committed（可能原因推斷犯罪）

  2. Misdemeanor committed in officer's presence（在執警人員面前犯下輕罪）

D. Arrest with Warrant—probable cause（有搜索票之逮捕）

E. Detention for Investigation—reasonable suspicion（調查時收押）

IV. THE EXCLUSIONARY RULE（證據排他法則）

  A. Motion to Suppress（提出消滅證據）

    1. Normally made before trial（審判前）

    2. Waived if not timely made（如未聲請視為放棄）

  B. Excludable Evidence（得排除之證據）

    1. Fruits of the poisonous tree（毒樹果實）

      a. Statements & evidence obtained during illegal arrest（非法逮捕）

      b. Witness discovered during illegal search（非法搜索）

    2. Independent Sources（獨立來源）

      a. Inevitable discovery（不可避免之發見事實）

      b. Voluntary statements（自願性之言詞）

  C. Harmless Error（輕微錯誤）：effect on verdict（對評決具影響）

  D. Reversible Error（重大錯誤）：得為上訴理由(de novo review)

V. INTERROGATION & CONFESSION（質詢與自白承認）

  A. Involuntary Confessions—inadmissible（非自願性自白）

    1. Coercion（脅迫）

    2. Not fully conscious (drug)（完全不知覺）（例如受葯物控制）

  B. Interrogation while in Custody: 質（詰）問

    1. Miranda v. Arizona (1966)—"I take fifth." (Miranda warning)「馬倫達」警告]

      a. Right to remain silent（保持緘默）

      b. Statements used against（呈堂證供）

c. Rights to attorney (counsel)（律師在場權）

d. Attorney appointed if the accused cannot afford（公設辯護律師）

2. Interrogation must cease on assertion of Miranda right.（如主張馬倫達權利，質詢應馬上終止）

VI. RIGHT TO COUNSEL（受律師有效幫助之權）

A. Sixth Amendment—criminal prosecution only（只適用刑事告訴案件）

B. Due Process is Separate Source of Right to Counsel（法律正當程序）

C. Equal Protection-Right to Counsel for Indigents（公平保障）

D. Effective Counsel（受律師有效幫助之權）

E. Waiver of Right（放棄）

VII. INITIATING PROSECUTION（起訴）

A. Indictment—grand jury (not applicable to states)（大陪審團提起公訴）

B. Information—complaint（起訴書）

C. Affidavit—under oath by citizens（宣誓書；舉發）

VIII GUILTY PLEAS（認罪）

A. Voluntary Waive（自願放棄）

B. Plea Bargain（認罪之協議）：被告與檢察官之協議（非與法官之協議）

IX. RIGHT TO IMPARTIAL JURY（受公正陪審團之權）

　A. Not required in Petty Offenses（輕微案件不適用）

　B. Unanimity－12 jurors in general（全體一致無異議之評決）

　　1. 12 persons jury need not be unanimous (11:1, 10:2, 9:3) in some states.（有些州得以11:1, 10:2或9:3評決之）

　　2. 6 persons jury must be unanimous in non-petty offense.（6人之評決必需全體通過）

　　3. 12 persons jury requires unanimity in federal courts.（聯邦評決應全體一致通過）

X. FAIR TRIAL（公平審判）

　A. Prejudicial Pretrial Publicity（審判前偏頗之公開）：不公平審判

　　1. Jury exposure to evidence（陪審員接觸證據）

　　2. The press（新聞媒體）

　　3. Change of venue（變更審判地）：得聲請之

　　4. "Gag" order（禁止公開命令）：法院得命令新聞記者不得公開評論或轉述

　B. Media in the Courtroom（媒體）：基本上可以進入法院聆聽審判

　C. Other Undue Influence（其他不當影響）

　　1. Threat of Mob violence（暴徒威脅）

　　2. Court has interest in outcome（法院對判決有利害關係）

　　3. Interference with jury deliberations（陪審之評議已遭干涉）

XI. CONFRONTATION OF WITNESS & COMPULSORY PRO-CESS (Evidence)（和證人對質程序）

  A. Right to Cross-examination（交互詰問）

  B. Confession by Co-defendants（共犯之自白）

  C. Prior Statements of Witness（證人以前之證詞）：得採為證據

    1. Counsel at preliminary examination（預審律師質詢之言詞）

    2. Recorded testimony（記錄之證詞）

    3. Unavailable witness（找不到證人時）

  D. Self-incrimination（自我控告）

    1. Applies in all proceeding (criminal, non-criminal) [所有民刑程序均可]

    2. Immunity（豁免權）

    3. No adverse inference（不會有不利之影響）

XII. TRIAL（審判）

  A. Burden of Proof（舉證責任）

  B. Presumption of Innocence（推定無罪）

  C. Corpus Delecti — some evidence of crime other than defendant's confession（直接客體證據：非自白之證據，例如屍體）

XIII. DOUBLE JEOPARDY（二次危險）

  A. Criminal proceeding only（只適用刑法）

  B. Separate sovereigns（不同之主權：與州系統獨立）

C. Separate offenses, same transaction （同樣事件，不同構成要件）

  1. Multiple witness （多數證人）

  2. Distinct property （不同財產）

  3. Related offenses （相關罪名）

D. Retrial after appeal（上訴後重審）: Insufficiency of evidence—reprosecution barred （證據不足不得重新起訴）

XIV. WRIT OF HABEAS CORPUS (You have the body) （人身自由保護令）

A. Applicable to states and federal court （州與聯邦均有）

B. No effect of collateral estoppel （一事不再理原則不適用之）

第九節　EVIDENCE （證據法）

I. DEFINITION—reasonably calculated to any admissible evidence （定義）

A. Material evidence—important （重要證據）

B. Relevant evidence—logic & legal relevance (具證據能力)，但下列情形不具證據能力：

  1. Liability Insurance (inadmissible) （責任保險）

  2. Subsequent Remedial Measures (inadmissible) （事後補救措施）

  3. Settlement Offers (inadmissible) （和解要約）

  *Exception: admission of facts with offer to pay medical ex-

penses（例外：和解係為付醫藥費）

4. Similar Act—admissible if probative value outweighs unfair prejudice（相類似行為）

5. Character（個性；人格）

  a. Civil cases—inadmissible unless directly in issue（民事上與本案直接關係不得採用人格證據）

  b. Criminal cases—刑事案件

  (1) Defendant may initiate his/her good character, while Prosecutor cannot initiate Defendant's bad character.（被告得舉證其人格善良，但檢察官不得提出被告不良之人格攻擊之）

  (2) D may introduce Victim's bad character except (past) rape offenses.（被告得主張受害人不良人格之證據，但不得舉證被害人過去之被強姦之罪名）

 C. Competent evidence（有證據能力之證據）

II. TYPES（型態）

 A. Direct evidence—直接證據

 B. Circumstance evidence—情況證據

 C. Best evidence rule—original documents (self-authenticating)（最好證據）

 D. Secondary evidence—OK if satisfactory explanation is given（次要證據）

 E. Parol evidence rule—口頭證據原則

 F. Dead Man Statute—inadmissible in civil cases only.（死人條

款）（死者所云在刑法上得為證據）

G. Opinion testimony — lay witness (relaxed) v. expert witness (strict)（意見）

Ⅲ. JUDICIAL NOTICE（司法常識）：顯而易知及利用管道即經證實之證據

A. 例如某年某月某日是否下雨？

B. 例如10月20日（1999年）是否為星期三？

Ⅳ. FORM OF EXAMINATION OF WITNESS（詰問證人型式）

A. Leading question: Yes/No question (inadmissible) except on cross-examination, loss of memory, or hostile witness（引導問題）：原則上禁止

B. Present recollection refreshed: Writing/memorandum or thing, but the unauthenticated writing cannot be introduced.（恢復目前記憶）

C. Past recollection recorded: insufficient recollection of any event, but the writing can be introduced if proper foundation is laid.（恢復過去記憶）

Ⅴ. CROSS-EXAMINATION（交互詰問）

A. Scope—limited to direct examination（只限直接質詢）

B. Impeachment v. credibility（彈劾 v. 可靠性）

　1. Prior inconsistent statements（以前不一致之言詞）

　2. Bias, hostility（偏見或敵意）

3. Prior conviction of crime: inadmissible if over 10 years except to show fraud or dishonesty（以前之罪名：逾十年不得舉證詐欺或不名譽之罪）

4. Specific instances—vicious immoral or criminal act (must be in good faith)（特別事件：舉證不道德或刑事犯罪行為需以善意為之）

5. Opinion or Reputation for truth（事實之意見評論與聲譽）

*Impeachment on collateral matter (not directly in issue) is inadmissible.（不相關本案之攻擊證據，不足採信）

VI. HEARSAY（傳聞證據）

A. Definition—out-of-court statements made by declarant offered to prove the matter asserted is inadmissible except (1) circumstantial evidence of state of mind, knowledge (2) effect on reasonable listeners (3) legal significant facts（傳聞證據不足採信，惟(1)情況證據(2)正當合理當事人之聆聽感覺(3)重要事實之傳聞得具證據能力）

B. Hearsay Exception I (availability of declarant is immaterial)（傳聞證據例外I）（證人在不在場不是重點，若符合下列即為足採）

1. Present sense impression: describe or explaining event while perceiving or immediately thereafter)（現在之形象）

2. Excited utterance: made under stress of startling event（激奮而發之話）

3. Then existing mental, emotional or physical emotion（那時之

心理身體情緒）

4. Statement made for medical treatment（為就醫而講的話）

5. Recorded recollection（有記錄之過去言詞）

6. Business record（商業記錄）：例如會計報表

7. Public record and reports（公開之記錄與報告）：例如政府公文書

8. Records of birth, death, or marriage（出生、死亡、結婚記錄）

9. Statements in document affecting interest in property（影響財產利益之言詞）

10. ancient documents (20 years at least)（20年以上之古老文件）

11. Market reports, commercial publications（市場報告、商業出版書籍）

12. Learned treatises（著名之論文）

13. Reputation as to character（個性之聲譽）

14. Judgment of previous conviction（先前罪名之判決）

15. Other exceptions in the interest of justice (catch-all provision)（其他公平情形）

C. Hearsay Exception II (declarant must be unavailable)（傳聞證據例外II）

1. Former testimony（證人必需不在場，傳聞證據始為足採）

2. Statement made under belief of impending death（相信自己將死亡而為之言詞）

3. Statement made against interest (penal interest requires cor-

roboration)（不利自己利益言詞）

4. Statement of personal or family history (family pedigree)（家族歷史之言詞）

5. Other exception in the interest of justice (another catch-all provision)（其他公平情形）

D. Hearsay within Hearsay—not excluded if each part is a valid exception（傳聞中之傳聞）（每一個傳聞均需具有證據能力）

Ⅶ. PRIVILEGE （特權）：不必出庭對下列之人彼此間為不利證詞

A. Attorney-Client privilege (confidential communication)（律師與客戶間特權）

B. Husband-Wife privilege (may not be compelled)（先生與太太之特權）

Ⅷ BURDEN OF PROOF （舉證責任）

A. Beyond a reasonable doubt (criminal evidence)（無合理懷疑證據）

B. Clear and convincing evidence (between A and C)（清晰具說服力）

C. Evidence of preponderance (more than 50%)（優勢證據）

1. Burden of going forward with evidence（轉移性舉證責任）

2. Burden of persuasion (proof): See A, B, C.（說服性舉證責任）

第十節 CIVIL PROCEDURE(民事訴訟法)

I. CIVIL LITIGATION(民事訴訟)

Federal Courts（聯邦法院）	審級區分	States（州法院）
U.S. Supreme Court	Supreme Court	---Supreme Court
U.S. Court of Appeals for---Circuit	Court of Appeals	Intermediate Courts(variety)
U.S. District Court	Trial Court	Variety of titles, e.g., superior court, circuit court, etc.

II. SUBJECT MATTER OF FEDERAL COURTS（聯邦法院之事務標的）

A. Constitutional Limitation: cases or controversies（爭議案件）

B. Federal Question: "arising under" federal constitution, laws, or treaty（聯邦問題）

C. Diversity: citizens (domicile) of different state（不同州民間之訴訟）

D. Subject Matter: more than $50,000 in dispute/suit （標的＞$50,000）

III. TYPES OF PERSONAL JURISDICTION（對人管轄型態）

A. In Personam jurisdiction (person)（對人）

1. Domicile（居所）

2. Citizen（公民）

3. Consent（同意）

4. Minimum contacts（最少接觸）

B. In rem jurisdiction (thing): presence of property in state（對物）

C. Quasi in rem jurisdiction (right as to specific property within the court's control)（準對物管轄）

   1. Dispute over preexisting rights in property（對財產以前爭議之權利）

   2. Ejectment（請求承租人遷讓房屋）

   3. Quiet title（確認所有權）

   4. Auto liability policy（汽車責任保險）

D. Subject matter: 事務管轄

Ⅳ. CIVIL PROCEDURE（民事訴訟程序）

A. Pleading — complaint (Pliantiff) v. Reply or Answer (Defendant)（起訴書←→答辯狀）

B. Joinder of parties（當事人追加訴訟）

   1. Indispensable parties（不可缺少之當事人）

   2. Necessary parties（必要之當事人）

   3. Proper parties（合理適當之當事人）

C. Joinder of claims（案件追加訴訟）：P代表原告，D代表被告

   1. Counterclaim (D v. P)（反訴）

   2. Cross-claims (D1 v. D2) [co-party] [ancillary jurisdiction]（交互訴訟）

3. Impleader (D1 v. 3rd party) [non-party] [ancillary jurisdiction]（追加第三人訴訟）

4. Intervention (3rd party joins the <u>P</u> v. <u>D</u> suit)（第三人參加訴訟）

5. Interpleader (stakeholder: e.g., insurance co. or trustee)（互爭權利訴訟）

D. Class action（集體訴訟）

1. Numerous (impracticable to join all)（人數眾多）

2. Common (question of law of fact)（相同問題）

3. Typical (of claim or defense)（典型問題）

4. Adequate (protected)（充分代表）

E. Discovery（發見證據）：以下情形不得強迫其提出證據

1. Privileged matter (not discoverable)（特權豁免事情）

2. Work-products of attorney (not discoverable)（律師工作產物）

3. Protected order by courts (not discoverable)（法院保護之證據）

F. Devices（方法）

1. Oral deposition（口頭質詢或詰問）

2. Written deposition (by court officer)（書面質詢或詰問）

3. Interrogation (usually adverse party only)（質問）

4. Subpoena duces tecum (compel nonparty to bring documents)（傳喚提出文件）

5. Physical/mental and blood examination ("good cause" test)（身體心理及驗血）

G. Pretrial conference (judge's discretion to order parties to appear)（預審）

H. Demurrer and motion to strike (merits of cause of action) v. dismissal（異議／抗告）

I. Motion to summary judgment (no dispute as to real/material issue of facts) [pretrial]（簡易判決）

J. Jury trial ($20 in civil cases)—jury as fact-determine (verdict)（陪審評決）

K. Judgment v. motion for a new trial (directed verdict ⟷ Judgment not withstanding of the verdict)（判決 v. 重審（指示評決⟷請求法官不顧評決逕行判決））

L. Appeal: for the losing party (reversible error)（上訴）

V. EFFECTS OF JUDGMENT（法院判決效力）

A. Res Judicata (claim preclusion)[案件既判力]

B. Collateral Estoppel (issue preclusion)[爭端既判力]

VI. RECOGNITION AND ENFORCEMENT OF JUDGMENT IN OTHER STATES（判決在他州之承認和執行）

A. Full Faith and Credit (comity to sister states)（完全信賴與信用）

B. No Full Faith and Credit to Foreign Country Judgment（對外國司法判決並無完全信賴原則適用）

第十一節 PROPERTY LAW（財產法）

I.REAL ESTATE (PROPERTY)[不動產]

  A.Freehold Estates（自由土地所有權之財產）：Inheritance（繼承）

    1.Fee Simple Absolute (infinite duration)[絕對單純繼承土地所有權]

    2.Determinable fee (possibility of reverter)（土地所有權人得終止的財產所有權：取回或不取回不動產均可）

    3.Fee Simple subject to condition subsequent (right of reentry)（附解除條件之不動產權：土地所有權人得逕行取回不動產為條件）

    4.Fee Simple subject to Executory Limitation (3rd party)（不動產權利受第三人日後履行之限制）

  B.Nonfreehold Estates [landlord-tenant]（非自由土地所有權之財產）

    1.Estate for years（年租賃）

    2.Periodic tenancy（定期租賃）

    3.Tenancy at will（不定期租賃）

    4.Sufferance (overstay＝periodic tenancy)[逾期租賃]

II.EASEMENT, RESTRICTIVE COVENANT, AND SERVITUDE（地役權；限制契約與地役承擔）：供役地(Detriment)←→需役地(Benefit)

A. Easement: right-of-way（地役權）

  1. Prescription (adverse possession)（得依時效取得）

  2. Implication (necessity)（推定）[需證明必要性]

    a. Common plan（共同計劃）

    b. Prior use（先前使用）

    c. Reasonable necessity (by grant)（合理必要性）

    d. Severance（分割）

  3. Grant (writing)（書面同意）

  4. Strict necessity (by reservation)（嚴格之必要性）

B. Restrictive Covenants（限制契約）

  1. "Touch & concern" the land (test affect legal relationship)（土地之重要之點）

  2. Intent（意向）

  3. Privity（契因）：私法契約之權利義務關係

  4. Notice（通知）

  5. Writing（書面）

C. Equitable Servitude（衡平之地役權）[privity not required]（不需證明契因關係）

  1. "Touch & concern" the land（土地重要之點）

  2. Intent（意向）

  3. Notice（通知）

  4. Writing（書面）

Ⅲ. ZONING（分區規劃）

A. Police Power—public morality, safety, general welfare（警

察權)

B. Taking—balance test v. character of governmental activity（徵收）

  1. 14th amendment: due process of law & equal protection

  2. 5th amendment: just compensation v. taking

Ⅳ. CONVEYANCE（轉讓財產）

A. Risk of Loss v. Equitable Conversion（危險負擔 v. 衡平占有）

  1. Buyer (majority)（買方）

  2. Seller (minority)（賣方）

  3. Possession test: when one who possesses or legal title passes（占有或所有權過戶）

B. Marketable Title（無瑕疵之所有權）

C. Covenants for Title [1–3 are present rights, while 4-6 future rights]（所有權保證條件）

  1. Seisin (one purports to convey) [取回權利]

  2. Right to convey (authority to convey) [移轉權利]

  3. Covenant v. encumbrances (title defects) [不得有負擔權利]

  4. Covenant for quiet enjoyment (future right) [排除他人干涉]

  5. Covenant of warranty (future rights) [瑕疵擔保]

  6. Covenant for further assurance (future rights) [確保權利]

D. Recording Act（登記法）

  1. Race Statute (test: who records first?)（登記條文：先登記為優先）

  2. Notice Statutes (test: who is bona fide purchaser without no-

tice?）（公告條文：以誰是不知情之善意購買人為優先）

3.Race/Notice Statute (test: BFP and 1st recorder prevail)（以善意購買人先登記者優先）

V.ADVERSE POSSESSION（時效取得）

A.Open & Notorious possession（公然公開占有）

B.Actual possession（實際占有）

C.Under claim of title（堅稱擁有所有權）

D.Hostile（惡意）

E.Continuous possession（繼續性占有）

VI.MORTGAGE（抵押）

A.Purchase Money Mortgage: title passes to buyer immediately（購買金額之抵押）

B.Conventional Mortgage: Default → Equitable redemption → Foreclosure→Statutory redemption（傳統抵押：違約→衡平回贖→取消回贖或棄權→法定回贖）

C.Land Sale Contract (installment contract)（不動產買賣契約：分期付款）

第十二節　BUSINESS　ASSOCIATION（商事法）

I.SOLE PROPRIETOR (entitled to residual interest/unlimited liability)[獨資：負無限責任]

II. PARTNERSHIP（合夥）

  A. General Partnership (single taxation)（出名合夥）

  B. Limited Partnership（有限合夥）

    1. At least one general partner (unlimited liability).[至少一人為無限責任股東，公司得為無限責任股東]

    2. Limited partners are responsible for their contribution only.[有限責任合夥人對出資額負有限責任]

    3. 一般出名合夥人(general partner)負無限責任，有限合夥人(limited partner)僅負有限責任。

III. CORPORATION（公司）

  A. Elements（構成要件）

    1. Continuity of life（無限生命）

    2. Centralized management（中央管理）

    3. Limited liability（有限責任）

    4. Easy transferability of shares/stocks（股份轉讓之自由）

  B. Shareholder's Rights（股東權利）

    1. Election of directors（董事之選舉）

    2. Vote (proxy) in merger, acquisition (take-over)（表決（委託書）權：合併、併購）

    3. Vote in sale of substantial assets（出售重要資產之表決）

    4. Amendment of certificate (or article) of incorporation or by-laws（章程／細則之修正）

    5. Right to vote（表決權）：一股一票

6. Right to derivative (on behalf of corp.) or direct (individual) suits（股東間接或直接訴訟權）

7. Right to inspect with reasonable particularity（具合理原因得檢查帳冊）

8. Appraisal right（評估權）

9. Shareholder's meeting（股東會）

C. Directors（董事）

1. Authority: "as he/she deems necessary, appropriate"（權限）

2. Business judgment rule: fiduciary duty（忠實義務：商業判斷原則）

  a. Ordinary prudent person with reasonable care（合理注意義務）

  b. Good faith（善意）

  c. Make disinterested decision（公正決定）

  d. In the best interest of corporation（為公司最佳利益）

3. Diversion of corporation opportunity prohibited except disclosure（競業禁止）

D. President (duty of inquiry)（董事長）

E. Officers（職員工）

IV. PIERCE CORPORATE VEIL（追究公司違法行為之責任）（無限責任）

A. Grounds（理由）

1. Commingle funds（侵占公司款）

2. Records not kept（未為記錄）

3. Disregard the formality（不符法定格式要件）

4. Undercapitalization（低於資本維持）

5. Fraud（詐欺）

B. Unlimited liability（公司與公司負責人負連帶責任）

V. S-CORPORATION v. C-CORPORATION（S－公司 v. C－公司）

A. S-Corporation（S－公司）

1. Single taxation ("flow through treatment") in corporate form
（單一課稅）

2. Only one class of stocks allowed（只能發行一種股份）

3. Less than 35 persons（低於35人）

4. Limited to U.S. citizens（限美國公民）

B. C-Corporation（C－公司）

1. Double taxation: profits & dividends are separately taxed（分
派盈餘二次課稅）

2. More than 35 persons（人數逾35人）

VI. DISSOLUTION (Corporation)[解散]

A. Voluntary (nonjudicial) Dissolution（任意解散）

1. A threshold of two-thirds of shares (New York): 2/3股東代
表出席

2. A vote of majority: 過半數同意

B. Involuntary (judicial) Dissolution（法定非自願解散）

1. Deadlock in management（管理意見不合）

2. Illegal, fraudulent, oppressive act（非法詐欺、壓迫等行為）

3. Deadlock in voting power（表決懸而未決情形）

4. Corporate assets misapplied or wasted（浪費公司資產）

C. Minority Shareholder's Right v. Dissolution（少數股東權利 v. 解散）

1. Shareholders of 20% of voting shares may petition if (B) is met.（逾總數達公司股份20%之股東得經表決聯合使公司解散）

2. 直接訴訟(Direct suit)：美國公司法允許股東得以自己名義對公司直接訴訟。

3. 間接訴訟(Derivative suits)：股東以公司名義起訴董監事。

第四章 案例實習(Legal Method)

請閱讀下列案例，這些案例為美國法學院或學習英美法典型之案件。第一次接觸英美法案例時，大部分學生均不知所措，但請務必一次又一次閱讀，方能知其祕訣。我們將於閱讀下列五個案件(cases)後，學習如何撰寫一份大綱(outline)，此對考試或了解cases有極大之幫助。

1. Read the case of Thomas v. Winchester and Winterbottom v. Wrigne. Read it first with no rule in mind as if you were reading a short story.

2. Read the case a second time with a view toward "briefing" the case. There are a variety of ways to brief a case. The main functions of a brief in law school are (a) to aid your understanding of the case now and (b) to aid your recollection of the case when outlining, studying for the exam, etc.

Use the following format for briefing the case: (F-IRAC approach)

(1)FACTS—a short, concise version of the facts of the dispute, including its procedural history (note that the case is on appeal to the highest court in New York; therefore, other courts have already acted on the case. Include briefly what those other courts have done.)

(2)ISSUE—a short statement of the principal question or question that the court addresses. (Framing a "Yes" or "No" question)

(3)RULE—What support does the court give for answering the issue as it does.

(4)ANALYSIS—Apply facts into law.

(5)CONCLUSION—Judgment for plaintiff or defendant.

第一節 THOMAS AND WIFE v. WINCHESTER

Court of Appeals of New York, 1852
6 N.Y. 397

Action in the supreme court, commenced in August, 1849, against Winchester and Gilbert, for injuries, sustained by Mrs. Thomas, from the effects of a quantity of extract of belladonna, administered to her by mistake as extract of dandelion.

In the complaint it was alleged, that the defendants from the year 1843, to the first of January, 1849, were engaged in putting up and vending certain vegetable extracts, at a store in the city of New York, designated as "108 John-street," and that the defendant Gilbert had for a long time previous thereto been so engaged, at the same place. That among the extracts so prepared and sold by them, were those respectively known as the.

Ruggles, Ch. J. deliver the opinion of the court. This is an action brought to recover damages from the defendant for negligently putting up, labeling and selling as and for the extract of dandelion, which is a simple and harmless medicine, a jar of the extract of belladonna, which is a deadly poison; by means of which the plaintiff Mary Ann Thomas, to whom, being sick, a dose of dandelion was prescribed by a physician, and a portion of the contents of the jar, was administered as and for the extract of dandelion, was greatly injured, etc. The facts proved were briefly these: Mrs. Thomas being in ill health, her physician prescribed for her a dose of dandelion. Her husband purchased what was believed to be the medicine prescribed, at the store of Dr. Foord, a physician and druggist in Cazenovia, Madison county, where the plaintiffs reside.

A small quantity of the medicine thus purchased was administered to "symptom" Mrs. Thomas on whom it produced very alarming effects; such as coldness of the surface and extremities, feebleness of circulation, spasms of the muscles, giddiness of the head, dilation of the pupils of the eyes, and derangement of the mind. She recovered, however, after some time, from its effects, although for a short time her life was thought to be in great danger. The medicine administered was belladonna, and not dandelion. The jar from which it was taken was labeled "1/2 lb. dandelion, prepared by A. Gilbert, No. 108 John-street, N.Y. Jar 8 oz. " It was sold for and believed by Dr. Foord to be the extract of dandelion from Jas. A. Aspinwall, a druggist at New York Aspinwall bought it of the defendant as extract of dandelion, believing it to be such. The defendant was engaged at No. 108

John-street, New York, in the manufacture and sale of certain veg-etable extracts for medicinal purpose, and in the purchase and sale of others. The extracts manufactured by him were put up in jars for sale, and those which he purchased were put up by him in like manner. The jars containing extracts manufactured by himself and those con-taining extracts purchased by him from others, were labeled alike. Both were labeled like the jar in question, as "prepared by A. Gilbert ." Gilbert was a person employed by the defendant at a salary, as an assistant in his business. The jars were labeled in Gilbert's name be-cause he had been previously engaged in the same business on his own account at No. 108 John-street, and probably because Gilbert's labels rendered the articles more salable. The extract contained in the jar sold to Aspinwall, and by him to Foord, was not manufactured by the defendant, but was purchased by him from another manufacturer of dealer. The extract of dandelion and the extract of belladonna re-semble each other in color, consistence, smell and taste; but may on careful examination be distinguished the one from the other by those who are well acquainted with these articles. Gilbert's labels were paid for by Winchester and used in his business with his knowledge and assent.

The defendant's counsel moved for a nonsuit 4 on the following grounds: That the action could not be sustained, as the defendant was the remote vendor of the article in question; and there was no connec-tion, transaction or privity between him and the plaintiffs, or either of them. Safety, to respond for his breach of duty to any one except the person he contracted with.

This was the ground on which the case of Winterbottom v. Wright, (10 Mees. & Welsb. 109) was decided. A contracted with the postmaster general to provide a coach to convey the mail bags along a certain line of road, and B and others also contracted to horse the coach along the same line. B and his co-contractors hired C, who was the plaintiff, to drive the coach. The coach, in consequence of some latent defect, broke down; the plaintiff was thrown from his seat and lamed. It was held that C could not maintain an action against A for the injury thus sustained. The reason of the decision is best stated by Baron Rolfe. A's duty to keep the coach in good condition, was a duty to the postmaster general, with whom he made his contract and not a duty to the driver employed by the owners of the horses.

But the case in hand stands of a different ground. The defendant was a dealer in poisonous drugs. Gilbert was his agent in preparing them for market. The death or great bodily harm of some person was the natural and almost inevitable consequence of the sale of belladonna by means of the false label.

Gilbert, the defendant's agent, would have been punishable for manslaughter if Mrs. Thomas had died in consequence of taking the falsely labeled medicine. Every man who, by his culpable negligence, causes the death of another, although without intent to kill, is guilty of manslaughter 2 R.S. 662 §19. A chemist who negligently sells laudanum in a phial labeled as paregoric, and thereby causes the death of a person to whom it is administered, is guilty of manslaugh-

ter. Tessymond's case, 1 Lewin's Crown Cases, 169. "So highly does the law value human life that it admits of no justification wherever life has been lost and the carelessness of negligence of one person has contributed to the death of another." Regina v. Swindall, 2 Car. & Kir. 232–3. And this rule applies not only where the death of one is occasioned by the negligent act of another, but where it is caused by the negligent omission of a duty of that other. 2 Car. & Kir. 368, 371. Although the defendant Winchester may not be answerable criminally for the negligence of his agent, there can be no doubt of his liability in a civil action, in which the act of the agent is to be regarded as the act of the principal.

In respect to the wrongful and criminal character of the negligence complained of this case differs widely from those put by the defendant's counsel. No such imminent danger existed in those cases.In the present case the sale of the poisonous article was made to a dealer in drugs, and not to a consumer. The injury therefore was not likely to fall on him, or on his vendee who was also a dealer; but much more likely to be visited on a remote purchaser as actually happened. The defendant's negligence put human life in imminent danger. Can it be said that there was no duty on the part of the defendant, to avoid the creation of that danger by the exercise of greater caution? Or that the exercise of that caution was a duty only to his immediate vendee, whose life was not endangered? The defendant's duty arose out of the nature of his business and the danger to others incident to its mismanagement. Nothing but mischief like that which actually happened could have been expected from sending the poison falsely labeled into the market; and the defendant is justly responsible for the probable consequence of the in upon the question whether, independent of the statute, the defendant would have been liable to these plaintiffs.

GRIDLEY, J. was not present when the cause was decided. All the other members of the court concurred in the opinion delivered by J. Ruggles. Judgment affirmed.

第二節　DEVLIN v. SMITH

Court of Appeals of New York, 1882
89 N.Y. 470

Appeal from judgment of the General Term of the Supreme Court, in the second judicial department, entered upon an order made December 12, 1881, which affirmed a judgment entered upon an order dismissing plaintiff's complaint on trial....

This action was brought to recover damages for alleged negligence, causing the death of Hugh Devlin, plaintiff's intestate.

Defendant Smith entered into a contract with the supervisors of the county of Kings, by which he agreed to paint the inside of the dome of the court-house in that county. Smith was not a scaffold-builder, and knew nothing of that business. He entered into a contract with defendant Stevenson, who was an experienced scaffold-builder,

and had been previously employed by Smith, to build the necessary scaffold. This was to be of the best of materials, and first-class in every way. Stevenson built the scaffold of poles, in sections. To the poles used for uprights, horizontal poles were lashed with ropes; these were called ledgers. Upon these ledgers, planks were placed, and upon the top of each section so constructed, was placed another similarly constructed. When the scaffolding reached the curve of the dome, it was necessary to lessen the width of the upper section. For this purpose a strip of plank was used as an upright to support the end of the shorter ledger. This upright was called a cripple; but instead of fastening the ledger to it by lashing it was fastened by nailing. The scaffold was ninety feet in height.

Devlin was a workman in Smith's company. He was working on the curve of the dome, and sitting on a plank laid upon a ledger which was nailed to an upright or cripple, as above described, when the ledger gave way and broke. He was precipitated to the floor below and so injured that he died soon after....

RAPALLO, J. Upon a careful review of all the testimony in this case, we are of opinion that there was sufficient evidence to require the submission to the jury of the question, whether the breaking down of the scaffold was attributable negligence in its construction. It appears that the ledger which supported the plank upon which the deceased was sitting broke down without any excessive weight being put upon it, and without any apparent cause sufficient to break a well-constructed scaffold. One witness on the part of the plaintiff, accustomed work on scaffolds and to see them built, testified that the upright which supported the end of the ledger should have been fastened to it by lashing with ropes, instead of by nailing, and that lashing would have made it stronger, giving as reasons for this opinion, that the springing of the planks when walked upon was liable to break nails or push them out, whereas lashings would only become tighter, and the witness testified that the kind of scaffold in question was generally fastened by lashing, and that it was not the proper way to support the end of the ledger which broke, with an uprights nailed to the ledger, and that the ledger in question was fastened by nailing.

Another, a carpenter and builder, testified, that when, on account of the carving of a dome, it became necessary to put in a cripple, the cripple as well as the main uprights should be tied to the ledgers with rope; that the springing of the scaffold will break nails.

The appearances after the breakage were described to the jury, and a model of the scaffold was exhibited to them. Testimony touching the same points was submitted on the part of the defendants, and we think that on the whole evidence it was a question of fact for the jury, and not of law for the court, whether or not the injury was the result of the negligent construction of the scaffold.

The question of contributory negligence on the part of the deceased was also one for the jury. They had before them the circumstances of the accident. It appeared that the deceased was sitting on a plank, performing the work for which the scaffold had been erected. He was washing the interior wall of the dome, preparatory to its being

painted. There was nothing to indicate that he was in an improper place, or that he unnecessarily exposed himself to danger, or did any act to contribute to the accident. It is suggested that he, or some of his fellow-servants, may have kicked against the upright or brace which supported the end of the ledger, and thus thrown it out of place, but there was no evidence which would entitle the court to assume that the accident occurred from any such cause. The case was, therefore, one in which the jury might have found from the evidence that the death was caused by the improper or negligent construction of the scaffold, and without any fault on the part of the deceased, and the remaining question is, whether, if those facts should be found, the defendants, or either of them, should be held liable in this action.

The defendant Smith claims that no negligence on his part was shown. He was a painter who had made a contract with the supervisors of Kings county to paint the interior of the dome of the county courthouse, and the deceased was a workman employed by him upon that work. As between Smith and the county, he was bound to furnish the necessary scaffolding; but he was not a scaffold-builder, nor had he any knowledge of the business of building scaffolds, or any experience therein. He did not undertake to build the scaffold in question himself, or by means of servants or workmen under his direction, but made a contract with the defendant Stevenson to erect the construction for a gross sum, and the work was done under that contract, by Stevenson, who employed his own workmen and superintended the job himself. Mr. Stevenson had been known to Smith as a scaffold builder since 1844. His experience had been very large, and Smith had employed him before, and on this occasion the contract with him was for a first-class scaffold. There is no evidence upon which to base any allegation of incompetence on the part of Stevenson, nor any charge of negligence on the part of Smith in selecting him as a contractor, nor is there any evidence that Smith knew, or had reason to know, of any defect in the scaffold.

An employer does not undertake absolutely with his employees for the sufficiency or safety of the implements and facilities furnished for their work, but only for the exercise of reasonable care in that respect, and where injury to an employee results from a defect in the implements furnished, knowledge of the defect must be brought home to the employer, or proof given that he omitted the exercise of proper care to discover it. Personal negligence is the gist of the action. [Citations omitted.]

Under the recent decisions in this State, it may be that if Smith had undertaken to erect the scaffold through agents, or workmen acting under his direction, he would have been liable for negligence on their part in doing the work, ... But in this case he did not so undertake. Stevenson was not the agent or servant of Smith, but an independent contractor for whose acts or omissions Smith was not liable. [Citation omitted.] Smith received the scaffold from his as a completed work, and we do not think that it was negligence to rely upon its sufficiency and permit his employees to go upon it for the purpose of performing their work. Stevenson was, as appears from the evidence,

much more competent than Smith to judge of its sufficiency. He had undertaken to construct a first-class scaffold, and had delivered it to Smith in performance of this contract, and we do not think that Smith is chargeable with negligence for accepting it without further examination. All that such an examination would have disclosed would have been that the upright was nailed to the ledger, and Smith, not being an expert, would have been justified in relying upon the judgment of Stevenson as to the propriety of that mode offsetting. The defect was not such as to admonish Smith or danger.

If any person was at fault in the matter it was the defendant Stevenson. It is contended, however, that even if through his negligence the scaffold was defective, he is not liable in this action because there was no privity between him and the deceased, and he owed no duty to the deceased, his obligation and duty being only to Smith, with whom he contracted.

As a general rule the builder of a structure for another party, under a contract with him, or one who sells an article of his own manufacture, is not liable to an action by a third party who uses the same with the consent of the owner of purchaser, for injuries resulting from a defect therein, caused by negligence. The liability of the builder or manufacturer for such defects, in general, only to the person with whom he contracted. But, notwithstanding this rule, liability to third parties has been held to exist when the defect is such as to render the article in itself imminently dangerous, and serious injury to any person using it is a natural and probable consequence of its use. As where a dealer in drugs carelessly labeled a deadly poison as a harmless medicine, it was held that he was liable not merely to the person to whom he sold it, but to the person who ultimately used it, though it had passed through many hands. This liability was held to rest, not upon any contract or direct privity between him and the party injured, but upon the duty which the law imposes on every one to avoid acts in their nature dangerous to the lives of others. (Thomas v. Winchester, 6 N.Y. 397) In that case Mayor, etc., v. Cunliff (2 N.Y. 165) was cited as an authority for the position that a builder is liable only to the party for whom he builds. Some of the examples there put by way of illustration were commented upon, and among others the case of one who builds a carriage carelessly and of defective materials, and sells it, and the purchaser lends it to a friend, and the carriage, by reason of its original defect, breaks down and the friend is injured, and the question is put, can he recover against the maker? The comments of Ruggles, Ch. J., upon this supposititious case, in Thomas v. Winchester, and the ground upon which he answers the question in the negative, show clearly the distinction between the two classes of cases. He says that in the case supposed, the obligation of the maker to build faithfully arises only out of his contract with the purchaser. The public have nothing to do with it. Misfortune to third persons, not parties to the contract, would not be a natural and necessary consequence of the builder's negligence, and such negligence is not an act imminently dangerous to human life.

Applying these tests to the question now before us, the solution

is not difficult. Stevenson undertook to build a scaffold ninety feet in height, for the express purpose of enabling the workmen of Smith to stand upon it to paint the interior of the dome. Any defect or negligence in its construction, which should cause it to give way, would naturally result in these men being precipitated from that great height. A stronger case where misfortune to third persons not parties to the contract would be a natural and necessary consequence of the builder's negligence, can hardly be supposed, nor is it easy to imagine a more apt illustration of a case where such negligence would be an act imminently dangerous to human life. These circumstances seem to us to bring the case fairly within the principle of Thomas v. Winchester.

The same principle was recognized in Coughtry v. The Globe Woolen Co. (56 N.Y. 124) and applied to the case of a scaffold. It is true there was in that case the additional fact that the scaffold was erected by the defendant upon its own premises, but the case did not depend wholly upon that point. The scaffold was erected under a contract between the defendant and the employers of the person killed. The deceased was not a party to that contract, and the same argument was made as is urged here on the part of the defendant, that the latter owed no duty to the deceased; but this court held that in view of the facts that the scaffold was upwards of fifty feet from the ground, and unless properly constructed was a most dangerous trap, imperiling the life of any person who might go upon it, and that its was erected for the very purpose of accommodating the workmen, of whom the person killed was one, there was a duty toward them resting upon the defendant, independent of the contract under which the structure was built, to use proper diligence in its construction. The additional fact that the structure was on the premises of the defendant was relied upon, but we think that, even in the absence of that nature, the liability can rest upon the principle of Thomas v. Winchester.

Loop v. Litchfield (42 N.Y. 351, 1 Am. Rep. 543) was decided upon the ground that the wheel which caused the injury was not in itself a dangerous instrument, and that the injury was not a natural consequence of the defect, or one reasonably to be anticipated. Losee v. Clute (51 N.Y. 494, 10 Am. Rep. 638) was distinguished from Thomas v. Winchester, upon the authority of Loop v. Litchfield.

We think there should be a new trial as to the defendant Stevenson, and that it will be for the jury to determine whether the death of the plaintiff's intestate was caused by negligence on the part of Stevenson in the construction of the scaffold.

The judgment should be affirmed, with costs, as to the defendant Smith, and reversed as to the defendant Stevenson, and a new trial ordered as to him, costs to abide the event.

ANDREWS, CH, J., DANFORTH and FINCH, JJ., concur; EARL, J., concurs as to defendant Smith and dissents as to defendant Stevenson. MILLER, J., absent; TRACY, J., not sitting.

Judgment accordingly.

第三節　LOOP v. LITCHFIELD

Court of Appeals of New York, 1870
42 N.Y. 351

HUNT, J. A piece of machinery already made and on hand, having defects which weaken it, is sold by the manufacturer to one who buys it for his own use. The defects are pointed out to the purchaser and are fully understood by him. This piece of machinery is used by the buyer for five years, and is then taken into the possession of a neighbor, who uses it for his own purposes. While so in use, it flies apart by reason of its original defects, and the person using it is killed. Is the seller, upon this state of facts, liable to the representatives of the deceased party? I omit at this stage of the inquiry the elements, that the deceased had no authority to use the machine; that he knew of the defects and that he did not exercise proper care in the management of the machine. Under the circumstances I have stated, does a liability exist, supposing that the use was careful, and that it was by permission of the owner of the machine? To maintain this liability, the appellants rely upon the case of Thomas v. Winchester (6 N.Y., 2 Seld., 397). In that case, the defendant was engaged in the manufacture and sale of vegetable extracts for medicinal purposes. The extracts were put up in jars with appropriate labels. The defendant sold the articles to Mr. Aspinwall, a druggist of New York. Aspinwall sold to Dr.

Foord, a physician and druggist of Cazenovia, where the plaintiff resided. Mrs. Thomas, one of the plaintiffs, being ill, her physician prescribed for her a dose of the extract of dandelion, which is a simple and harmless medicine. The article furnished by Dr. Foord in response to this prescription was the extract of belladonna, a deadly poison. The jar from which this medicine was taken was labeled "1/2 lb. dandelion, prepared by A. Gilbert, 108 John St., N.Y., Jar 8 oz.," and thus labeled was sold to Dr. Foord. He relied upon the label, believing the medicine to be dandelion, and sold and delivered it to the plaintiffs as such. Mrs. Thomas suffered a severe illness by reason of this mistake. It was conceded by the counsel in that case and held by the court, that there was no privity of contract between Winchester and Thomas, and that there could be no recovery upon that ground. The court illustrates the argument by the case of a wagon built by A, who sells it to B, who hires it to C, who, in consequence of negligence in the building, is overturned and injured. C cannot recover against A, the builder. It is added: "Misfortune to third persons, not parties to the contract, would not be a natural and necessary consequence of the builder's negligence, and such negligence is not an act imminently dangerous to human life." So, if a horse, defectively shoed, is hired to another, and by reason of the negligent shoeing, the horse stumbles, the rider is thrown and injured, no action lies against the Smith. In these and numerous other cases put in the books, the answer to the action is, that there is no contract with the party injured, and no duty arising to him by the party guilty of negligence. "But,"

the learned judge says "the case in hand stands on a different ground. The defendant was a dealer in poisonous drugs. Gilbert was his agent in preparing them for market. The death or great bodily harm of some person was the natural and almost inevitable consequence of the sale of belladonna by means of the false label." "The defendant's neglect puts human life in imminent danger. Can it be said that there was no duty on the part of the defendant to avoid the creation of that danger by the exercise of greater caution?"

The appellants recognize the principle of this decision, and seek to bring their case within it, by asserting that the fly wheel in question was a dangerous instrument. Poison is a dangerous subject. Gunpowder is the same. A torpedo is a dangerous instrument, as is a spring gun, a loaded rifle or the like. They are instruments and articles in their nature calculated to do injury to mankind, and generally intended to accomplish that purpose. They are essentially, and in their elements, instruments of danger. Not so, however, an iron wheel, a few feet in diameter and a few inches in thickness although one part may be weaker than another. If the article is abused by too long use, or by applying too much weight or speed, an injury may occur, as it may from an ordinary carriage wheel, a wagon axle, or the common chair in which we sit. There is scarcely an object in art or nature, from which an injury may not occur under such circumstances. Yet they are not in their nature sources of danger, nor can they, with any regard to the accurate use of language, be called dangerous instruments. That an injury actually occurred by the breaking of a carriage axle, the failure of the carriage body, the falling to pieces of a chair or sofa, or the bursting of a fly wheel, does not in the least alter its character.

It is suggested that it is no more dangerous or illegal to label a deadly poison as a harmless medicine than to conceal a defect in a machine and paint it over so that it will appear sound. Waiving the point that there was no concealment, but the defect was fully explained to the purchaser, I answer, that the decision in Thomas v. Winchester was based upon the idea that the negligent sale of poisons is both at common law and by statute an indictable offense. If the act in that case had been done by the defendant instead of his agent, and the death of Mrs. Thomas had ensued, the defendant would have been guilty of manslaughter, as held by the court. The injury in that case was a natural result of the act. It was just what was to have been expected from putting falsely labeled poisons in the market, to be used by whomever should need the true articles. It was in its nature an act imminently dangerous to the lives of others. Not so here. The bursting of the wheel and the injury to human life was not the natural result or the expected consequence of the manufacture and sale of the wheel. Every use of the counterfeit medicines would be necessarily injurious, while this wheel was in fact used with safety for five years.

It is said that the verdict of the jury established the fact that this wheel was a dangerous instrument. I do not see how this can be, when there is no such allegation in the complaint, and no such question was submitted to the jury. "The court stated to the counsel that

the only question on which they would go to the jury would be that of negligence. Whether in the manufacture and sale of this article, the defendants are guilty of negligence, which negligence produced the injury complained of." If the action had been for negligence in constructing a carriage, sold by the defendants to Collister, by him lent to the deceased, which had been broken down, through the negligence of its construction, it might have been contended with the same propriety, that the finding of those facts by the jury established that a carriage was a dangerous instrument, and thereby the liability of the defendants became fixed. The jury found simply that there was negligence in the construction of the wheel, and that the injury resulted therefrom. It is quite illogical to deduce from this, the conclusion that the wheel was itself a dangerous instrument.

Upon the facts as stated, assuming that the deceased had no knowledge of the defects complained of, and assuming that he was in the rightful and lawful use of the machine, I am of the opinion that the verdict cannot be sustained. The facts constitute no cause of action.

The case contains the element, that the deceased was himself personally aware of the defects complained of. Collister testifies that he pointed them out to him, and conferred with him in relation to their effect. Instead of submitting this question of knowledge to the jury, the judge charged, "that if they find from the evidence, that the defendants made this defective wheel for use, and that it broke by reason of the defect, the defendants are liable for the defect to whoever used it." To which the defendant excepted.

The question is also presented of the effect of the circumstance, that the deceased was engaged in the use of the machine, without the permission of the owner. Having reached the conclusion, that there can be no recovery independent of these difficulties, it would not be profitable to spend time in their discussion. It is only necessary to say, that in my judgment, they are very important elements, and that, were the plaintiffs otherwise entitled to recover, they would merit the gravest consideration.

I cannot say that there was error in the charge, on the subject of negligence. It was not submitted with clearness, certainly, nor in the most appreciable form. The question is rather, what care the deceased was bound to exercise, than what negligence would be excused. The charge stated, that the "defendants, were not exonerated by slight negligence on the part of the deceased, although if he had used the utmost possible care, the accident would not have happened." This is equivalent to a charge, that the deceased was not bound to use the utmost possible care and was free from objection. The deceased was bound to exercise that care and attention in and about the business he was engaged in, that prudent, discreet, and sensible men are accustomed to bestow under like circumstances. The utmost possible care is not required. Indeed, its exercise would required an extent of time and caution that would terminate half the business of the world. (Sheridan v. Brooklyn, 36 N.Y. 43; Wells v. Long Island, 32 Barb. 398, aff'd, 34 N.Y. 670; Button v. Hudson River Co., 28 N.Y. 258; Curran v. Warren Co., 36 N.Y. 153; Milton v. Hudson S.B. Co., 37

N.Y. 212; Owen v. Hudson River Co., 35, 516.)

The order of the General Term should be affirmed, and judgment absolute given for the defendants.

All concur. Judgment affirmed, and judgment absolute ordered for the defendants.

第四節　LOSEE v. CLUTE

Commission of Appeals of New York, 1873
51 N.Y. 494

Appeal from judgment of the General Term of the Supreme Court in the fourth judicial district, affirming a judgment entered upon an order dismissing plaintiff's complaint on the trial.

The action was brought to recover damages caused to the property of the plaintiff by the explosion of a steam boiler while the same was owned and being used by the Saratoga Paper Company at their mill situated in the village of Schuylerville, Saratoga County and State of New York, on the thirteenth day of February, 1863, by means whereof the boiler was thrown on to the plaintiff's premises and through several of his buildings, thereby injuring and damaging the same.

The defendants, Clute, were made parties defendants to the action with the Saratoga Paper Company and Coe S. Buchanan and Daniel A. Bullard, trustees and agent of said company, on the ground that they were the manufacturers of the boiler, and made the same out of poor and brittle iron and in a negligent and defective manner, in consequence of which negligence said explosion occurred.

At the close of the evidence the complaint was dismissed as to the defendants Clute.

The facts, so far as they are material to the decision in this court, are sufficiently stated in the opinion....

LOTT, CH, C. It appears by the case that the defendants Clute manufactured the boiler in question for the Saratoga Paper Company, in which they were stockholders, for the purposes and uses to which it was subsequently applied by it; and the testimony tended to show that it was constructed improperly and of poor iron, that the said defendants, knew at the time that it was to be used in the immediate vicinity of and adjacent to dwelling-houses and stores in a village, so that, in case of an explosion while in use, it would be likely to be destructive to human life and adjacent property, and that, in consequence of the negligence of the said defendants in the improper construction of the boiler, the explosion that took place occurred and damaged the plaintiff's property. The evidence also tended to show that the boiler was tested by the company to its satisfaction, and then accepted, and was thereafter used by it for about three months prior to the explosion, and that after such test and acceptance the said defendants had nothing whatever to do with the boiler, and had no care or management of it at the time of the explosion, but that the company had the sole and exclusive ownership, management and conduct of it.

In determining whether the complaint was properly dismissed, we must assume all the facts which the evidence tended to show as established, and the question is thereby presented whether the defendants have incurred any liability to the plaintiff. They contracted with the company, and did what was done by them for it and to its satisfaction, and when the boiler was accepted they ceased to have any further control over it or its management, and all responsibility for what was subsequently done with it revolved upon the company and those having charge of it, and the case falls within the principle decided by the Court of Appeals in The Mayor, etc., of Albany v. Cunliff (2 Comst. 165), which is, that at the most an architect or builder of a work is answerable only to his employees for any want of care or skill in the execution thereof, and he is not liable for accidents or injuries which may occur after the execution of the work; and the opinions published in that case clearly show that there is no ground of liability by the defendants to the plaintiff in this action. They owed him no duty whatever at the time of the explosion either growing out of contract or imposed by law.

It may be proper to refer to the case of Thomas v. Winchester (2 Selden, 397), cited by the appellant's counsel, and I deem it sufficient to say that the opinion of Hunt, J., in Loop v. Lithchfield (42 N.Y. 351) clearly shows that the principle decided in that case has no application to this.

It appears from these considerations that the complaint was properly dismissed, and it follows that there was no case made for the consideration of the jury, and, consequently, there was no error in the refusal to submit it to them.

There was an exception taken to the exclusion of evidence to show that two persons were killed by this boiler in passing through a dwelling-house in its course, but as it is not urged on this appeal, it is, I presume, abandoned; but if not, it was matter, as the judge held at the trial, wholly immaterial to the issue between the parties in this action.

There is, for the reasons stated, no ground for the reversal of the judgment. It must, therefore, be a affirmed, with costs.

All concur.

Judgment affirmed.

第五節 MacPHERSON v. BUICK MO-TOR CO.

Court of Appeals of New York, 1916
217 N.Y. 382, 111 N.E. 1950

Appeal, by permission, from a judgment of the Appellate Division of the Supreme Court in the third judicial department, entered January 8, 1914, affirming a judgment in favor of plaintiff entered upon a verdict.

The nature of the action and the facts, so far as material, are stated in the opinion....

CARDOZO, J. The defendant is a manufacturer of automobiles. He sold an automobile to a retail dealer. The retail dealer resold to the plaintiff. While the plaintiff was in the car, it suddenly collapsed. He was thrown out and injured. One of the wheels was made of defective wood, and its spokes crumbled into fragments. The wheel was not made by the defendant; it was bought from another manufacturer. There is evidence, however, that its defects could've been discovered by reasonable inspection, and that inspection was omitted. There is no claim that the defendant knew of the defect and willfully concealed it. The case, in other words, is not brought within the rule of Kuelling v. Lean Mfg. Co. (183 N.Y. 78, 75 N.E. 1098). The charge is one, not of fraud, but of negligence. The question to be determined is whether the defendant owed a duty of care and vigilance to any one but the immediate purchaser.

The foundations of this branch of the law, at least in this state, were laid in Thomas v. Winchester (6 N.Y. 397). A poison was falsely labeled. The sale was made to a druggist, who in turn sold to a customer. The customer recovered damages from the seller who affixed the label. "The defendant's negligence," it was said, "put human life in imminent danger." A poison falsely labeled is likely to injure any one who gets it. Because the danger is to be foreseen, there is a duty to avoid the injury. Cases were cited by way of illustration in which manufacturers were not subject to any duty irrespective of contract. The distinction was said to be that their conduct, though negligent, was not likely to result in injury to any one except the purchaser. We are not required to say whether the chance of injury was always as remote as the distinction assumes. Some of the illustrations might be rejected today. The principle of the distinction for present purposes is an important thing.

Thomas v. Winchester became quickly a landmark of the law. In the application of its principle there may at times have been uncertainty or even error. There has never in this state been doubt or disavowal of the principle itself. The chief cases are well known, yet to recall some of them will be helpful. Loop v. Litchfield (42 N.Y. 351) is the earliest. It was the case of a defect in a small balance wheel used on a circular saw. The manufacturer pointed out the defect to the buyer, who wished a cheap article and was ready to assume the risk. The risk can hardly have been an imminent one, for the wheel lasted five years before it broke. In the meanwhile the buyer had made a lease of the machinery. It was held that the manufacturer was not answerable to the lessee. Loop v. Litchfield was followed in Losee v. Clute (51 N.Y. 494), the case of the explosion of a steam boiler. That decision has been criticized (Thompson on Negligence, 233; Shearman & Readfield on Negligence [6th ed.], §117), but it must be confined to its special facts. It was put upon the ground that the risk of injury was too remote. The buyer in that case had not only accepted the boiler, but had tested it. The manufacturer knew that his own test was not the final one. The finality of the test has bearing on the measure of diligence owing to persons other than the purchaser (Bevin, Negligence, 3d ed., pp. 50, 51, 54; Wharton, Negligence, 2d

ed., §134).

These early cases suggest a narrow construction of the rule. Later cases, however, evince a more liberal spirit. First in importance is Devlin v. Smith (89 N.Y. 470). The defendant, a contractor, built a scaffold for a painter. The painter's servants were injured. The contractor was held liable. He knew that the scaffold, if improperly constructed, was a most dangerous trap. He knew that it was to be used by the workmen. He was building it for that very purpose. Building it for their use, he owed them a duty, irrespective of his contract with their master, to build it with care.

From Devlin v. Smith we pass over intermediate cases and turn to the latest case in this court in which Thomas v. Winchester was followed. That case is Statler v. Ray Mfg. Co. (195 N.Y. 478, 480, 88 N.E. 1063). The defendant manufactured a large coffee urn. It was installed in a restaurant. When heated, the urn exploded and injured the plaintiff. We held that the manufacturer was liable. We said that the urn "was of such a character inherently that, when applied to the purposes for which it was designed, it was liable to become a source of great danger to many people if not carefully and properly constructed."

It may be that Devlin v. Smith and Statler v. Ray Mfg. Co. have extended the rule of Thomas v. Winchester. If so, this court is committed to the extension. The defendant argues that things imminently dangerous to life are poisonous explosives, deadly weapons-thing whose normal function is to injure or destroy. But whatever the rule in Thomas v. Winchester may once have been, it has no longer that restricted meaning. A scaffold (Devlin v. Smith, supra) is not inherently a destructive instrument. It becomes destructive only if imperfectly constructed. A large coffee urn (Statler v. Ray Mfg. Co., supra) may have within itself, if negligently made, the potency of danger, yet no one thinks of it as an implement whose normal function is destruction. What is true of the coffee urn is equally true of bottles of aerated water (Torgeson v. Schultz, 192 N.Y. 156, 84 N.E. 956). We have mentioned only cases in this court. But the rule has received a like extension in our courts of intermediate appeal. In Burke v. Ireland (26 App. Div. 487, 50 N.Y.S. 369), in an opinion by Cullen, J., it was applied to a builder who constructed a defective building; in Kahner v. Otis Elevator Co. (96 App. Div. 169, 89 N.Y.S. 185) to the manufacturer of an elevator; in Davies v. Pelham Hod Elevating Co. (65 Hun, 573, 20 N.Y.S. 523; affirmed in this court without opinion, 146 N.Y. 363) to a contractor who furnished a defective rope with knowledge of the purpose for which the rope was to be used. We are not required at this time either to approve or to disapprove the application of the rule that was made in these cases. It is enough that they help to characterize the trend of judicial thought.

Devlin v. Smith was decided in 1882. A year later a very similar case came before the Court of Appeal in England (Heaven v. Pender, L.R. [11 Q.B.D.] 503). We find in the opinion of Brett, M. R., afterwards Lord Esher (p. 510), the same conception of a duty, irrespective of contract, imposed upon the manufacturer by the law itself:

"Whenever one person supplies goods, or machinery, or the like, for the purpose of their being used by another person under such circumstances that every one of ordinary sense would, if he thought, recognize at once that unless he used ordinary care and skill with regard to the condition of the thing supplied or the mode of supplying it, there will be danger of injury to the person or property of him for whose use the thing is supplied, and who is to use it, a duty arises to use ordinary care and skill as to the condition or manner of supplying such thing." He then points out that for a neglect of such ordinary care of skill whereby injury happens, the appropriate remedy is an action for negligence. The right to enforce this liability is not to be confined to the immediate buyer. The right, he says, extends to the persons or class of persons for whose use the thing is supplied. It is enough that the goods "would in all discovering any defect which might exist," and that the thing supplied is of such a nature "that a neglect of ordinary care or skill as to its condition or the manner of supplying it would probably cause danger to the person or property of the person for whose use it was supplied, and who was about to use it." On the other hand, he would exclude a case "in which the goods are supplied under circumstances in which it would be a chance by whom they would be used or whether they would be used or not, or whether they would be used before there would probably be means of observing any defect," or where the goods are of such a nature that "a want of care or skill as to their condition or the manner of supplying them would not probably produce danger of injury to person or property."

What was said by Lord Esher in that case did not command the full assent of his associates. His opinion has been criticized "as requiring every man to take affirmative precautions to protect his neighbors as well as to refrain from injuring them" (Bohlen, Affirmative Obligations in the Law of Torts, 44 Am. Law Reg. [N.S.] 341). It may not be an accurate exposition of the law of England. Perhaps it may need some qualification even in our own state. Like most attempts at comprehensive definition, it may involve errors of inclusion and of exclusion. But its tests and standards, at least in their underlying principles, with whatever qualifications may be called for as they are applied to varying conditions, are the tests and standards of our law.

We hold, then, that the principle of Thomas v. Winchester is not limited to poisons, explosives, and things of like nature, to things which in their normal operation are implements of destruction. If the nature of a thing is such that it is reasonably certain to place life and limb in peril when negligently made, it is then a thing of danger. Its nature gives warning of the consequences to be expected. If to the element of danger there is added knowledge thing will be used by persons other than the purchaser, and used without new test, then, irrespective of contract, the manufacturer of this thing of danger is under a duty to make it carefully. That is as far as we are required to go for the decision of this case. There must be knowledge of a danger, not merely possible, but probable. It is possible to use almost anything in a way that will make it dangerous if defective. That is not enough to charge the manufacturer with a duty independent of his contract.

Whether a given thing is dangerous may be sometimes a question for the court and sometimes a question for the jury. There must also be knowledge that in the usual course of events the danger will be shared by others than the buyer. Such knowledge may often be inferred from the nature of the transaction. But it is possible that even knowledge of the danger and of the use will not always be enough. The proximity or remoteness of the relation is a factor to be considered. We are dealing now with the liability of the manufacturer of the finished product, who puts it on the market to be used without inspection by his customers. If he is negligent, where danger is to be foreseen, a liability will follow. We are not required at this time to say that it is legitimate to go back of the manufacturer of the finished product and hold the manufacturers of the component parts. To make their negligence a cause of imminent danger, an independent cause must often intervene; the manufacturer of the finished product must also fail in his duty of inspection. If may be than in those circumstances the negligence of the earlier members of the series is too remote to constitute, as to the ultimate user, an actionable wrong (Beven on Negligence [3d ed.], 50, 51, 54; Wharton on Negligence [2d ed.], §134; Leeds v. N.Y. Tel. Co., 178 N.Y. 118, 70 N.E. 219; Sweet v. Perkins, 196 N.Y. 482, 90 N.E. 50; Hayes v. Hyde Park, 153 Mass. 514, 516, 27 N.E. 522). We leave that question open. We shall have to deal with it when it arises. The difficulty which it suggests is not present in this case. There is here no break in the chain of cause and effect. In such circumstances, the presence of a known danger, attendant upon a

known use, makes vigilance a duty. We have put aside the notion that the duty to safeguard life and limb, when the consequences of negligence may be foreseen, grows out of contract and nothing else. [We have put the source of the obligation where it ought to be. We have put its source in law.]

From this survey of the decisions, there thus emerges a definition of the duty of a manufacturer which enables us to measure this defendant's liability. Beyond all question, the nature of an automobile gives warning of probable danger if its construction is defective. This automobile was designed to go fifty miles an hour. Unless its wheels were sound and strong, injury was almost most certain. It was as much a thing of danger as a defective engine for a railroad. The defendant knew the danger. It knew also that the car would be used by persons other than the buyer. This was apparent from its size; there were seats for three persons. It was apparent also from the fact that the buyer was a dealer in cars, who bought to resell. The maker of this car supplied it for the use of purchasers from the dealer just as plainly as the contractor in Devlin v. Smith supplied the scaffold for use by the servants of the owner. The dealer was indeed the one person of whom it might be said with some approach to certainty that by him the car would not be used. Yet the defendant would have us say that he was the one person whom it was under a legal duty to protect. The law does not lead us to so inconsequent a conclusion. Precedents drawn from the days of travel by stage coach do not fit the conditions of travel today. The principle that the danger must be imminent does

not change, but the things subject to the principle do change. They are whatever the needs of life in a developing civilization require them to be.

In reaching this conclusion, we do not ignore the decisions to the contrary in other jurisdictions. It was held in Cadillac M.C. Co. v. Johnson (221 F. 801) that an automobile is not within the rule of Thomas v. Winchester. There was, however, a vigorous dissent. Opposed to that decision is one of the Court of Appeals of Kentucky (Olds Motor Works v. Shaffer, 145 Ky. 616, 140 S.W. 1047). The earlier cases are summarized by Judge Sanborn in Huset v. J. I. Case Threshing Machine Co. (120 F. 865). Some of them, at first sight inconsistent with our conclusion, may be reconciled upon the ground that the negligence was too remote, and that another cause had intervened. But even when they cannot be reconciled, the difference is rather in the application of the principle than in the principle itself. Judge Sanborn says, for example, that the contractor who builds a bridge, or the manufacturer who builds a car, cannot ordinarily foresee injury to others is to be foreseen not merely as a possibility, but as an almost inevitable result. Indeed, Judge Sanborn concedes that his view is not to be reconciled with our decision in Devlin v. Smith (supra). The doctrine of that decision has now become the settled law of this state, and we have no desire to depart from it.

In England the limits of the rule are still unsettled. Winterbottom v. Wright (10 M. & W. 109) is often cited. The defendant undertook to provide a mail coach to carry the mail bags. The coach broke down from latent defects in its construction. The defendant, however, was not the manufacturer. The court held that he was not liable for injuries to a passenger. The case was decided on a demurrer to the declaration. Lord Esher points out in Heaven v. Pender that the form of the declaration was subject to criticism. It did not fairly suggest the existence of a duty abide from the special contract which was the plaintiff's main reliance. At all events, in Heaven v. Pender, the defendant, a dock owner, who put up a staging outside a ship, was held liable to the servants of the shipowner. In Elliott v. Hall (15 Q.B.D. 315) the defendant sent out a defective truck laden with goods which he had sold. The buyer's servants unloaded it, and were injured because of the defects. It was held that the defendant was under a duty "not to be guilty of negligence with regard to the state and condition of the truck." There seems to have been a return to the doctrine of Winterbottom v. Wright in Earl v. Lubbock (L.R. [1905] 1 K.B. 253). In that case, however, as in the earlier one, the defendant was not the manufacturer. He had merely made a contract to keep the van in repair. A later case (White v. Steadman, L.R. [1913], 3 K.B. 340, 348) emphasizes that element. A livery stable keeper who sent out a vicious horse was held liable not merely to his customer but also to another occupant of the carriage, and Thomas v. Winchester was cited and followed. It was again cited and followed in Dominion Natural Gas Co. v. Collins (L.R. [1909] A.C. 640, 646). From these cases a consistent principle is with difficulty extracted. The English courts, however, agree with ours in holding that one who invites another to

make use of an appliance is bound to the exercise of reasonable care
(Caledonian Ry. Co. v. Mulholland, L.R. [1898] A.C. 216, 227; In-
dermaur v. Dames, L.R. [1 C.P.] 274). That at bottom is the underlying principle of Devlin v. Smith. The contractor who builds the scaffold invites the owner's workmen to use it. The manufacturer who
sells the automobile to the retail dealer invites the dealer's customers
to use it. The invitation is addressed in the one case to determinate
persons and in the other to an indeterminate class, but in each case it
is equally plain, and in each its consequences must be the same.

There is nothing anomalous in a rule which imposes upon A,
who has contracted with B, a duty to C and D and others according as
he knows or does not know that the subject-matter of the contract is
intended for their use. We may find an analogy in the law which
measures the liability of landlords. If A leases to B a tumble-down
house he is not liable in the absence of fraud, to B; suggests who enter
it and are injured. This is because B is then under the duty to repair it,
the lessor has the right to suppose that he will fulfill that duty, and if
he omits to do so, his guests must look to him (Bohlen, supra, at
p.276). But if A leases a building to be used by the lessee at once as a
place of public entertainment, the rule is different. There injury to
persons other than the lessee is to be foreseen, and foresight of the
consequences involves the creation of a duty (Junkermann v. Tilyou
R. Co., 213 N.Y. 404, 108 N.E. 190, and cases there cited).

In this view of the defendant's liability there is nothing inconsistent with the theory of liability on which the case was tried. It is true

that the court told the jury that "an automobile is not an inherently dangerous vehicle." The meaning, however, is made plain by the context. The meaning is that danger is not to be expected when the vehicle is well constructed. The court left it to the jury to say whether the defendant ought to have foreseen that the car, negligently constructed, would become "imminently dangerous." Subtle distinctions are drawn by the defendant between things inherently dangerous and things imminently dangerous, but the case does not turn upon these verbal niceties. If danger was to be expected as reasonably certain, there was a duty of vigilance, and this whether you call the danger inherent or imminent. In varying forms that thought was put before the jury. We do not say that the court would not have been justified in ruling as a matter of law that the car was a dangerous thing. If there was any error it was none of which the defendant can complain.

We think the defendant was not absolved from a duty of inspection because it bought the wheels from a reputable manufacturer. It was not merely a dealer in automobiles. It was a manufacturer of automobiles. It was responsible for the finished product. It was not at liberty to put the finished product on the market without subjecting the component parts to ordinary and simple tests (Richmond & Danville R.R. Co. v. Elliott, 149 U.S. 266, 272, 13 S. Ct. 837). Under the charge of the trial judge nothing more was required of it. The obligation to inspect must vary with the nature of the thing to be inspected. The more probable the danger, the greater the need of caution. There is little analogy between this case and Carlson v. Phoenix

Bridge Co. (132 N.Y. 273, 30 N.E. 750), where the defendant bought a tool for a servant's use. The making of tools was not the business in which the master was engaged. Reliance on the skill of the manufacturer was proper and almost inevitable. But that is not the defendant's situation. Both by its relation to the work and by the nature of its business, it is charged with a stricter duty.

Other rulings complained of have been considered, but no error has been found in them.

The judgment should be affirmed with costs.

WILLARD BARTLETT, CH. J. (dissenting) The plaintiff was injured in consequence of the collapse of a wheel of an automobile manufactured by the defendant corporation which sold it to a firm of automobile dealers in Schenectary, who in turn sold the car to the plaintiff. The wheel was purchased by the Buick Motor Company, ready made, from the Imperial Wheel Company of Flint, Michigan, a reputable manufacturer of automobile wheels which had furnished the defendant with eighty thousand wheels, none of which had proved to be made of defective wood prior to the accident in the present case. The defendant relied upon the wheel manufacturer to make all necessary tests as to the strength of the material therein and made no such tests itself. The present suit is an action for negligence brought by the subvendee of the motor car against the manufacturer as the original vendor. The evidence warranted a finding by the jury that the wheel which collapsed was defective when it left the hands of the defendant. The auto mobile was being prudently operated the time of the accident and was moving at a speed of only eight miles an hour. There was no allegation of proof of any actual knowledge of the defect on the part of the defendant of any suggestion that any element of fraud or deceit or misrepresentation entered into the sale.

The theory upon which the case was submitted to the jury by the learned judge who presided at the trial was that, although an automobile is not an inherently dangerous vehicle, it may become such if equipped with a weak wheel; and that if the motor car in question, when it was put upon the market was in itself inherently dangerous by reason of its being equipped with a weak wheel, the defendant was chargeable with a knowledge of the defect so far as it might be discovered by a reasonable inspection and the application of reasonable test. This liability, it was further held, was not limited to the original vendee, but extended to a subvendee like the plaintiff, who was not a party to the original contract of sale.

I think that these rulings, which have been approved by the Appellate Division, extend the liability of the vendor of a manufactured article further than any case which has yet received sanction of this court. It has hereto fore been held in this state that the liability of the vendor of a manufactured article for negligence arising out of the existence of defects therein does not extend to strangers injured in consequence of such defects but is confined to the immediate vendee. The exceptions to this general rule which have thus far been recognized in New York are cases in which the article sold was of such character that danger to life or limb was involved in the ordinary us

there of; in other words, where article sold was inherently dangerous. As has already been pointed out, the learned trial judge instructed the jury that an automobile is not an inherently dangerous vehicle.

The late Chief Justice Colley of Michigan, one of the most learned and accurate of American law writers, states the general rule thus: "The general rule is that a contractor, manufacturer, vendor, or furnisher of an article is not liable to third parties who have no contractual relations with him for negligence in the construction, manufacturing, or sale of such article."

The leading English authority in support of this rule, to which all the later cases on the same subject refer, is Winterbottom v. Wright (10 Meeson & Welsby, 109), which was an action by the driver of a stage coach against a contractor who had agreed with the postmaster general to provide and keep the vehicle in repair for the purpose of conveying the royal mail over a prescribed route. The coach broke down and upset, injuring the driver, who sought to recover against the contractor on account of its defective construction. The Court of Exchequer denied him any right of recovery on the ground that there was no privity of contract between the parties, the agreement having been made with the postmaster general alone. "If the plaintiff can sue," said Lord Abinger, the Cief Baron, "every passenger or even any person passing along the road, who was injured by the upsetting of the coach, might bring a similar action. Unless we confine the operation of such contracts as this to the parties who enter into them, the most absurd and outrageous consequences, to which I can see no limit, would ensue."

The doctrine of that decision was recognized as the law of this state by the leading New York case of Thomas v. Winchester (6 N.Y. 397, 408), which, however, involved an exception to the general rule. There the defendant, who was a dealer in medicines, sold to a druggist a quantity of belladonna, which is a deadly poison, negligently labeled as extract of dandelion. The druggist in good faith used the poison in filling a prescription calling for the harmless dandelion extract and the plaintiff for whom the prescription was put up was poisoned by the belladonna. This court held that the original vendor was liable for the injuries suffered by the patient. Chief Judge Ruggles, who delivered the opinion of the court, distinguished between an act of negligence imminently dangerous to the lives of others and one that is not so, saying: "If A builds a wagon and sells it to B, who sells it to C and C hires it to D, who in consequence of the gross negligence of A in building the wagon is overturned and injured, D cannot recover damages against A, the builder. A's obligation to build the wagon faithfully, arises solely out of his contract with B. The public have nothing to do with it. So, for the same reason, if a horse be defectively shod by a smith, and a person hiring the horse from the owner is thrown and injured in consequence of the smith's negligence in shoeing; the smith is not liable for the injury."

In Torgeson v. Schultz (192 N.Y. 156, 159, 84 N.E. 956) the defendant was the vendor of bottles of aerated water which were charged under high pressure and likely to explode unless used with

precaution when exposed to sudden changes of temperature. The plaintiff, who was a servant of the purchaser, was injured by the exploding of one of these bottles. There was evidence tending to show that it had not been properly tested in order to insure users against such accidents. We held that the defendant corporation was liable notwithstanding the absence of any contract relation between it and the plaintiff "under the doctrine of Thomas v. Winchester (supra), and similar cases based upon the duty of the vendor of an article dangerous in its nature, or likely to become so in the course of the ordinary usage to be contemplated by the vendor, either to exercise due care to warn users of the danger or to take reasonable care to prevent the article sold from proving dangerous when subjected only to customary usage." The character of the exception to the general rule limiting liability for negligence to the original parties to the contract of sale, was still more clearly stated by Judge Hiscock, writing for the court in Statler v. Ray Manufacturing Co. (195 N.Y. 478, 482, 88 X.E. 1063), where he said that "in the case of an article of an inherently dangerous nature, a manufacturer may become liable for a negligent construction which, when added to the inherent character of the appliance, makes it immediately dangerous, and causes or contributes to a resulting injury not necessarily incident to the use of such an article if properly constructed, but naturally following from a defective construction." In that case the injuries were inflicted by the explosion of a battery of steam-driven coffee urns, constituting an appliance liable to become dangerous in the course of ordinary usage.

The case of Devlin v. Smith (89 N.Y. 470) is cited as an authority in conflict with the view that the liability of the manufacturer and vendor extends to third parties only when the article manufactured and sold is inherently dangerous. In that case the builder of a scaffold ninety feet high which was erected for the purpose of enabling painters to stand upon it, was held to be liable to the administratrix of a painter who fell therefrom and was killed, being at the time in the employ of the person for whom the scaffold was built. It is said that the scaffold if properly constructed was not inherently dangerous; and hence that this decision affirms the existence of liability in the case of an article not dangerous in itself but made so only in consequence of negligent construction. Whatever logical force there may be in this view it seems to me clear from the language of Judge Rapallo, who wrote the opinion of the court, that the scaffold was deemed to be an inherently dangerous structure; and that the case was decided as it was because the court entertained that view. Otherwise he would hardly have said, as he did, that the circumstances seemed to bring the case fairly within the principle of Thomas v. Winchester.

I do not see how we can uphold the judgment in the present case without overruling what has been so often said by this court and other courts of like authority in reference to the absence of any liability for negligence on the part of the original vendor of an ordinary carriage to any one except his immediate vendee. The absence of such liability was the very point actually decided in the English case of Winterbottom v. Wright (supra), and the illustration quoted from the opinion

of Chief Judge Ruggles in Thomas v. Winchester (supra) assumes that the law on the subject was so plain that the statement would be accepted almost as a matter of course. In the case at bar the defective when on an automobile moving only eight miles an hour was not any more dangerous to the occupants of the car than a similarly defective wheel would be to the occupants of a carriage drawn by a horse at the same speed; and yet unless the courts have been all wrong on this question up to the present time there would be no liability to strangers to the original sale in the case of the horse-drawn carriage.

The rule upon which, in my judgment, the determination of this case depends, and the recognized exceptions thereto, were discussed by Circuit Judge Sanborn of the United States Circuit Court of Appeals in the Eighth Circuit in Huset v. J. I. Case Threshing Machine Co. (120 F. 865) in an opinion which reviews all the leading American and English decisions on the subject up to the time when it was rendered (1903). I have already discussed the leading New York cases,but as to the rest I feel that I can add nothing to the learning of that opinion or the cogency of its reasoning. I have examined the cases to which Judge Sanborn refers but if I were to discuss them at length I should be forced merely to paraphrase his language, as a study of the authorities he cites has led me to the same conclusion; and the repetition of what has already been so well said would contribute nothing to the advantage of the bench, the bar or the individual litigants whose case is before us.

A few cases decided since his opinion was written, however,

may be noticed. In Earl v. Lubbock (L.R. 1905 [1 K.B. Div.] 253) the Court of Appeal in 1904 considered and approved the propositions of law laid down by the Court of Exchequer in Winterbottom v. Wright (supra), declaring that the decision in that case, since the year 1842, had stood the test of repeated discussion. The master of the rolls approved the principle laid down by Lord Abinger as based upon sound reasoning; and all the members of the court agreed that his decision was a controlling authority which must be followed. That the Federal courts still adhere to the general rule, as I have stated it, appears by the decision of the Circuit Court of Appeals in the Second Circuit, in March, 1915, in the case of Cadillac Motor Car Co. v. Johnson (221 F. 801). That case, like this was an action by a subvendee against a manufacturer of automobiles for negligence in failing to discover that one of its wheels was defective, the court holding that such an action could not be maintained. It is true there was a dissenting opinion in that case, but it was based chiefly on the proposition that rules applicable to stage coaches are archaic when applied to automobiles and that if the law did not afford a remedy to strangers to the contract the law should be changed. If this be true, the change should be effected by the legislature and not by the courts. A perusal of the opinion in that case and in the Huset case will disclose how uniformly the courts throughout this country have adhered to the rule and how consistently they have refused to broaden the scope of the exceptions. I think we should adhere to it in the case at bar and, therefore, I vote for a reversal of this judgment.

HISCOCK, CHASE, and CHDDEBACK, JJ., concur with
CARDOZO, J., and HOGAN, J., concurs is result; WILLARD
BARTLETT, CH. J., reads dissenting opinion; POUND, J., not
voting.

Judgment affirmed.

第六節　EXPLANATION（說明）

閱讀上述案例後，我們得知這些案例重點在於製造人產品之
法律責任(Product liability)，　茲將上述案件的重要事實與法律內
容，節錄如下：

一、MANUFACTURER'S DUTY（製造人之責任）

1. A defective boiler is not imminently dangerous. (Losee)

2. A manufacturer owes a duty of reasonable care to his immediate
   purchaser. (Thomas, Winterbottom)

3. In determining whether product imminently dangerous, we have to
   analyze whether or not it is dangerous when properly manufactured. (Loop, Losee)

4. Manufacturer's contractual promises are not made to people not in
   privity. (Winterbottom)

5. A gun is imminently dangerous. (Thomas, dicta)

6. Manufacturers do not owe duty of care to someone not in privity.
   (Winterbottom)

7. Poison is imminently dangerous. (Thomas) [Cf: conflict with 1]

8. A defective flywheel is not imminently dangerous. (Loop) [Cp: 8]

9. Manufacturers owe duty of reasonable care to person not in privity if the product is imminently dangerous. (Thomas) [Cf: conflict with 4] [exception]

10. Immediate purchasers can hold manufacturers to their contractual promises. (Winterbottom) [Contract]

11. Products are imminently dangerous if death or injury is natural and probable consequence of their intended use. (Thomas)

Summary: You need to rearrange the above principles in order to get a well-organized outline as follows: (The following is a suggestive sample of legal outline only.)

經過以上之整理，我們遂一把已知的法院判決內容，以大綱 (Brief or Outline)之方式呈現如下：

二、MANUFACTURER'S DUTY (SUMMARY)（綜合整理）

I. IN CONTRACT（契約）

  A. Immediate purchaser: can hold manufacturers liable to their contractual promises (#10)（直接之購買者）

  B. Those not in privity: contractual promises are not made to such person and cannot be sued on by those not in privity (#4)（沒有契因關係之購買者，不得主張製造人之責任）

II. IN TORT（侵權行為）

  A. Immediate purchaser: A manufacturer owes a duty of reasonable care to immediate purchaser. (#2)（直接之購買者）

B. Those not in privity: Manufacturers owes no duty of care to those not in privity. (#6)（沒有契因關係之購買者）

  1. Exceptoin: such duty is owed if the product is "imminently dangerous." (#7)（例外）

  2. Definition: "imminently dangerous" is variously defined as whether or not death or injury is a natural and probable consequence of product's use when it is properly made.（法院判決文字）

  3. Application of definition

    a. includes guns, poison (#5, #7)

    b. excludes defective boiler, defective flywheel (#1, #8)

綜上，由上之演習是否有較清晰之觀念？英美法案例之閱讀要訣，應先大略閱讀一遍，了解前面第一頁之事實後，再看最後一頁判決(但需注意有時最後頁之編排是反對意見說)， 推論判決是原告或被告勝訴，再接下去看全部詳細內文分析部分，何者是原告與被告主張(Plaintiff's Contention v. Defendant's Contention)，比較雙方提出之案件，找出結論。看完案例後一定要作Brief，否則以後想再重頭看一次，已無時間或記憶已模糊。複習時只看以前作過之Brief，通常可節省時間並達成事半功倍之效率。

第五章　BRIEF示範

這次我們再以一案例，使學習者充分掌握如何以FACTS，ISSUE，RULE，ANALYSIS及CONCLUSION寫一份以IRAC為基礎之BRIEF：

第一節　PEOPLE v. VOLPE et al.

Kings County Court
June 22, 1953

SOBEL, Judge.

The defendants move on the grand jury minutes for dismissal of the inducement. The indictment charges conspiracy (for which crime a prima facie case is established) and attempted robbery.

There is no doubt that the defendants jointly planned a robbery. There is no doubt that they committed overt acts tending towards the commission of a robbery. The only question is whether these acts reached the stage of an "attempt". The statute and the cases draw a line between those acts which are too remote and those which are proximate and near to the consummation.

The rule of law has been variously stated. "There must be dan-

gerous proximity to success," Hyde v. U.S. 225 U.S. 347, 32 S.Ct. 793, 810, 56 L.Ed. 1114; "very near," Commonwealth v. Peaslee, 177 Mass. 267, 59 N.E. 55; "it must be such as would naturally effect that result, unless prevented by some extraneous cause." People v. Mills, 178 N.Y. 274, 70 N.E. 786, 790, 67 L.R.A. 131; "The act or acts must come or advance very near to the accomplishment of the intended crime," People v. Rizzo, 246 N.Y. 334, 339, 158 N.E. 888, 889, 55 A.L.R. 711.

It should be noted that the shadowy line of demarcation between remote and proximate acts will vary with the nature of the crime intended. See People v. Bennett, 182 App. Div. 871, 170 N.Y.S. 718, affirmed 224 N.Y. 594, 120 N.E. 871, attempted bribery; People v. Mills, 178 N.Y. 274, 70 N.E. 786, 67 L.R.A. 131, attempted bribery; People v. Gardner, 144 N.Y. 119, 38 N.E. 1003, 28 L.R.A. 699, attempted extortion; People v. Moran, 123 N.Y. 254, 25 N.E. 412, 10 L.R.A. 109, attempted larceny; People v. Spolasco, 33 Misc. 22, 67 N.Y.S. 1114, attempted larceny.

It should also be noted that the cases impose a less rigid test of proximity where nothing but " interruption " by the police or other extraneous cause prevents the consummation of the crime. This class of cases is discussed in People v. Sullivan, 173 N.Y. 122, 65 N.E. 989, 993, 63 L.R.A. 353. There the Court said:

" Whenever the acts of a person have gone to the extent of placing it in his power to commit the offense unless interrupted, and nothing but such interruption prevents his present commission of the offense, at least then he is guilty of an attempt to commit the offense, whatever may be the rule as to his conduct before it reached that stage. " See also discussion of same principle of law in People v. O'Connell, 60 Hun.109, 14 N.Y.S. 485.

The problem is best stated by Judge Cane in People v. Rizzo, 246 N.Y. 334, at page 337, 158 N.E. 888, at page 889:

" The method of committing or attempting crime varies in each case, so that the difficulty, if any, is not with this rule of law regarding an attempt, which is well understood, but with its application to the facts. As I have said before, minds differ over proximity and the nearness of the approach. "

Thus it is clear that the test in each case is factual one depending upon the nature of the crime attempted, the nature of the interruption which prevented consummation, and the degree of proximity or nearness to consummation.

In the Rizzo case, supra, the defendants planned to rob one Rao, a pay roll clerk. The defendants, two of whom had firearms, started out in an automobile looking for him. They went to the bank and to various buildings under construction by Rao's firm. During this time they were followed by the police. When they were arrested their intended victim was nowhere near the scene of the arrest. In short, the defendants were looking for Rao, but they had not seen or discovered him up to the time they were arrested. The Court held that these facts did not constitute an attempt.

In People v. Gormley, 222 App. Div. 256, 225 N.Y.S. 653, 656,

affirmed without opinion 248 N.Y. 583, 162 N.E. 533, the facts were that defendants planned a robbery of a paymaster. For nearly an hour before their arrest the defendants all fully armed, waited in a stolen car outside the bank. Their arrest just before the arrival of their victim alone prevented them from consummating their crime. To all of this the defendants confessed. During trial the defendants pleaded guilty to the attempt. They appealed when their subsequent motion to withdraw their pleas was denied. In distinguishing the Rizzo case, the Court said:

" In view of the aggravated circumstances of this case, and of the defendants' pleas of guilty, a majority of this court feels that the judgment of conviction should be affirmed. We regard the admitted facts in the case here to much more strongly prove the guilt of the defendants of the crime charged in the indictment than did those upon which the defendant Rizzo and his confederates were convicted. Beyond that, we are confronted upon this appeal with a peculiar situation, which we think clearly distinguishes this case from the Rizzo case. The defend & ants, during the progress of the trial, withdrew their former pleas of not guilty, and each pleaded guilty to the charge in the indictment. At the time of such pleas, the evidence had not been closed. Who can say that further facts might have been revealed before the trial was ended, which might have shown the defendants' guilt? Who can say that the defendants themselves did not know of circumstances, in addition to those already established at the trial, that impelled them to plead guilty to the crime charged? In the Rizzo

Case the defendants were convicted upon the proof that they had committed acts which, in the view of the Court of Appeals, did not constitute the crime for which they were convicted. Here the defendants did not plead guilty to the commission of any specific acts, but, generally, that they were guilty of the crime charged, to wit, attempted robbery in the first degree. The trial upon the indictment ended with their pleas of guilty. We are of the opinion that the trial court was fully justified, under the proven facts and under the pleas of the defendants, in rendering the judgment of conviction, and in imposing state prison sentences thereon."

In the instant case most of the proof upon which the People rely was obtained by means of telephone taps. On several occasions the defendants discussed robbing their victim, X, a jeweler, over the phone.

On February 19th, the following conversation took place between Volpe, one of the conspirators and Masciale, the alleged finger man.

"M—You call up the house on 80th Street.

"V—Yeah. I figured the wife answered.

"M—Oh yeah.

"V—And I asked him is he home—she said no, he's not at home. So what time will he be home? She says: Well, I don't know; you might catch him about nine-thirty." But I couldn't find out what time he comes home you know. About what time does he come home?

"M—Let's see now—I'd say about eight, eight thirty.

"V—He comes home that late?

"M—Sure.

"V—All right, all right. Maybe tonight or tomorrow night."

Later the same day, another conversation was overheard between defendants Vople and Conigliano.

"V—Hello. Listen—I called that party up.

"C—Yeah.

"V—And he says about eight—eight thirty now.

"C—Tonight, huh?

"V—Yeah, now.

"C—Yeah.

"V—He's going to check on it; try to get more information and call back at six o'clock tonight, see.

"C—Well, tonight it'll be over.

"C—Yeah.

"V—All right. Er—listen, you should get Chick's car No.?

"C—Yeah, I'll try.

"V—Oh. We got to have something like that Joey.

"C—Yeah, huh.

"V—Oh sure.

"C—H'm'm; well, can't we—we could just as we take his too you know. Oke, we need that anyway, yeah.

"V—Gee.

"C—Well, I'll get it.

"V—All right. What time now shall I see you?

"C—Listen, what time is this guy going to let you know?

"V—About six.

"C—Six, huh? I'll be down there about six thirty, seven o'clock.

"V—Seven o'clock.

"C—Seven o'clock I'll meet you in—er—in the place there.

Later, the same day a conversation between Vople and Masciale was overheard.

"M—Er—I couldn't find out—I didn't bother calling up there—you know?

"V—Uh, uh.

"M—See if he answer the phone over there and I start talking, you know—er—he may recognize my voice or something.

"V—Yeah. So what time do you think I got—to meet—my—Jerry at seven.

"M—You know what he should do Nick?

"V—Yeah.

"M—Er—I know if—if you go into the place there—and once you see them leave there—he'll be heading right home that guy.

"V—Uh, uh.

"M—You're not going to have anything with you, are you?

"V—I don't know. I don't think so.

"M—Because you don't need anything.

"V—Uh, uh. All right.

"M—Yeah.

"V—How big is he?

"M—Oh, he's about your height. He's got gray hair. He's about your height, Nick. He's got a big nose.

"V—All right.

"M—See?

"V—We'll both sit there and wait until the car pulls up.

"M—Yeah—er—did you see the house yet?

"V—Yeah.

"M—Yeah. He's got—he's got a big alley way, you know.

"V—Yeah.

"M—There's two alleys connected with one like.

"V—Yeah—uh—one from each house.

"M—Yeah, see.

"V—All right. Well, here's what we'll do. We'll go over there and wait. If nothing happens, then we'll make an arrangement that tomorrow night we'll go over there.

"M—Why sure, you just go over there—er—you wait for him to come out there. He's always got that—er—it's the brief case you got to grab.

"V—Yeah, K know that.

"M—That suitcase there.

"V—Yeah.

"M—That's the thing you got to grab. If you can get his keys naturally—er—unless—unless you gonna just—you know take right off.

"V—We might have a car."

That night, February 19th, Volpe and Conigliano were observed to meet at 7:20 P.M. They boarded a bus and at 7:35 reached the residence of the victim X on 80th Street. They walked into the driveway about 10 feet, stayed there from between 5 and 10 minutes and then walked up the block to 13th Avenue to 80th Street and approach to within 100 feet of the victim's residence. This continued until about 8:45 P.M. They then left the neighborhood.

There was some testimony that the victim returned to his home about an hour later than usual that evening.

A subsequent telephone conversation was overheard on February 21st between Vople and Conigliano.

"C—Well, what do we want to do?

"V—Well, nothing. I said Chappie is working on that thing, you're trying to find out just what's what.

"C—Monday no good?

"V—Monday night? Oh, no. Monday's a holiday, but" C—Yeah.

"V—We'll have to wait till Tuesday.

"C—So—. You don't know nothing yet. Nothing else you found out?

"V—No—. I'll give him a ring again tonight. But I mean if you want that thing—this guy—he'll hold it."

There are subsequent telephone conversations indicating that the defendants learned that their telephone conversations had been

tapped. They were arrested March 1, 1953, after it had become clear that they had abandoned their purpose to commit the hold up.

Such is the pertinent factual testimony before the Grand Jury. On this motion, I must interpret the facts in their aspects most favorable to the People. But even if I assume that on February 19th the defend-ants intended to commit the robbery if their victim appeared, yet on the basis of the Rizzo and Gormley cases, supra, I must hold that there is insufficient proof of over facts carrying the crime proximately or dangerously close to consummation. We have here more than the Rizzo case but none of the "aggravated circumstances" of the Gormley case. The defendants were not armed. They had no stolen automobile or any automobile. They never approached closer to the premises than about 100 feet at the proximate time when the evidence shows they might reasonably expect their victim to return to his home. Their victim was nowhere near the scene of the intended crime when the overt acts were committed.

Basically, the test is a factual one—and as Judge Crane stated, minds differ over proximity and nearness of the approach. I believe that there is insufficient evidence to establish an attempt. But, it would be unfair to dispose of this issue on the law during trial and thus deprive the People of the right to appellate review. The interests of justice is best served by this intermediate determination.

The motion is granted to the extent only of dismissing those counts of the indictment which charge the defendants with attempted robbery and included crimes. Motion is denied with respect to the

conspiracy count. Submit order.

第二節　CASE BRIEFS: FIRAC公式

仔細閱讀下列說明，你將學會利用FIRAC公式，整理案例：

You will learn legal reasoning and substantive law in law school by analyzing the appellate decisions included in your textbooks. This teaching device is called the case method.（案例教育）

To prepare for class you will be expected to brief assigned cases. A brief is an organized, written summary of the important elements of a judicial opinion. In addition to class discussions, briefs will be helpful in review and exam preparation.

This discussion is introductory in nature and designed to help you during your first few days of classes.

You must carefully read the assigned case to get an overall understanding of the facts and decision. Be sure to look up all terms you do not understand in a legal dictionary. The leading one is *Black's Law Dictionary*. *Baron Law Dictionary* is another choice.

After you have read the case, go back and begin to identify the different elements. A case brief will usually contain four basic elements: facts, issue, decision, and reasons. The elements are explained below.

1. Facts: State only the facts which are essential to the decision. The case may say "a thirty-five-year-old woman slipped and fell on a wet floor in the A & P grocery store on Fifth Avenue." Your brief

needs only to state "a woman fell on a wet floor in a grocery store."

2. Issue: Forming a statement of the issue involved in a decision is probably the hardest part of briefing a case. Identify exactly what the court decided without being too broad or too narrow.

Too Broad: Did the defendant assault plaintiff?; Is there a contract?

Too Narrow: Can the plaintiff, a tenant in the defendant's apartment, recover for assault when the defendant threatened to shoot movers with a pistol he was carrying if they moved any furniture and also threatened to shoot the plaintiff?

Good Issue: Does a threat, that the plaintiff has reason to believe the defendant has the ability to carry out, constitute assault?

3. Rule (Reason): The precedents, logic, dictum, and policy the court relied upon to render its decision.

4. Analysis: Apply facts into law (combine 1 and 3).

5. Conclusion: Judgment for P or D.

第三節　BRIEF EXAMPLE: PEOPLE v. VOLPE

正式的Brief應具有下列之要素：即FIRAC之公式。以People v. Volpe之案件為例。

<u>People v. Volpe</u>

FACTS: The state uses the tapped telephone discussions of three defendants (Ds) regarding robbing a jeweler as evidence in an action for attempted robbery and conspiracy. After learning that jeweler would probably come home about 8:00 p.m., two Ds stood in intended victim's driveway at about 7:35 p.m. for 5–10 minutes. Ds walked up the street and back to the house every 15 minutes. They did this until 8:45 and left the neighborhood. The victim returned home about 9 p.m., an hour later than usual. During later phone conversations, Ds' discussion over that their phones had been taped. They are arrested days after they had abandoned their purpose to commit the holdup (robbery).

ISSUE: Did Ds attempt to rob the jeweler by their acts of planning robbery on telephone, waiting at intended victim's telephone, and returning every 15 minutes for about an hour constitute an attempt? (NO)

RULE: To constitute an attempt, an act must be near to the consummation (completion) of the crime. At **common law**, the act must have dangerous proximity to the success of crimes. But for the police's interruption, the crimes would have been completed. Under **Model Penal Code** (MPC), the act must be beyond "substantial step" to be considered (as) an attempt.

ANALYSIS: In determining whether these acts reached the stage of attempt, Courts must look to the nature of crimes attempted, nature of interruption, and nearness to the consummation. **Here** (in the present care), there are no enough facts bringing the crimes close to consummation. Unlike the D in Rizzo, Ds here were not armed.

Although they planned to rob, there were no aggravating circumstances such as a stolen car or any getaway car as they were in Gormley. **Even if** Ds did commit acts tending towards commission of robbery, they never got closed to the home than 100 feet and their victim was not home at the time of these acts.

CONCLUSION: Therefore, D's act did not reach the stage of attempt. (J→D) If I were the judge, I'll find D not Guilty.

CONCURRING OPINION: (optional)（判決主文協同意見法官之意見）

DISSENTING OPINION: (optional) （判決主文反對意見法官之意見）

NOTE:

1. Under Model Penal Code (MPC) section 5.01 of American Law Institute, a person is guilty of an attempt to commit a crime (robbery here) if he purposely does or omits to do anything that, under the circumstances as believes them to be, is an act or omission constituting a substantial step in a course of conduct planned to culminate in his commission of the crime.

2. MPC, completed in 1962, plays an important role in the widespread revision and codification of substantive criminal law of the U.S. It is safe to say that over thirty five states were influenced in some parts by the position taken in the MPC.

3. Computer search:

  （1）West Law (WL): Ex: find 2 N.Y. 2d. 10

  （2）Lexis/Nexus: Ex: Lexsee 2 N.Y. 10

＊以上NOTES為學生上課時，認為老師之解說有助於本案，而自
　行抄錄之memo。

附錄一：美國ABA承認和不承認之法學院

U.S. Law Schools
Approved by the
American Bar Association
(美國律師協會ABA承認之學校)

University of Akron
School of Law
Akron, OH 44325–2901

University of Alabama
School of Law
101 Paul Brant Drive
Tuscaloosa, AL 35487

Albany Law School
of Union University
80 New Scotland Avenue
Albany, NY 12208

American University
Washington College of Law
4400 Massachusetts Avenue,
N.W.
Washington, DC 20016

University of Arizona
College of Law
Tucson, AZ 85721C

Arizona State University
College of Law
Tempe, AZ 85287–7906

University of Arkansas—
Fayetteville
School of Law
Fayetteville, AR 72701

University of Arkansas—
Little Rock
School of Law
1201 McAlmont
Little Rock, AR 72202–5142

University of Baltimore
School of Law
1420 North Charles Street
Baltimore, MD 21201

Baylor University
School of Law
P.O. Box 97288
Waco, TX 76798–7288

Boston College
Law School
885 Centre Street
Newton, MA 02159C

Boston University
School of Law
765 Commonwealth Avenue
Boston, MA 02215

Bridgeport School of Law
at Quinnipiac College
303 University Avenue
Bridgeport, CT 06604

Brigham Young University
J. Ruben Clark Law School
340 JRCB
Provo, UT 84602

Brooklyn Law School
250 Joralemon Street
Brooklyn NY 11201

University of California—
Berkeley
School of Law
220 Boalt Hall
Berkeley, CA 94720

University of California—
Davis
School of Law
King Hall
Davis, CA 95616–5201

University of California
Hastings College of Law
200 McAllister Street
San Francisco, CA 94102C

University of California—
Los Angeles
School of Law
71 Dodd Hall
405 Hilgard Avenue
Los Angeles, CA 90024–1476

California Western
School of Law
350 Cedar Street
San Diego, CA 92101

Campbell University
School of Law
Box 158
Buies Creek, NC 27506

Capital University
Law School
665 South High Street

Columbus, OH 43215

Benjamin N. Cardozo
School of Law
Yeshiva University
55 Fifth Avenue
New York, NY 10003

Case Western Reserve
University
School of Law
11075 East Boulevard
Cleveland, OH 44106C

Catholic University
America School of Law
Washington, DC 20064

Catholic University of
Puerto Rico
School of Law
Ponce, PR 00732

Chicago-Kent Law School
Mimois Institute of

Technology
565 West Adams
Street
Chicago,
IL 60661-3691

University of Chicago
Law School
1111 East 60th Street
Chicago, IL 60637

University of Cincinnati
College of Law
M.L. 40
Cincinnati, OH 45221

Cleveland State University
Marshall College of Law
Cleveland, OH 44115

University of Colorado
School of Law
Campus Box 403
Boulder, CO 80309-0403C

Columbia University
School of Law
435 West 116th Street
New York, NY 10027

University of Connecticut
School of Law
55 Elizabeth Street
Hartford, CT 06105-2296

Cornell Law School
College Avenue
240 Myron Taylor Hall
Ithaca, NY 14853-4901

Creighton University
School of Law
2133 California Street
Omaha, NE 68178-0340

University of Dayton
School of Law
300 College Park
Dayton, OH 45469-1320

University of Denver

College of Law

37039 East 18th Street

Denver, CO 80220

Depaul University

College of Law

25 East Jackson Boulevard

Chicago, IL 60604C

University of Detroit

Mercy School of Law

651 East Jefferson Avenue

Detroit, MI 48226

Detroit College of Law

130 East Elizabeth Street

Detroit, MI 48201

Dickinson School of Law

150 South College Street

Carlisle, PA 17013

District of Columbia

School of Law

719 13th Street NW

Washington, DC 20005

Drake University

Law School

Cartwright Hall

27th & Carpenter

Des Moins, IA 50311

Duke University

School of Law

University Tower

3101 Petty Road

Suite 207

Durham, NC 27706

Duquesne University

School of Law

900 Locust Street

Pittsburgh, PA 15282C

Emory University

School of Law

Gambrell Hall

Atlanta, GA 30322

University of Florida
College of Law
164 Holland Hall
Gainesville, FL 32611

Florida State University
College of Law
425 W. Jefferson Street
Tallahassee, FL 32306–1034

Fordham University
School of Law
140 West 62nd Street
New York, NY 10023

Franklin Pierce
Law Center
2 White Street
Concord, NH 03301

George Mason University
School of Law
3401 North Fairfax Drive
Arlington, VA 22201–4498

George Washington University
National Law Center
Stockton Hall, Room 101
Washington, DC 20052C

Georgetown University
Law Center
600 New Jersey Avenue,
N.W.
Washington, DC 20001

University of Georgia
School of Law
Athens, GA 30602

Georgia State University
College of Law
University Plaza
Atlanta, GA 30303–3092

Golden Gate University
School of Law
536 Mission Street
San Francisco, CA 94105

Gonzaga University
School of Law
Box 3528
Spokane, WA 99220

Hamline University
School of Law
1536 Hewitt Avenue
St. Paul, MN 55104

Harvard University
Law School
1563 Massachusetts Avenue
Cambridge, MA 02138C

University of Hawaii
William S. Richardson
School of Law
2515 Dole Street
Honolulu, HI 96822

Hofstra University
School of Law
1000 Fulton Avenue
Hempstead, NY 11550

University of Houston
Law Center
4800 Calhoun Road
Houston, TX 77004–6391

Howard University
School of Law
2900 Van Ness Street, N.W.
Washington, DC 20008

University of Idaho
College of Law
Moscow, ID 83843

University of Illinois
College of Law
504 East Pennsylvania Avenue
Champaign, IL 61820

Indiana University—
Bloomington
School of Law
Bloomington, IN 47405C

Indiana University—
Indianapolis
School of Law
735 West New York Street
Indianapolis, IN 46202

Inter American University
School of Law
P.O. Box 8897
Santurce, PR 00910

University of Iowa
College of Law
276 Boyd Law Building
Melrose at Byington
Streets
Iowa City,IA 52242

John Marshall Law School
315 South Plymouth Court
Chicago, IL 60604

University of Kansas
School of Law
Lawrencee, KS 66045

University of Kentucky
College of Law
Lexington, KY 40506–0048

Lewis and Clark College
Northwestern School of Law
10015 Terwilliger
Boulevard
Portland, OR 97219C

Louisiana State University
Paul M. Hebert Law Center
Baton Rouge, LA 70803

University of Louisville
School of Law
Belknap Campus
Louisville, KY 40292

Loyola Law School—
Los Angeles
1441 West Olympic
Boulevard
Box 15019
Los Angeles, CA 90015–3980

Loyola University—Chicago
School of Law
One East Delaware, Suite
300
Chicago, IL 60611

Loyola University—
New Orleans
School of Law
7214 St. Charles Avenue
Box 904
New Orleans, LA 701198

University of Maine
School of Law
246 Deering Avenue
Portland, ME 04102C

Marquette University
Law School
1103 West Wisconsin Avenue
Milwaukee, WI 53233

University of Maryland
School of Law

500 West Baltimore Street
Baltimore, MD 21201

University of the Pacific
McGeorge School of Law
3200 Fifth Avenue
Sacramento, CA 95817

Memphis State University
Cecil C. Humphreys
School of Law
Memphis, TN 38152

Mercer University
Walter F. George
School of Law
1021 Georgia Avenue
Macon, GA 31201–6709

University of Miami
School of Law
P.O. Box 248087
Coral Gables,
FL 33124–8087C

University of Michigan
Law School
625 South State Street,
Room 320 Ann Arbor,
MI 48109–1215

University of Minnesota
Law School
229 19th Avenue
South Minneapolis, MN 55455

University of Mississippi
School of Law
University, MS38677

Mississippi College
School of Law
151 East Griffith Street
Jackson, MS 39201

University of
Missouri—Columbia
School of Law
Law Building
Columbia, MO 65211

University of Missouri—
Kansas City
School of Law
5100 Rockhill Road
Kansas City, MO 64110

University of Montana
School of Law
Missoula, MT 59812C

University of Nebraska
College of Law
42nd & Fair Streets
Lincoln, NE 68583–0902

New England School of Law
154 Stuart Street
Boston, MA 02116

University of New Mexico
School of Law
1117 Stanford Drive, N.E.
Albuquerque, NM 87131

CUNY Law School
at Queens College
65–21 Main Street
Flushing, NY 11367

SUNY at Buffalo
School of Law
312 O'Brien Hall
Buffalo, NY 14260

New York Law School
57 Worth Street
New York, NY 10013

New York University
School of Law
40 Washington Square South
New York, NY 10012C

University of North
Carolina
School of Law
CB 3380
Chapel Hill, NC 27599–3380

North Carolina Central
University
School of Law
1512 South Alston Avenue
Durham, NC 27707

University of North Dakota
School of Law
P.O. Box 9003
Grand Forks, ND 58202

Northeastern University
School of Law
400 Huntington Avenue
Boston, MA 02115

Northern Illinois
University
College of Law
Dekalb, IL 60115

Northern Kentucky
University
Salmon P. Chase College of
Law

Nunn Hall, Room 530
Highland Heights, KY
41099–6031C

Northwestern University
School of Law
357 East Chicago Avenue
Chicago, IL 60611

Notre Dame Law School
Notre Dame, IN 46556

Nova University
Shepard Broad Law Center
3305 College Avenue
Fort Laudredale, FL 33314

Ohio Northern University
Pettit College of Law
525 S. Main Street
Ada, OH 45810

Ohio State University
College of Law
1659 North High Street

Columbus, OH 43210

University of Oklahoma
Law Center
300 Timberdell Road
Norman, OK 73019

Oklahoma City University
Law School
P.O. Box 61310
Oklahoma City, OK
73146–1310C

University of Oregon
School of Law
1101 Kincaid Street
Eugene, OR 97403

Pace University
School of Law
78 North Broadway
White Plains, NY 10603

University of Pennsylvania
Law School

3400 Chestnut Street
Philadelphia, PA 19104

Pepperdine University
School of Law
24255 Pacific Coast
Highway Malibu, CA 90263

University of Pittsburgh
School of Law
3900 Forbes Avenue
Pittsburgh, PA 15260

University of Puerto Rico
School of Law
Rio Pedras, PR 15260

University of Puerto Rico
School of Law
Rio Pedras, PR 00931C

University of Puget Sound/Seattle
School of Law
950 Broadway Plaza

Tacoma, WA 98402

Regent University
School of Law
1000 Centeville Turnpike
Virginia Beach, VA 23464

University of Richmond
T. C. Williams School of Law
University of Richmond,
VA 23173

Rutgers University— Camden
School of Law
P.O. Box 93650
Camden, NJ 08101–3650

Rutgers University—Newark
School of Law
15 Washington Street
Newark, NJ 07102

St. John's University
School of Law

Fromkes Hall
Grand Central &
Utopia Parkways
Jamaica, NY 11439C

St. Louis University
School of Law
3700 Lindell Boulevard
St. Louis, MO 63108

St. Mary's University of
San Antnio
School of Law
One Camino Santa Maria
San Antonio, TX 78228–8601

St. Thomas University
School of Law
16400 N.W. 32nd Avenue
Miami, FL 33054

Samford University
Cumberland School of Law
800 Lakeshore Drive
Birmingham, AL 35229

University of San Diego
School of Law
2199 Fullton Street
San Francisco,
CA 94117–1080

Santa Clara University
School of Law
Santa Clara, CA 95053

Seton Hall University
School of Law
One Newark Center
Newark, NJ 07102–5210C

University of South
Carolina
School of Law
Main & Green Streets
Columbia, SC 29208

University of South Dakota
School of Law
414 East Clark Street
Vermillion, SD 57069–2390

South Texas College of Law
1303 San Jacinto
Houston, TX 77002–7006

University of Southern
California
Law Center
University Park MC 0071
Los Angeles, CA 90089–0071

Southern Illinois University
School of Law
Carbondale, IL 62901

Southern Methodist University
School of Law
3315 Daniel Avenue
Dallas, TX 75275–0116

Southern University
Law Center
P.O. Box 9294
Baton Rouge, LA 70813C

Southwestern University
School of Law
675 South Westmoreland
Avenue
Los Angeles, CA 90005–3992

Stanford Law School
Stanford, CA 94305

Steson University
College of Law
1401 61st Street South
St. Petersburg, FL 33707

Suffolk University
Law School
41 Temple Street
Boston, MA 02114

Syracuse University
College of Law
Syracuse, NY 13244–1030

Temple University
School of Law

1719 North Broad Street,
Khein Hall, Room 516
Philadelphia, PA 19122

University of Tennessee
College of Law
1505 West Cumberland
Avenue
Knoxville, TN 37996–1800C

University of Texas
School of Law
727 East 26th Street
Austin, TX 78705

Texas Southern University
Thurgood Marshall
School of Law
3100 Cleburne Avenue
Houston, TX 77004

Texas Tech University
School of Law
Lubbock, TX 79409

**Thomas M. Cooley Law
School**
507 South Grand Avenue
Lansing, MI 48901

University of Toledo
College of Law
Toledo, OH 4606

Touro College
Jacob D. Fuchsberg Law
Center
300 Nassau Road
Huntington, NY 11743

Tulane University
School of Law
6801 Freret Street
New Orleans, LA 70118C

University of Tulsa
College of Law
3120 East Fourth Place
Tulsa, OK 74104

University of Utah
College of Law
101 Law Building
Salt Lake City, UT 84112

Valparaiso University
School of Law
Valparaiso, IN 46383

Vanderbilt University
School of Law
21st Avenue
South Nashville, TN 37240

Vermont Law School
P.O. Box 96
South Royalton, VT 05068

Villanova University
School of Law
Villlanova, PA 19085

University of Virginia
School of Law
North Grounds

Charlottesvillee, VA 22901C

Wake Forest University
School of Law
Corner Wingate Drive &
Carsinell Drive
Winston-Salem, NC 27109

Washburm University
School of Law
Topeka, KS 66621

University of Washington
School of Law
1100 N.E. Campus Parkway
JB-20
Seattle, WA 98105

Washington and Lee
University
School of Law
Lewis Hall
Lexington, VA 24450

Washington University
School of Law
One Brookings Drive
Campus Box 1120
St. Louis, MO 63130

Wayne State University
Law School
468 West Ferry
Detroit, MI 48202C

West Virginia University
College of Law
P.O. Box 6130
Morgantown, WV 26506

Western New England
College School of Law
1215 Wibraham Road
Springfield, MA 01119–9989

Whitier College
School of Law
5353 West Third Street
Los Angeles, CA 90020

Widener University
School of Law
P.O. Box 7474, Concord
Pike Wilmington, DE 19803

Willamette University
College of Law
245 Winter Street, S.E.
Salem, Or 97301

College of William and
Mary Marshall—Wythe
School of Law
Willamsburg, VA 23185

William Mitchell
College of Law
875 Summit Avenue
St. Paul, MN 55105C

University of Wisconsin
Law School
Madison, WI 53706

University of Wyoming
College of Law
University Station
P.O. Box 3035
Laramie, WY 82071–3035

Yale Law School
127 Wall Street
Drawer 401A, Yale Station
New Haven, CT 06520

U.S. Law Schools
Not Approved by the
American Bar Association
(美國律師協會ABA不承認
之學校)

American College of Law
401 South Brea Boulevard
Brea, CA 93621

CAL Northern School of Law
2515 Dominic Drive
Chico, CA 95928C

California Pacific
School of Law
1600 Truxton Avenue
Suite 100
Bakersfield, CA 93301

California Southern Law
School
3775 Elizabeth Street
Riverside, CA 92506

Central California College
School of Law
925 N. Street #110
Fresno, CA 93721

CLEO—Council on Legal
Education Opportunity
1800 M Street, N.W.
Suite 290, North Lobby
Washington, DC 20036

Empire College
3033 Cleveland Avenue
Suite 102

Santa Rosa, CA 95401–2185

Glendale University
College of Law
220 North Glendale Avenue
Glendale, CA 91206C

Humphreys College of Law
6650 Inglewood Avenue
Stockton, CA 95207

John F. Kennedy University
School of Law
12 Altarinda Road
Walnut Creek, CA 94563

Jones School of Law
5345 Atlanta Highway
Montgomery, AL 36193

University of La Verne
College of Law
Encino Campus
5445 Balboa Boulevard
Encino, CA 91316

University of La Verne
College of Law
1950 3rd Street
Sacramento, CA 95816

Lincoln University
The Law School
2160 Lundy Avenue
San Jose, CA 95131

Massachusetts School of Law
500 Federal Street
Andover, MA 01810C

Monterey College of Law
498 Pearl Street
Monterey, CA 93940

National University
School of Law
8380 Miramar Road
San Diego, CA 92126–4431

New College of California
School of Law
50 Fell Street
San Francisco, CA 94102

University of Northern California
Lorenzo Patino School of Law
816 H Street
Sacramento, CA 95814

Oakland College of Law
436 14th Street
Suite 411
Oakland, CA 94612–2703

Peninsula University
Law School
436 Dell Avenue
Mountain View, CA 94043

Roger Williams University
School of Law
One Old Ferry Road
Bristol, RI 02809C

San Francisco Law School
3385 East Shields Avenue
Fresno, CA 93726

Santa Barbara College of Law
911 Tremonto Road
Santa Barbara, VA 93103

Simon Greenleaf School of Law
3855 East LaPalma Avenue
Anaheim, CA 92807

Southern California College of Law
595 West Lambert Road
Brea, CA 92621

Southern New England School of Law
874 Purchase Street
New Bedford, MA 02740–6232

Ventura College of Law
4475 Market Street
Ventura, CA 93003

University of West Los Angeles
1155 W. Arbor
Vitae Street
Los Angeles, CA
90301–2902C

Western State
University–Irvine
College of Law
16485 Laguna Cayon Road
Irvine, CA 92718

Western State University
Fullerton College of Law
1111 North State College
Boulevard
Fullerton, CA 92631

Western State University–
San Diego
College of Law
2121 San Diego Avenue
San Diego, CA 92110C

附錄二：美國法律碩博士研究課程之學校

Director of the M.C.L. Program
Admissions Office
University of Alabama (http://www.law.ua.edu/)
School of Law
101 Paul Brant Drive East
Box 1435
Tuscaloosa, Al 35401
U.S.A.
M.C.L.

Graduate International Legal Studies Program
American University (http://www.wcl.american.edu/pub/wcl.htm)
Washington College of Law
4400 Massachusetts Avenue, N.W.
Washington, DC 20016
U.S.A.
LL.M.—International Law

Director of the M.C.L. Degree Program
California Western School of Law (http://www.cwsl.edu/)
350 Cedar Street

San Diego, CA 92101

U.S.A.

M.C.L.

Admissions Office

University of California at Berkeley (http://www.sims.berkeley.edu)

Boalt Hall School of Law

Berkeley, CA 94720

U.S.A.

LL.M., J.S.D.

IP—Intellectual Property Law (Master)

Admissions Office

University of California at Los Angeles (http://www.law.ucla.edu/)

School of Law

405 Hilgard Avenue

Los Angeles, CA 90024–1476

U.S.A.

LL.M. (for non-United States law school graduates only);

LL.M. (two-year program)—teaching Public International Law and Institutions (for minority and women scholars)

IP

Catholic University of Puerto Rico

School of Law

Ponce, PR 00732

U.S.A.

Spanish doctorate in Civil Law (in cooperation with Valladolid University, Spain);

LL.M.—Comparative Law (courses conducted in Spanish)

Graduate Student Affairs

University of Chicago (http://www.lib.uchicago.edu/law/)

Law School

1111 East 60th Street

Chicago, IL 60637

U.S.A.

D.C.L., M.C.L., J.S.D., LL.M.– International Law (for non-United States law school graduates only) Columbia University (http://www. columbia.edu/cu/law/bulletin9596/)

School of Law

Graduate Legal Studies

435 West 116th Street

New York, NY 10027

U.S.A.

J.S.D., LL.M.—International and Comparative Law (among others); IP

Dickinson School of Law (http://www.dsl.edu)

150 South College Street

Carlisle, PA 17013

U.S.A.

M.C.L.

Graduate Law Programs

Fordham University (http://www.fordham.edu/law/cle/
law_main.html)

School of Law

140 West 62nd Street

New York, NY 10023

U.S.A.

LL.M.—International Business and Trade Law

Dean of Admissions

William S. Richardson

School of Law

University of Hawaii at Manoa (http://gopher.hawaii.edu/11/student/
cat)

2515 Dole Street

Honolulu, HI 96822

M.C.L./LL.M.—Pacific and Asian Legal Studies
(program in formation as of 1990)

Director, Post-J.D. Programs

George Washington University (http://www.law.gwu.edu/)

National Law Center

2000 H Street, N.W.

Washington, DC 20052

U.S.A.

LL.M.—International Law;

M.C.L.

IP

Graduate Admissions Coordinator

Georgetown University (http://www.ll.georgetown.edu)

Law Center

600 New Jersey Avenue, N.W.

Washington, DC 20001

U.S.A.

LL.M.—International Law;

D.C.L., M.C.L.

Harvard University (http://www.law.harvard.edu/)

Law School

Graduate Program in International Legal Studies

Cambridge, MA 02138

U.S.A.

S.J.D., LL.M. — Comparative Jurisprudence, Public International Law (among others)

University of Houston (http://www.law.uh.edu/)

Law Center

4800 Calhoun Road

Houston, TX 77004

U.S.A.

LL.M.—International Economic Law

IP

Director of Graduate Programs

Howard University (http://www.law.howard.edu/)

School of Law

2900 Van Ness Street, N.W.

Washington, DC 20008

U.S.A.

M.C.J.

Graduate Studies Program

University of Illinois (http://www.law.uiuc.edu/)

College of Law

504 East Pennsylvania avenue

Champaign, IL 61820

U.S.A.

LL.M.—International Law; M.C.L.

Illinois Institute of Technology

Chicago-Kent College of Law (http://www.kentlaw.edu)

77 South Wacker Drive

Chicago, IL 60606

U.S.A.

M.A.L.S./LL.M. (for non–United States law school graduates only;

new law center address beginning January 1992:

565 West Adams Street)

Chicago, IL 60606

U.S.A.

Law School Admissions

Indiana University at Bloomington (http://www.law.indiana.edu)

School of Law

Third Street and Indiana Avenue

Bloomington, IN 47405

U.S.A.

M.C.L., LL.M.

University of Iowa (http://www.uiowa.edu/~lawcoll/)

College of Law

Iowa City, IA 52242

U.S.A.

M.C.L.

Associate Director

Foreign Graduate Programs

University of Miami (http://www.law.miami.edu/)

School of Law

P.O. Box 248087

1311 Miller Drive

Coral Gables, FL 33124

U.S.A.

LL.M.—International Law

Graduate Office

University of Michigan (http://www.law.umich.edu/)

Law School

Hutchins Hall

Ann Arbor, MI 48109–1215

U.S.A.

S.J.D., LL.M., M.C.L.

Committee on Admissions

New York University (http://www.nyu.edu/law/)

School of Law—Global Law School

Vanderbilt Hall 419

40 Washington Square South

New York, NY 10012

U.S.A.

LL.M.—International Law, International Tax Law

M.C.J.—Inter-American Law—Comparative Law [now changed to LL.M. (C.J.)]

IP

Northwestern University (http://nuinfo.nwu.edu/lawschool)

School of Law

357 East Chicago Avenue

Chicago, IL 60611–3069

U.S.A.

LL.M.—International and Comparative Law (among others)

Notre Dame Law School (http://www.nd.edu/~ndlaw/)

Notre Dame, IN 46556

U.S.A.

LL.M.—International Law; M.C.L. (course of study for both programs is nor mally completed at Notre Dame's London Law Center in England)

Graduate Admissions Office

University of the Pacific

McGeorge School of Law (http://www.uop.edu/law/)

3200 Fifth Avenue

Sacramento, CA 95817

U.S.A.

LL.M.—Transnational Business Law

Southern Methodist University (http://www.smu.edu/~law/)
School of Law
Dallas, TX 75275
U.S.A.
S.J.D., M.C.L., LL.M.—International Law

Temple University (http://astro.ocis.temple.edu/~law/)
School of Law
1719 North Broad Street
Philadelphia, PA 19122
U.S.A.
LL.M.—International Law

University of Texas (http://www.law.utexas.edu/)
School of Law
727 East 26th Street
Austin, TX 78705
U.S.A.
M.C.J.

University of San Diego (http://www.acusd.edu/~usdlaw/)
School of Law
Alcala Park

San Diego, CA 92110

U.S.A.

M.C.L., LL.M.—International Law

Assistant Director

Law School Admissions

Graduate Study Program

Tulane University (http://www.law.tulane.edu/)

School of Law

Joseph Merrick Jones Hall

6801 Freet Street

New Orleans, LA 70118

U.S.A.

M.C.L., LL.M.—Admiralty Law

Director

Graduate Program

University of Virginia (http://www.virginia.edu/~law/)

School of Law

Charlottesville, VA 22901

U.S.A.

LL.M., S.J.D.—International Law

Graduate Admissions

University of Washington (http://felix.law.washington.edu/

CondonHome.html)

School of Law

Condon Hall 316, JB-20

1100 N.E. Campus Parkway

Seattle, WA 98105

U.S.A.

Ph.D.—Comparative Law (with emphasis on East Asia);

LL.M.—East Asian Law

Director, Graduate Programs

Yale Law School (http://elsinore.cis.yale.edu/lawweb/lawschool/ylsfd.htm)

127 Wall Street

Yale Station

Drawer 401A

New Haven, CT 06520

U.S.A.

J.S.D., LL.M.—Law School Teaching

＊其他有IP (Intellectual Property Law)智慧財產權領域之學校如下：

　⑴Boston University School of Law:參見前JD學校住址

　⑵Cornell University Law School:/www.law.cornell.edu

　⑶Franklin Pierce Law Center:/www.fplc.edu

　⑷The John Marshall Law School:/www.jmls.edu

(5)Stanford Law School:/www-leland.stanford.edu/group/law

　　智慧財產權領域愈來愈重要，建議可專攻此領域，相信將來企業界或法律實務界應有很大之需求。IP範圍包含電子商務、商標、專利、著作權、營業祕密與積體電路等半導體相關領域。電腦與科技領域亦屬之，例如網際網路之法律，頗值吾人研究。

附錄三： 學位縮寫一覽表

B.C.L.	—Bachelor of Civil Law
D.C.L.	—Doctor of Comparative Law
D.Jur.	—Doctor of Jurisprudence
D.Phil.	—Doctor of Philosophy
Dr.Jur.	—Doctor of Jurisprudence
G.D.I.L.	—Graduate Diploma in International Law
J.D.	—Juris Doctor
J.S.D.	—Doctor of Juridical Science
J.S.M.	—Master of the Science of Law
LL.D.	—Doctor of Law
LL.M.	—Master of Law
M.A.	—Master of Arts
M.A.L.S.	—Master of American Legal Studies
M.C.J.	—Master of Comparative Jurisprudence
M.C.L.	—Master of Comparative Law
M.E.L.S.	—Master of European Legal Studies
M.I.C.L.	—Master of International and Comparative Law
M.I.L.	—Master of International Law
M.I.P.	—Master of Intellectual Property Law
M.L.	—Master of Law
M.L.I.	—Master of Arts or Science in Legal Institutions
M.Phil.	—Master of Philosophy
MM.L. & S.	—Master of Marine Law and Science
Ph.D.	—Doctor of Philosophy
S.J.D.	—Doctor of Juridical Science;
	—Doctor of Jurisprudence;
	—Doctor of the Science of Law

附錄四：The Top 25 Law Schools（前廿五名學校）

Here are the law schools with the highest scores according to the recent U.S. News survey:

Rank/School（排行／學校）	Overall Score（分數）
1. YALE UNIVERSITY（耶魯大學）	100.0
2. HARVARD UNIVERSITY（哈佛大學）	94.9
3. STANDFORD UNIVERSITY（史丹福大學）	93.6
4. COLUMBIA UNIVERSITY（哥倫比亞大學）	92.8
5. NEW YORK UNIVERSITY（紐約大學）	90.8
6. UNIVERSITY OF CHICAGO（芝加哥大學）	87.7
7. UNIVERSITY OF MICHIGAN（密西根大學）	86.4
8. UNIVERSITY OF VIRGINIA（維吉尼亞大學）	85.0
9. DUKE UNIVERSITY (D.C.)	83.7
10. UNIVERSITY OF PENNSYLVANIA	82.2
11. GEORGETOWN UNIVERSITY (D.C.)	81.4
12. UNIVERSITY OF CALIFORNIA AT BERKELEY	81.2
13. NORTHWESTERN UNIVERSITY	80.2
14. CORNELL UNIVERSITY	77.2
15. UNIVERSITY OF TEXAS	73.0
16. VANDERBILT UNIVERSITY (Tenn.)	71.2
17. UNIVERSITY OF CALIFORNIA AT LOS ANGELES	70.2
18. UNIVERSITY OF SOUTHERN CALIFORNIA	67.5
19. UNIVERSITY OF CALIFORNIA-HASTINGS	66.2
20. UNIVERSITY OF NOTRE DAME	64.3
21. UNIVERSITY OF MINNESOTA	64.2

22.	BOSTON COLLEGE	62.9
23.	UNIVERSITY OF WASHINGTON	62.9
24.	GEORGE WASHINGTON UNIVERSITY (D.C.)	62.5
25.	UNIVERSITY OF IOWA	62.4

*上述學校每年排行榜會因ABA之評鑑而有變動，不過前15名學
校大致不變。

附錄五： 法律用語和字彙

一、一般用語

abortion (illegal)： 非法墮胎

abortion (legal)： 合法墮胎

acceptance： 承諾

accessories after the fact： 事後從犯

accessories before the fact： 事前從犯

accommodation party： 借款當事人；保兌人（共同發票人或背書人）

accusation： 控告

accusatory pleading： 起訴／告訴狀

acquitted： 無罪

actual cash value： 實際現金價值

add-on sale： 一種如債務人遲延給付分期付款即可立即占有抵押物的條款

adjudicate： 宣判

administrative agencies： 行政代理人或機關

administrator： 管理人

adultery： 通姦

adversary system： 兩造辯論主義

affirmative action： 積極行動

agency shop agreement： 受僱人和工會之集體協定

aid and abet： 幫助和教唆

allegations of fact: 闡明事實

amicus curiae: 法院之朋友；非原告或被告之當事人提出有利於
一造之辯護

amnesty: 大赦(＝pardon)

amortization: 讓渡；攤銷

annulment: 無效

answer: 答辯

antenuptial agreement: 婚前協議

appellant: 上訴人

appellate courts: 上訴法院

appellee: 被上訴人

appraised value: 經評估價值

arbitration: 仲裁

arraignment: 提審傳喚

arrest: 逮捕

arson: 縱火罪

articles of incorporation: 公司章程或稱certificate of incorporation

assault (criminal): 攻擊威脅（刑法）

assault (civil): 攻擊威脅（民法）

asset: 資產

assigned risk: 被分擔之危險

assumption of loan: 承擔借款

assumption of risk: 承擔風險

attachment: 扣押

attempt: 未遂

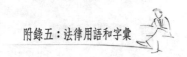

at law: 法律（理）

attractive nuisance doctrine: 有吸引力之危害（對小孩）主義

auction sale: 拍賣

automobile insurance: 汽車保險

automobile medical payments coverage: 汽車醫藥付款保險額（包含乘客）

bail: 保釋（金）

balance sheet: 資產負債表

balloon payment: 貸款一次付清之付款(lump sum payment)

bankruptcy: 破產

bar association: 律師公會

bargaining unit: 團（集）體協約部門

battery: 毆擊

bearer: 持（執）票人

beneficiary: 受益人

benefit of the bargain: 交易利益（期待利益）

Better Business Bureau: 美好企業局（自願私人機構協助商務部揭發不實虛偽買賣）

bigamy: 重婚

bill of exchange: 匯票(＝draft)

Bill of Rights: 憲法所保障之基本權利

blank: 空白

board of directors: 董事會

bodily injury and property damage insurance: 人身受傷和財產受損保險

bond：債券

booking：逮捕（＝arrest）

breach of contract：違約

breach of legal duty：違反法定責任

briefs：上訴狀；簡單書狀

burden of proof：舉證責任

burglary：夜間侵入住宅罪

business invitee：商業性質之受邀者（有金錢利益者）

busing：載運小孩至他校以達族群融合的目的

buy and sell agreement：買賣同意書

by-laws：附則；細則；法規

cancel (contract)：解除（契約）

capital gain：資本利得

capital punishment：死刑

carrying charge：一定期間信用購物之利息費用

case：案件

case citation：案件引證處

case-in-chief：主要案件

cashier's check：銀行保付支票

cash sale transaction：現金買賣交易

casualty insurance：意外險

cause of action：訴因

caveat emptor：買方注意當心

caveat venditor：賣方注意當心

certificate of deposit：定期存款證明

certificate of incorporation： 章程

certificate of ownership： 所有權書狀

certificate of registration： 登記證明書

certified check： 保付支票

certiorari： 聲請調閱卷宗或覆審（向聯邦最高法院申請cert.）

challenge of juror： 反對（某）陪審員

charter： 證書；執照；規章；憲章；特權；包租；備船

check： 支票

civil action： 民事訴訟

civil law： 民法

class action： 集體訴訟

clemency： 政府赦免刑事處罰之德政

close corporation： 未上市由一人或少數人所擁有之公司(＝close held co.)

closing costs： 手續費（購物相關費用），例如檢查費，公證費，移轉登記費，貸款費，檢查白蟻費，保險費等

codicil： 遺囑修改附錄

cohabitation： 同居

collateral： 抵押物；附屬的（不相關的）；間接附帶的

collaterals： 抵押物

collective bargaining： 團體協約

collision insurance： 碰撞保險

commercial paper： 商業票據

commercial property： 商業財產

common law： 習慣法

common law marriage: 習慣法之婚姻（同居）

common stock: 普通股

community property: 共有財產

commutation: 轉換（commutation of fines in lieu of fines: 易科罰金）

comparative negligence: 相對過失

competent parties: 有行為能力（資格）之當事人

complaint (civil): 訴狀（民事）

complaint (criminal): 訴狀（刑事）

composition of creditors: 債權人之組成

comprehensive insurance: 全險

compensatory: 賠償的

conciliation: 和解

condominium: 公寓(condo)

consequential: 因果關係的；特殊的

conservatorship: 監護權

consideration: 約因；對價

consortium: 配偶之權利；合夥；國際性協議

conspiracy: 共犯（謀）

constitution: 憲法

consumerism: 消費者主義

contempt of court: 藐視法庭

contingent beneficiary: 不確定受益人（臨時或第一受益人）

contingent fee: 律師抽成比例報酬（如1/3 或 1/4）或後酬

contract: 契約

contributing to the delinquency of a minor：成年人幫助未成年人
之不法行為

contributory negligence：可歸責之過失

conversion：侵佔

convicted：犯罪；被判罪刑

cooperative apartment：互助公寓(co-op)

copyright：著作權

coroner's jury corporation corpus：驗屍法醫

corpus delicti：犯罪屍（遺）體；犯罪事實

corrective advertising：矯正廣告使其正確

co-sign：共同簽名

court：法院

cover：封面；包含

creative labor：創造能力（發明物品）

credit card：信用卡

credit sale：信用買賣

crime：犯罪

criminal action：刑事訴訟

criminal intent：刑事犯意

criminal law：刑法

criminal negligence：刑事過失

cumulative voting：累積投票

damages：賠償

dangerous instrumentality：危險之工具（媒介；分支機構）

dangerous propensity：危險傾向

death taxes：死亡稅

decedent：死者(＝deceased)

deceit：詐欺(＝fraud)

declamatory judgment：宣示判決；法律關係判決；確認之判決

decree of dissolution：解散命令

deductible clause：扣除條款

deed：契據；讓與；證書

deed of reconveyance：再移轉契據

deed of trust：信託契據（證書）

de facto：事實上

defamation of character：毀損名譽

default：債務不履行

default judgment：一造缺席判決

defective or voidable marriage：瑕疵或得撤銷婚姻

defendant：被告

deficiency judgment：不足額判決

deficit：赤字；不足清償

de jure：法律上

demand paper：要求文件

demurrer：異議

deposit receipt：寄存收據

deposition：詰（質）詢（口頭或書面）

depreciated value：貶低之價值

depreciation：貶值

diminished capacity：減輕責任能力

directors：董事

disability income insurance：殘障收入保險

disbarment：撤銷律師資格

discovery procedures：發見證據程序

dishonor：不兌現

dissolution：解散

divided interest：分歧之利益

dividend：利潤

divorce：離婚

donee：受贈人

dower and curtesy：寡婦和鰥夫（財產）

draft (military)：徵兵（軍中）

draft：匯票(＝bill of exchange)

drawee：付款人

drawer：發票人(＝maker)

due process of law：法律正當程序

duress：脅迫

duty (legal)：法律責任

dwelling and contents：房屋和所有物格式（火險）

easement：地役權

economic strike：經濟罷工

emancipation：脫離父母獨立生活的未成年人（自立）

embezzlement：瀆職；侵佔

eminent domain：國家徵用（收）權

employment contract：僱傭契約

enact：立法

endorsements (policy)：背書；贊助

endowment life insurance：養老保險

entrapment：陷害；誘捕（騙）

entrepreneur：企業家

equitable owner：衡平法之所有人

equal protection clause：平等保障條款

equitable title：衡平法的所有權

equity：衡平；權益

escrow：由第三人信託之保管契約；履約保證（不動產買賣）

estate planning：遺產之規劃

estate tax：遺產稅

evidence：證據

excess liability：超額責任

exclusive agency listing：獨家公開登刊買賣權

exclusive right to sell listing：獨家專屬公開登錄賣出權

executive branch：行政單位（總統）

executive privilege：行政特權

executor：執行人

expatriation：移居外國；放逐

express powers：明示授權

express warranty：明示瑕疵擔保責任

expulsion：驅逐出境(＝deportation)

extortion：威脅

fair comment：公正評論

false imprisonment：不法監禁

family income policy：家庭收入政策

FDIC：聯邦儲蓄保險公司

federal：聯邦

federal register：聯邦法律和行政法規登記彙編

federal reporter：聯邦上訴法院意見和判決彙編

federal supplement：聯邦地方法院意見和判決彙編

fee, fee simple：無條件繼承不動產權（自由土地所有權）

fee simple determinable：有限制的無條件繼承不動產權（條件式）

felon：犯重罪之人

felony：重罪

fiduciary relationship：信（受）託關係

financial responsibility law：財務責任法案

financial statement：財務報表

find：判決（評決）

first degree murder：一級謀殺罪

formal will：正式遺囑

form prescribed by law：依法規定格式

fornication：私通罪（與一方有婚之人通姦）

franchise：特許

franchisee：被特許之人

franchisor：授權特許之人

fraud：詐欺

fringe benefits：非薪資之直接或間接利益（員工）

garnishment：扣押債務人財產

general：一般

general partner：一般合夥人

general partnership：一般合夥

genuine assent：真實之同意

gift from decedent's estate：遺贈

gift tax：贈與稅

good faith：善意(＝bona fide)

grand jury：大陪審團（16～23人）

grand theft：重大竊盜罪

group life insurance policy：團體人身（壽）保險

guaranty：保證

guardian ad literm：法定監護人

guardianship：監護

guest：客人；乘客

guest statutes：汽車乘客條款(國際私法中乘客受傷之賠償條款)

habeas corpus：人身自由

health insurance：健康保險

hearsay：傳聞

heirs：繼承人

hoard：累積閒錢；戰時屯積貨物

holder in due course (HDC) — holder through a holder in due course：善意持（執）票人

holographic will：親筆遺囑

homeowners insurance：房屋擁有人保險

hostile fire：意外之火

hung jury：懸而不決之陪審決議(6:6)

immaterial：不重要的

immunity from prosecution：免訴權

implied powers：隱示之權利

incest：亂倫；雞姦

incompetent：沒有證據能力的

income statement：損益表

incontestable clause：不可抗告條款

indemnification：賠償

indemnify：補償損失

independent contractor：獨立承攬人

indeterminate sentence law：不定期刑法案

incidental：偶然的

liquidated：清償的；約定的

indictment：公訴；起訴（由大陪審團提起）

indorsement：背書；簽名；保證

industrial life insurance policy：工業人身保險單

inflation：通貨膨脹

information：起訴書（由檢察官提起）；資料；訊息

infraction：違法

inheritance tax：繼承稅（遺產稅）

injunction：強制令

in equity：衡平

in loco parentis：代位父母親行使權利

insurable interest：財務損失之保險利益

insured：被保險人；保險的；要保人

insurer：保險人；承保人；保險公司

intentional infliction of mental disturbance：故意侵害精神致使錯亂

intentional tort：故意侵權

interest：利益；利息；權益

interspousal immunity：配偶間之豁免權

interstate commerce：州際間之商務

inter-vivos gift：生前贈與

intestacy：未立遺囑死亡

intestate law：未立遺囑之法律

intrastate commerce：州內商務

invest：投資

investment companies：投資公司

involuntary manslaughter：非自願性過失殺人

irrelevant：不相關的

irresistible impulse：不能抗拒之衝動

irrevocable trust：不得撤銷之信託

joint tenancy：共同共有人(＝with right of survivorship)（共有人繼承人不得繼承，繼承權屬其他共有人所有）

judge：法官

judgment：判決

judgment-proof：判決證明

judicial branch：司法單位（聯邦最高法院）

jurisdiction: 管轄權

jury: 陪審團 （一般為12人或6人）

jury (grand): 大陪審團 （16～23人）

jury (trial): 陪審團

justices: 大法官 （9人）

juvenile court: 少年法院

kidnapping: 綁架

laches: 時效罹於消滅(＝statute of limitation)

land contract: 不動產契約

landlord: 出租人 （房東）

larceny: 竊盜罪

last will: 最後遺書

law: 法律

lease: 租賃

leasehold: 租賃權

legal owner: 法律上之所有人

legal separation: 法定分 （別） 居

legal tender: 法定貨幣 （tender: 提供；投標；償還）

legislative branch: 立法單位 （國會: 參議員和眾議員）

legitimization: 合法性

letter of instructions: 指示書

liability: 責任

libel: 毀謗 （書面）

licensee: 被允許之人 （社會上之朋友）；被授權人

lien: 留置權；抵押權；質權

life estate：終身財產

life insurance：人身（壽）保險

life tenant：終身租借人

limited defenses：有限之抗辯事由

limited liability：有限責任

limited partner：有限責任合夥人

limited partnership：有限合夥

limited payment life insurance：有限付款人身保險

lineals：直系親屬

listing agreement：公開登刊買賣協議

litigation：訴訟

load：負荷

loan shark：高利貸(＝usury)

loan value：貸款價值

magistrates：行政法官；小額訴訟承辦法官

maker：發票人

malice aforethought：預謀之惡意

malicious prosecution：惡意起訴

manslaughter：過失殺人

marital deduction：婚姻扣減

market value：市價

mayhem：重傷害罪

mechanic's lien：技術人員優先權

mediation：調停

medical payments insurance：醫療付款保險

minor：未成年人；微小的

misdemeanor：輕罪

misrepresentation：不實之虛偽陳述

mistrial：誤審

mobile home：流動的房屋

moot question：已不具爭論之問題

motion：申請；提議

motion to produce：向法院申請提出

motive：動機

multiple listing：多頭登刊買賣

murder：謀殺

mutual fund：共同基金

nominal or token：名義或象徵

naturalization：歸化

negative injunction：「不得為」之禁止令

negligence：過失

net worth：淨值

no-fault divorce：無過失離婚

no-fault insurance：無過失保險

nolo contendere (plea)：不願辯護但不承認有罪之申訴

note：本票；票據

notice of dishonor：拒絕付款之通知

nullification of marriage：婚姻之無效

nuncupative will：口頭遺書；口述遺書

obscene：淫穢的

occupancy：佔據

offer：要約

officers：警員（察）

opening statements：開始陳述之話

open listing：公開登刊買賣

ordinances：命令；條例

ordinary life insurance：一般人身保險

owner：業主；所有人

pardon：大赦

parole：假釋

parol evidence rule：口頭證據原則

participating preferred stock：參與優先股

partnership：合夥

patent：專利

paternity proceeding：確認生父程序

peremptory challenge：絕對強制迴避（無需理由指明某一陪審員迴避）

perjury：偽證罪

petty theft：輕微竊盜

picketing：示威

pilferage：小偷行為

pimping：略誘女性從事娼妓

plaintiff：原告

plea：訴；抗辯；請願

pleadings：訴訟程序；訴狀（原告）；答辯（被告）

police power: 警察權（公共福利、安全或道德提昇）；治安權（州之權限）

policy: 政策

power of appointment: 指定權；任命權；委任狀

power of attorney: 委託書；授權書；委任書

preemption: 優先購買權

preferred stock: 優先股

preliminary hearing: 預審（刑事調查庭）

premium: 保險費

presentment for payment: 提示付款

pretermitted heir statute: 遺漏繼承人法例

pretrial proceedings: 預審（審判前）程序

prima facie: 表面（初步）

primary liability: 主要責任

principal: 主要的；校長；本金

punitive or exemplary: 懲罰性或示範的

prior restraint: 事前限制

privilege against self-incrimination: 不得自我控制之特權

privileged communication: 有特權之通信或對話（豁免權）

privity of contract: 契因；相互關係

probate: 認證

probation: 緩刑；監獄

procedural law: 程序法

process: 程序；過程

process server: 傳票送達員

profit：利潤

promissory note：本票

property：財產

personal property：動產

prosecutor：檢察官（＝District Attorney)(D.A.)

prospectus：募股章程；說明書；計畫書；發起書

proximate cause：法律原因

proxy：委託書

public defender：公設辯護人

purchasing power of the dollar：購買力

qualified：合格的

quasi：準

question of fact：事實問題

question of law：法律問題

quitclaim deed：放棄對所有財產權利之契據（任何瑕疵一併移轉）

rape (forcible)：強姦（暴力）

rape (statutory)：準強姦（法定）

real property：不動產

reasonable man：合理人

recognizance：承認

registered buyer—owner：登記之買方——所有人

reinstate：重述；復職

relevant：相關的

remainderman：繼承權

remedies：救濟

rent：房租

rental agreement：租金協議

replacement value：替代價值

replevin：追回原物之訴

repossession：再佔有

reprieve：緩刑(＝reprieval or probation)

request for admission of facts：要求承認事實

rescission：解除

residual powers：剩餘權限

restrictive：限制的

res ipsa loquitur：不證自明原則(things speak for itself)

respondeat superior：代理責任（主僕關係）

restitution：恢復原狀(＝status quo)

retainer fee：預聘律師費(＝deposit)

retaliatory eviction：報復性驅逐房客

reverse discrimination：反歧視

reversionary interest：回復利益；期待權

revocable trust：得撤銷之信託

right (legal)：權利

right of retraction：撤回權(withdraw/reject)

rights (civil)：權利（民法）

rights (fundamental)：權利(重要)

right-to-work laws：有權工作法案

robbery：強盜罪

Roman civil law: 羅馬大陸法

sale on approval: 條件買賣——買方在購買前先行佔有使用該物

sales contract: 買賣契約

satisfaction of judgment: 清償判決

search and seizure: 搜索和扣押

secondary boycott: 第二次抵制

secondary liability: 第二順位責任

secured loan: 有擔保之貸款

special: 特別的

securities: 有價證券；保證；產權證明（複數）

security agreement: 擔保協議

seduction: 誘姦

segregation: 分開

self-defense: 自我防衛

self-incrimination: 自我控告

separate property: 分別財產

sex crimes: 性犯罪（sexual harassment: 性騷擾）

sex perversion: 性變態

shareholder: 股東

shoplifting: 順手牽羊偷竊

sight draft: 見票即付匯票

sitdown strike: 靜坐抗議

slander: 口頭毀謗（libel: 書面毀謗）

small claims court: 小額訴訟法院

sole proprietorship: 獨資

solicitation: 教唆

sovereign immunity: 主權豁免權

special: 特殊的

specific performance: 特別履行

standard fire policy: 標準火險

stare decisis: 維持先前判決(precedent)

statutes: 法條

statutes of limitations: 消滅時效

stock: 股票；股份

stock dividend: 股利

stockholder: 股東(＝shareholder)

stock split: 股票分割

strict (product) liability: 絕對（產品）責任

strike: 罷工抗議

subornation of perjury: 說明他人偽證

subpoena: 傳票（喚）

subrogation: 代位

substantive law: 實質法律

summons: 傳票

tax rate: 稅率

tax shelter: 避稅天堂

tenancy in common: 共有（共有人繼承人可繼承）(no right of survivorship) (inheritable)

tenancy by the entirety: 共有人（夫妻間）

testamentary trust: 遺囑信託

testator: 立遺囑人

theft: 竊盜

time draft: 定（註）期匯票

title: 所有權；權狀；產權書

title insurance: 所有權狀保險

tort: 侵權

tortfeasor: 侵權行為人

trade acceptance: 商業承兌（匯票）

trademark: 商標

trade name: 商品

treble: 三倍

trespass: 非法侵害（人）

trial: 審判

trial courts: 審判法院

trust: 信託

unconscionable contract: 顯不公平契約

undue influence: 不當影響

uninsured motorist insurance: 未保與摩托車撞擊之保險

union: 工會

universal defenses: 法定抗辯事由

unlawful detainer: 非法扣留押金

unsecured loan: 未擔保之貸款

unwritten law: 習慣法(＝common law)

usury: 高利貸

valid: 有效的；合法的

venue (change of): 改變審判地

verdict: 評決（陪審團）(deliberation: 評議)

vicarious liability: 代理（表）責任

void: 無效

voidable: 效力未定的；得撤銷的

voir dire: 預先審核陪審員或證人之資格

voluntary arbitration: 自願性仲裁

waive: 放棄

warrant: 逮捕或搜索狀

warranty: 瑕疵擔保

white collar crimes: 白領犯罪

will: 遺囑

workers' compensation: 勞工賠償法

writ of execution: 執行令

written interrogatories: 書面質（詰）問

二、契約用語

acceptance: 承諾

administration: 實施

affidavit: 宣誓

agency: 經銷

annex: 附件(enclosure)

application: 適用

arbitration: 仲裁

assignment: 讓與

authority：主管機關（當局）

bidder：投標人

bid bond：押標金

bill of exchange：匯票

breach of contract：違約

calendar day：日曆天

common provision：通則

consideration：對價

considering：鑑於

consolidation (A＋B＝C or A or B)：合併

contractor：承攬人

corresponded application：準用

damages：賠償

default：債務不履行

delegation：承擔

distributor：總代理（經銷）

drawing：圖形

establishment：規定

ex officio：依職權

gazette：公報

grace period：除斥期間（延展期間）

guarantor：連帶保證人

item：項(paragraph, clause)

joint venture：合資企業

leave the motion without cognizance：不審理

liquidated damages: 約定違約賠償金

may: 得

merger (asset or shares): 購併

motion: 申請

non-restroactive: 不溯及既往

notary public: 公證人

noting: 鑒於

offer: 要約

offeree: 要約相對人（承諾人）

offeror: 要約人

option: 選擇權

owner: 業主

part: 篇

partnership: 合夥

pending: 未定的（繫屬中）

performance bond: 履約保證金

power of attorney: 委任狀

power of appointment (authorization): 授權書

promissory estoppel: 禁止反言

provided that: 如(if)

proviso (exception): 但書

provisional: 臨時的，暫時的

public notice: 公告

quantum meriut (service rendered): 勞務所得

recognizing: 咸認

repeal：取消

rescission：解除契約

restitution (status quo)：回復原狀

retroactive：溯及既往

representative：代表

revoke：撤銷（回）

save for：除…之外(exempt from)

section：條(article)

security deposit：訂金

standardization contract：定型化契約

statute of limitation：消滅時效

subject matter：標的

subparagraph：款

subcontractor：次承攬人

surety：一般保證人

taking into account：顧及

understanding：諒解書(memo)

void (invalid)：無效

voidable：得撤銷；效力未定的

withdraw：撤回

working day：工作日

三、刑法用語

abandon：中止(犯) (＝renunciation)

abandonment：遺棄罪

abduct：略誘

abortion：墮胎

accomplice：從犯(＝abettor or accessory)

accountant(CPA)：會計師

admonition：訓誡

adultery：通姦

aggravating circumstance：酌加

AIDS：愛滋病

ammunition：子彈

annul：使無效(＝void)

arbitrator：仲裁人

arson：縱火

attachment：假扣押

attempt：未遂

barred：消滅(＝elapse)

breach of contract：違約

breach of trust：背信罪

calamity：災難

cannon：砲(加儂)

capital sentence：死刑

carnal：肉體(欲)的

clergyman：牧師

cocaine：高根(古柯鹼)

combined punishment for several offenses：數罪併罰

concealment of offender：藏匿人犯

confiscation：沒收(＝taking)

conspiracy：共犯(謀)

conversion：侵占(misappropriation)

corpus：屍體

counterfeit currency：偽造貨幣

counterfeit valuable security：偽造有價證券

cremate：火葬

criminal liability：刑事責任

criminal provision：刑法分則

default of contract：債務不履行

deportation：驅逐出境

deprivation of civil right：褫奪公權

destruction of evidence：湮滅證據

detention：拘役

disciplinary punishment：懲戒處分

discretion：職權(自由心證)

drug：藥

druggist：藥商

duress：脅迫

element of crime：構成要件

emergency defense：緊急避難

execution：執行

extortion：恐嚇(＝blackmail or intimidate)

false weights and measures：偽造度量衡

felony：重罪

fines：罰金(commuted to fines：易科罰金)

forge instrument(seal)：偽造文書(印文)

fraud：詐欺

gambling：賭博(＝wagering)

gay：男同性戀

general provision：總則

guardian：監護人

hearing：調查審問庭

heroin：海洛因

homicide：殺人罪(kill)

ignorance：不知；無知

immigration：移民(入境)

injunction：強制令

insanity：心神喪失；精神耗弱

insult：侮辱

intentional：故意的

interpreter：通譯

interrupt：中斷

investigation：調查(偵查)

judge(justice)：法官(大法官)

jurisdiction：管轄權

jury：陪審團

kidnap：綁架(for ransom＝贖金)

knowledge：明知

larceny：竊盜(＝steal)

lesbian：女同性戀

libel：書面毀謗

life sentence：無期徒刑

magistrate：行政官

malfeasance：瀆職罪

manslaughter：過失殺人

misdemeanor：輕罪

mistake：錯誤

mitigating circumstance：酌減

morphine：嗎啡

murder：謀殺

negligence：過失

notary public：公證人

offense against external security of the state：外患罪

offense against internal security of the state：內亂罪

offense of interference with relations with other states：妨害國交罪

offense：罪

opium：鴉片

overt：公然的(＝obvious)

parole：假釋(＝conditional release)

peace preservation measures：保安處分

perjury：偽證罪

pharmacist：藥劑師

piracy：海盜罪

poison：毒

pot：大麻

privacy：隱私權

probation：緩刑

promulgate：公佈

prosecution：起訴

prosecutor：檢察官

provided：假設

proviso：但書

provocation：激怒

public danger：公共危險罪

public morality：公共道德

public official：公務員

purpose：故意

quarantine：檢疫

rape：強姦

receiving stolen property：贓物罪

recidivism：累犯

reckless：魯莽草率

reformatory educatory：感化教育

revoke：撤銷

robbery：強奪罪

self defense：正當防衛

sentence：刑

service：勞役(＝labor)

sexual harassment：性騷擾

shrine：廟寺(＝temple)

slander：口頭毀謗

solicitation：教唆

specific performance：特別履行令

statute of limitation：時效

successive acts：連續行為

suicide：自殺

tribunal：法庭

usury：高利貸(＝shark loan)

venereal disease：性病(V.D.)

victim：受害人

witness：證人

參考書目(BIBLIOGRAPHY)

英文部分

1. A. Kritzer, *International Contract Manual* (1993)

2. A. Dworsky, *User's Guide to A Uniform System of Citation* (1988)

3. *A Uniform System of Citation* (Published and Distributed by Harvard Law Review Association)

4. Baird, Eisenberg & Jackson, *Commercial and Debtor—Creditor Law* (1989)

5. Boyce & Perkin, *Criminal Law and Procedure* (1991)

6. Kadish & Schhullhofer, *Criminal Law and its Process* (5th ed. 1989)

7. Kamisar, LaFave & Israel, *Modern Criminal Procedure* (1990)

8. LaFave & Israel, *Criminal Procedure* (1991)

9. LaFave & Scot, *Criminal Law* (1886)

10. Lee, Toms & Cheng, *Cases and Materials on Criminal Law & Enforcement* (1986)

11. Lee & Israel, *Criminal Procedure* (1991)

12. Low & Jeffrey & Bonnie, *Criminal Law* (1986)

13. L. Fuller & M. Eisenberg, *Basic Contract Law* (5th ed. 1993)

14. *Model Penal Code*: American Law Institute (1985)

15. P. Low, *Criminal Law* (1990)

16. R. Hamilton, A. Rau & R. Weintraub, *Contract* (1984)

17. Whitebread & Slobogin, *Criminal Procedure* (1993)

18. Makdisi, *Law School Orientation* (1986)

19. Hay, *An Introduction to U.S. Law* (1988)

20. Coughlin, *Your Introduction to LAW* (1983)

21. Steven, *Law Dictionary*, Barron (1984)

22. Robert, *How and When To Be Your Own Lawyer, Avery* (1993)

23. Bantam Doubleday Deel, *The Official Guide to U.S. Law Schools* (1994)

24. Delaney, *How to do Your Best on Law School Exams* (1988)

25. Fleming, *The Essay Examination Writing Workbook* (1987)

26. Bodenheimer, Oakley & Love, *An Introduction to the Anglo-American Legal System*, West Publishing Co. (1988)

27. UWLA (unpublished law handouts of the Mini Law School compendium); NYU (unpublished law handouts); Valparaiso University (unpublished law handouts of professor Berner & Vance).

中文部分

1. 蔣耀祖，《中美司法制度比較》，臺灣商務印書館，臺北，民國六十五年。

2. 何孝元，《中國債法與英美法之比較》。

3. 陶龍生，《美國法律與移民指南》，食貨出版社，臺北，民國八十一年。

4. 《法律英漢辭典》，五南公司，民國七十七年。

5. 《法律名詞辭典》，五州出版社，民國八十五年。
6. 《法律問題上線》，永然文化，民國八十六年。

從身旁事物開始學習的

生活英語

你是否一

　　學了多年的英文，卻在離開學校後又原封不動地還給老師？

　　遇上了老外，第一反應是想要逃之夭夭？

　　常常下定決心「要救回我的英文」，卻又將花大錢買來的英語教材束之高閣？

　　本書藉由學習身旁事物的英文用法，並在實際生活中不斷運用，使英文的生活用語能自然地留在腦海裡，是最具效果的英語學習法！

　　不僅可以讓你輕鬆掌握日常生活語彙，更可有效加強你的會話實戰能力，相信在每天實踐的過程中，你還會發現意想不到的樂趣呢！

定價160元

英語自然學習法

你將會發現：學英語竟然可以這麼自自然然、輕輕鬆鬆！

英文自然學習法（一）

針對被動語態、時態、進行式與完成式、Wh-疑問句與關係詞等重點分析解說，讓你輕鬆掌握英文文法的竅門。

定價160元

英文自然學習法（二）

打破死背介系詞意義和片語的方式，將介系詞的各種衍伸用法連繫起來，讓你自然掌握介系詞的感覺和精神。

定價190元

英文自然學習法（三）

運用「兔子和鴨子」的原理，解說PRESSURE的MUST、POWER的WILL、UP / DOWN / OUT / OFF等用法的基本感覺，以及所衍伸出各式各樣精采豐富的意思，讓你簡單輕鬆活用英語！

定價170元

專為需要經常查最新詞彙的你設計

三民 袖珍英漢辭典

15.5×8cm，1000頁

* 收錄詞條高達58,000字，從最新的專業術語、時事用詞到日常生活所需詞彙全部網羅！
* 輕巧便利的口袋型設計，最適於外出攜帶！
* 字義解釋詳盡，是輔助新生代學習英語、吸收新知的最佳利器！

定價280元

出國旅行者的良伴

三民 簡明英漢辭典

16.5×8.5cm，700頁

* 收錄57,000字，最常用、常用字以*特別標示，內容深入淺出而豐富。
* 口袋型設計，輕巧便利。
* 附簡明英美地圖，是出國旅遊者最佳良伴。

定價260元

你可知道

rubberneck 可不是「塑膠脖子」，而是指「好奇的人」？

four-and-two 可不是「四跟二」，而是「三明治」？

eighty-eight 可不是「八十八」，而是「鋼琴鍵盤」？

我們說「永遠的二十五歲」用來表示「永遠年輕」，而美國人說的卻是「永遠的二十一歲」（perpetual 21）！

美國日常語辭典

一本伴你暢遊美國的最佳工具書！

21×15cm，500頁

◎ 描寫美國真實面貌，讓你不只學好美語，更進一步了解美國社會與文化！

◎ 廣泛蒐集美國人日常生活的語彙，從日常生活的角度出發，自日常用品、飲食文化、文學、藝術、到常見俚語，帶領你感受美語及其所代表的文化內涵，讓學習美語的過程不再只是背誦單字和強記文法句型的單調練習。

定價580元

老外會怎麼說？

作者以留美多年所接觸的英語為基礎，指出以文法為中心的學校英語在會話上的種種不自然表達方式，並從發音、詞彙、文法等各個層面，帶您瞭解最生動自然的英語。

（定價130元）

輕鬆高爾夫英語

不管打不打高爾夫，講英語都嘛會通！全世界有十多億人在講英語，公車、學校、馬路、球場、銀行、醫院、事務所…專業的、生活的，處處都是英語。說英語不分場合，學英語當然也不應自我設限！你或許不打高爾夫，但那不該是阻撓你拓展見聞的理由；當然，如果你是高爾夫球友，那更是要一讀為快！

本書忠實呈現了球場上各種狀況場景對話，讓你一書在手，不管打不打高爾夫，講英語都嘛會通！

（定價170元）